GREAT PREACHING ON
THE SECOND COMING

GREAT PREACHING ON

THE SECOND COMING

COMPILED BY
CURTIS HUTSON

SWORD of the LORD
PUBLISHERS
P.O.BOX 1099, MURFREESBORO, TN 37133

Printed and Bound in the United States of America

Preface

Here are the answers to what lies ahead!

The alert Christian of today is vitally interested in Bible prophecy. He wants to know just how the prophecies set forth in the Bible relate to him and recent developments throughout the world. He wants an answer to:

> Why did the Jews expect Christ to set up a literal kingdom on earth? Will the Antichrist come before the rapture? Will Christians have to go through the Great Tribulation? What is the Mark of the Beast? What has to happen before the kingdom of Christ begins on earth? Is it possible to know if we are in the last days? Can Christ return before the Gospel is preached in all the world? Has God cast the Jews away forever, or will they yet be reunited in their own land? How many of the Bible prophecies are yet to be fulfilled? And, what can I believe about the future when so many disagree?

There has been so much false teaching, so much speculation and guesswork, so much arguing about incidental points, that many good people have missed the sweetness of God's teaching here.

Our aim in this volume is to clear up that teaching and answer these questions—and a host of others—which so many are confused about today. We can know what God has planned, what He has promised about Christ's coming again and His reign over the whole earth. God has a program; He will carry it out; and He has clearly revealed that program in great detail in His Word.

This volume places prophecies in their right order. There is no guesswork, no setting of dates for Christ's return. Many books in recent days have been written in defense of these truths, but we do not recall any that are more convincing than this collection of fifteen sermons by well-known authors who adhere strictly to the Bible, fifteen messages picked as the best from fifty-two years of issues of THE SWORD OF THE LORD. The reader will come to love "that blessed hope" and to see the coming of Christ in its true relationship with the Jew, the Gentile, and the church of God.

Powerful preaching! Will convict the unsaved and will certainly search the hearts of slothful Christians to get busy in the Master's vineyard, for we know not the day nor the hour when our Lord will return.

Curtis Hutson, Editor
THE SWORD OF THE LORD

Table of Contents

I. M. HALDEMAN
1845-1933

ABOUT THE MAN:

Dr. Haldeman was long pastor of First Baptist Church, New York, and one of the foremost of Bible expositors.

His best-known work was *The Tabernacle Priesthood and Offerings.* With great wealth of detail, he shows how the framework, the coverings, the curtains, the hangings, the priesthood, the robes and the offerings of the Tabernacle in the wilderness prefigured the Person, the work and the glory of Christ.

Another well-known volume was *How to Study the Bible.* Dr. Haldeman believed that the New Testament is a fulfillment of the Old, that each book of the entire Bible finds place and value by the law of growth—and by a moral and spiritual logic.

In *Christian Science in the Light of Holy Scripture,* Dr. Haldeman states his case with legal exactness—first, calling as witness the words of the scientists, then calling as witness the words of the Bible. The reader must act as jury and decide whether the witnesses agree or whether they are flatly contradictory. It shows the naked deformity of Christian Science.

Other books by this great Bible scholar include: *The Coming of Christ; Ten Sermons on the Second Coming; Christ, Christianity and the Bible; Can the Dead Communicate With the Living,* etc.

I.

Christ's Second Coming

I. M. HALDEMAN

A Profound Address Before the Ministerial Association of New York City

"Unto them that look for him shall he appear the second time."—
Heb. 9:28.

If the value of a doctrine were to be judged by the frequency of its
mention, then easily the second coming of our Lord would be the most
important doctrine in the Word of God; it will be admitted that the atonement is the core of the Gospel, the crimson reservoir out of which flow
forth the streams of gladness that fill the whole area of the divine commission. Yet this sublime word occurs but once in the New Testament,
and there, when faithfully translated, is not atonement at all but recon-
ciliation, something quite different and apart from atonement. On the
other hand, the doctrine of the second coming in this same New Testament is mentioned on an average of at least once in thirty verses.

When you turn to the Old Testament, you find that the seventh man
who ever lived on the earth, the seventh man from Adam, even Enoch,
spoke of the second coming, saying: "Behold, the Lord cometh with
ten thousands of his saints."

From Genesis to Malachi the book is filled with the doctrine.

It is set forth in type, figure, symbol, parable, story, illustration and
direct statement. The Spirit seems to exhaust human vocabulary in the
vain endeavor to proclaim it. The noblest prose and the most exalted
poetry the world ever knew break like waves upon the shore and at
times seem to turn into mist in utter helplessness to express the coming
glory.

The stars of Heaven pale, break loose from their orbits and fall, the
waves of the sea roar, the floods lift up their voices, the mountains bow

down at His presence, the trees of the wood clap their hands, and every voice in Heaven and earth cries out: "Behold, He cometh! He cometh!—the King!" And by the time you have reached Malachi and leaned across four centuries of prophetic silence, your ears are full of the footsteps of the coming King.

I. CHRIST'S SECOND COMING TAUGHT THROUGHOUT NEW TESTAMENT

The moment you enter the New Testament, John the Baptist is heard speaking not of the first advent but of the second; and when the starlight of Bethlehem, the mystery of the manger, and the apprenticeship of thirty years are passed and the Christ sets forth upon His mission, His lips are full, not of the first advent but of the second. Indeed I do not know that He ever spoke directly of His first advent, but His lips were continually full of the second. So filled was He with the thought of it that on one occasion He took His disciples up into the mountain height; and there on the background of the dark and black midnight was transfigured before them till His garments shone whiter than any fuller on earth could whiten them, blazing forth in the beauty of His essential light till they saw Him as their glorious and coming King. And the Apostle Peter, speaking of that supreme event, declares in his epistle that the Lord manifested Himself not only as their King, but set forth in full detail the manner and fashion of the coming kingdom.

When He stood before His judges He was not careful to speak of that marvelous moment when the angels of God saluted Him upon His mother's breast; but lifting up His voice, warned them that the hour was at hand when they should see Him coming on the bosom of the clouds in great power and glory.

When for the last time He passed through the Temple, He so spoke of coming days that His disciples sought Him out privately and entreated Him that He explain to them the import of His words. And sitting down there upon the Mount of Olives where the whole city and the vista of the centuried years lay before Him, He unfolded to them event after event, with Judaea and Jerusalem as the arena and center of their emphasis until they beheld the climax of His second coming.

Just before the solemn tragedy when He would comfort the hearts of His sorrowing followers, sorrowing because of the shadowing hour of separation, He takes them to the window of the little Upper Room and, bidding them look out on the illimitable sweep of the nightly heavens, lifts Himself to the level of Godhead and declares that He is going into that upper country to prepare a place for them, and that, when He has completed it, He will come again and receive them unto Himself.

After the tragedy, when He has risen from the dead, lined the grave with the light of His own immortality and ascended Heavenwards, two angels stand by the up-looking disciples and say unto them:

"Ye men of Galilee, why stand ye gazing up into heaven? this same Jesus, which is taken up from you into heaven, shall so come in like manner as ye have seen him go into heaven."—Acts 1:11.

On the day of Pentecost the Apostle Peter preaches to the Jews that this Man of Nazareth whom they killed and whom God had raised from the dead, was none other than their own Messiah; and that if they would repent, confess His death and resurrection, God would give them the times of refreshing promised in the prophets and would send Jesus Christ to them a second time.

Throughout the Acts while the apostles lift up the crucified Lord to the vision of faith, they are always careful to declare that God raised Him from the dead and will send Him back.

When you pass into the epistle, you are confronted on the very threshold with the testimony that the Son of God is coming again. The epistle to the Romans is divided into three sections: doctrinal, dispensational and hortatory. Each section ends with the declaration that Christ is coming.

Chapter 8 is the climax of one of the most stupendous and hopeful lines of argument ever written; and the climax of this chapter is the second coming of Christ.

Chapter 11 is the climax of an argument concerning the dispensational distinction between Israel and the church; and the climax of that dispensational argument is the second coming of Christ.

Chapter 16 is the climax of exhortations and regulations concerning the simple details of Christian life and obligation. And the climax of this chapter is the second coming of Christ.

Chapter 1 of the primary epistle to the Corinthians tells us that as Christians we come behind in no gift, our spiritual equipment is perfect: therefore we ought to be in the constant attitude of waiting for our Lord as stewards who will not be ashamed to meet Him.

The climax of chapter 15 is the argument for the resurrection of the dead; and the initial and climax of that argument is the coming of Christ. Taking the whole race and sweeping it up into Adam for death, the apostle declares that the race thus dying and dead shall come forth again in Christ both to salvation and damnation, but every man in his own order, and particularly, as described, they that are Christ's at His coming, thus declaring that the first resurrection—the resurrection of the saints of God—will take place at the coming. In the second epistle to the same church, Christ is seen coming to set up that judgment seat at which each Christian is to be manifested for reward.

In the epistle to the Galatians, we get no mention of the second coming because there the apostle has us on the cross, crucified with Christ.

We get no mention of this great event in the epistle to the Ephesians because there we are seen as risen and seated with Christ in heavenly places. We are there as those who have already ascended in the anticipation of the Spirit, as that church which He has raised, translated and presented to Himself without spot or wrinkle or any such thing.

In the first epistle written to the Gentiles, the epistle to the Thessalonians, the Apostle Paul testifies that these converts had "turned to God from idols to serve the living and true God; And to wait for his Son from heaven, even Jesus, which delivered us from the wrath to come." It is a notorious fact that each chapter of these two epistles to the Thessalonians closes with the declaration that Christ is coming.

In writing to Timothy he laces the two epistles together with the coming of Christ. In Titus he represents that coming as the blessed hope. The whole aim of the epistle to the Hebrews is to set up the types, figures and shadows of truth and let us see how they all melt into the white light of fulfillment in Christ as their perfect Antitype, at His second coming.

James, with all the conservatism of Jerusalem and the bondage of the law upon him, lifts up his voice and declares that the Lord is coming.

Peter testifies that the second coming of Christ is the one thing that appeals to faith and love, and in his second epistle warns the believer that the time will come, if the Lord should tarry, when scoffers will arise in the very midst, and in the name of Christ Himself scoff and mock at the doctrine of the second coming, saying, "Where is the promise of his coming?"

In his threefold and family epistle, the Apostle John sounds the chord of "Home, Sweet Home" in the exalted utterances concerning the coming of Him whom he lovingly describes as "The Coming One."

Jude quotes Enoch, and thus binds the New Testament back to the Old, making the whole Bible but one testimony as to the coming of the King.

The book of the Revelation is written by the Apostle John. It is called in our Bible the Revelation of St. John the Divine. Its proper title is, "The Revelation," that is to say, the revealing, the manifestation "of Christ." It might well be called in English "The Book of the Second Advent," since its one subject from the first to the last of its chapters is the second coming of Christ. The book is like the roof of some mighty cathedral, each of the 22 chapters like a panel in the roof, each panel filled with a scenic representation of the coming Christ.

So important is the doctrine to our Lord Himself that He practically puts His own signature to this book which specially speaks of it, openly and unqualifiedly avouching that He is its cause and inspiration and attaching to it what He does not do to any other portion of Scripture, namely, a threefold blessing: blessing to him who reads it, to those who hear it read, and to those who keep its "sayings."

As the book closes, the Spirit and the bride say, "Come"; and he who has heard the Lord's declaration that He is coming is commanded to say, "Come"; while the voice of Christ as the last utterance out of Heaven earthward, is saying: "Behold, I am coming quickly."

Thus from Genesis to Revelation this doctrine of the second coming is inwrought with the warp and woof of the inspired Word and lies as thick upon its pages as the autumn leaves; and he who keeps his ears alert as he opens its pages may hear the rustling of the footsteps of the coming King.

From all this, it is evident that the coming of Christ is the predominantly mentioned doctrine in the Word of God.

How is it, then, that faithful preachers, those who claim to love their Lord, neglect it, make it the "neglected theme," send it into the background and rarely mention it except with an apology as to its uselessness; giving the impression indeed that he who does preach it is guilty of some offense, if not against decency and order, at least, against wisdom and knowledge?

II. CHRIST'S SECOND COMING BOUND UP WITH EVERY FUNDAMENTAL DOCTRINE OF THE BIBLE

Not only is this doctrine the predominantly mentioned one of the

Bible; it is also the one bound up with every other doctrine of the Word of God—so bound up that it cannot be neglected without disaster to the whole body of truth.

It is bound up with every fundamental doctrine.

It is bound up with the doctrine of the resurrection.

Victory over death, the change from corruption to incorruption, from mortality to immortality, the resurrection, transfiguration and translation of the church, are wholly and alone at the coming of Christ.

It is bound up with the doctrine of the divine sonship in believers, even as it is written:

"Beloved, now are we the sons of God, and it doth not yet appear what we shall be: but we know that, when he shall appear, we shall be like him; for we shall see him as he is."—I John 3:2.

It is bound up with the doctrine of the deliverance of creation from the bondage of corruption.

If you will put your ear to the breast of old Mother Earth, you will hear her travail, groans and cries as she seeks to bring forth a world into the light of peace, beyond the agony of human suffering and the stain of sin. If you listen, throughout her borders, in all the operation of her laws, you will hear the protest against that condition of existence where birth is followed by death, where hope is chased by despair, where defeat, night and silence end the scene. The apostle represents this groaning and protesting creation like one on the "tip-toe of expectation," craning the neck and looking forward to that hour when she shall be delivered from her bondage and be manifested into the "glorious liberty of the sons of God" at the coming of our Lord Jesus Christ.

It is bound up with the doctrine of the deliverance of God and Christ over Satan.

Jesus Christ died that He might destroy "him that had the power of death, that is, the devil." But this consummation devoutly to be wished for cannot take place till the door in Heaven opens and the Lord Christ, with His ascended church, shall come forth like an army with banners to lay hold on that old serpent, which is the Devil and Satan, and bind him for a thousand years.

It is bound up with the doctrine of the recognition of the dead, as it is written: "Then," in the day of the Lord's coming, "we shall know even as we are known." Wherefore the apostle writes to the Thessalonians that they will be his crown and rejoicing, whether by resurrection or translation, in the presence of our Lord Jesus Christ at His coming.

III. CHRIST'S SECOND COMING CONNECTED WITH EVERY EXHORTATION TO CHRISTIAN LIVING

It is bound up with every exhortation to Christian living.

When he exhorts to faithfulness in the breaking of bread, he does so by saying unto them: "Ye do show the Lord's death till he come," thus making manifest that this ordinance is to be observed in the light of the Lord's coming and that each time we gather at the table, whether we know it or not, we are proclaiming that the second coming of Christ is the *terminus ad quem* of Christian pilgrimage.

When the apostle exhorts to Christian liberality, he does so by the coming of the Lord.

When he inspires to holy living, he says, "I pray God your whole spirit and soul and body be preserved blameless unto the coming of our Lord Jesus Christ."

When he comforts those who mourn above their Christian dead, he does so by the fact of the second coming, telling them,

"The Lord himself shall descend from heaven with a shout, with the voice of the archangel, and with the trump of God: and the dead in Christ shall rise first: Then we which are alive and remain shall be caught up together with them in the clouds, to meet the Lord in the air."

And then speaking by inspiration he adds, "Wherefore COMFORT one another with these words"—that is to say, the blessed words that the Lord is coming to bring the dead and the living saints together in His presence.

Does the apostle see that "perilous times" are at hand in which there shall be a form of godliness but denying the power thereof, an hour coming when the church will no longer endure sound doctrine but heaping to themselves teachers who shall tickle their ears, be turned away from the truth and unto fables? And when he desires to exhort the Christian minister to be faithful among the faithless found, he does so by the coming of Christ, saying:

"I charge thee therefore before God, and the Lord Jesus Christ, who shall judge the quick and the dead and by [such is the true rendering] *HIS APPEARING and his kingdom; PREACH THE WORD."*

Does he see the time approaching when there shall be a great apostasy, a great falling away, and Antichrist seated in the Temple of God showing himself that he is God? And when he would comfort the minds of the followers of the truth as against the lie, he does so by declaring that the Lord is coming in His might and power to destroy with the breath of His lips this last masterpiece of Satan.

Does the Apostle James see that in the closing hours of this dispensation, capital and labor shall look at each other with scowling faces and clenched hands?

Does he see that rich men shall heap up treasures for the last days, that there will be an immense accumulation of wealth in the hands of the few, and that the rust of unused money shall eat like a gangrene in the hands of those who hold it?

Does he see that the lawful wage of the laborer by unjust combination is kept back from him, and does he hear the voice of that injustice crying in the ears of the Lord of Sabaoth?

Does he see that impatience at this injustice is unnerving the hearts of those who confess the name of Christ, and that the temptation to take justice in their own hands is gaining ground?

And when he would counsel them not to be guilty of such treason against the profession they have made as the followers of a rejected Christ, he does so by saying unto them: "Be patient, therefore, brethren, unto the coming of the Lord." Again: "The coming of the Lord draweth nigh." And this climax: "Behold, the judge standeth before the door."

When he would exhort the Christian pastors to faithfulness in that most solemn and arduous of tasks—the shepherding of the flock—the Apostle Peter does so by announcing to them that when Christ "the chief Shepherd shall appear, ye shall receive a crown of glory that fadeth not away."

When the Apostle Jude exhorts to stand by the faith once delivered to the saints, he does so by quoting the testimony of Enoch, the seventh from Adam, that the Lord with ten thousands of His saints is coming.

If the prophets of the Old Testament announce in joyful accents that there shall be a time when the knowledge of the Lord will cover the earth as the waters cover the face of the deep, they do so by declaring in unbroken symmetry of speech that this era of righteousness and splendor will be introduced by the coming of the Holy One of Israel, even the Lord Jesus Christ.

Does the Lord Jesus Christ Himself foretell the end of this age as a terrific crisis in the world's history?

Does He announce with all the ex-cathedra authority of headquarter's truth, with all the incontrovertible authority of Him who is the truth and no lie that the end of this age will be in wars, in the multiplication of lawlessness, the mob element rising and falling in its emotions with cries like the roaring of the seas, and men's hearts failing them with fear for looking after the things that are coming on the earth?

Does He raise the question whether *faith,* the faith, shall abide to the end?

And when He would give comfort in the darkness which His words seem to inspire, He does so by assuring us that in the deepest hour of the earth's spiritual midnight, He will Himself come as the Light of the world, that Light without which the earth must abide in its darkness forever.

In short, the coming of Christ, considered as a testimony, is so bound up with the varied doctrines of the Word of God that it is impossible to neglect it without producing a fatal lack of emphasis in any doctrine preached.

Let the preacher lose sight of the fact that Christ is coming back to this world as a glorified Man, the Man who was raised from the dead in the body in which He died, and it will not be long before he will lose sight of the veritable resurrection of Christ; and losing sight of that immortal body on the throne, the transition to the moment when the incarnation is to be seen only as an incident and not as the perpetual incorporation of the eternal God, will not be long deferred. Nor will it be long before such a preacher will find himself upon the threshold of that unecclesiastical but all-pervading unitarianism which finds no need either of incarnation or resurrection.

So bound up with the body of truth is this testimony of the second coming that there are doctrines which cannot be fully presented without holding them up in the light of it.

This is illustrated in the doctrine of atonement and may be demonstrated by looking at the type in the wilderness.

On the great day of atonement, after he had offered the sacrifice on the altar, the high priest went within the veil into the most holy place to make atonement (and let it be remembered that the atonement was not made on the altar but within the veil as the type of Heaven and that, in fulfillment of that type, the Lord Jesus Christ did not make atonement on the cross but in Heaven after His resurrection). The high priest, let it be repeated, went within the veil to make atonement; and not till he came out the second time and not till the man who had led away the live goat came back in the sight of all the people without that sin offering, could it be said that the atonement was complete and justified to the expectation of the people.

Now says the apostle referring to this event, as only a shadow, and bringing into the mind of his hearers the substance, "So Christ was once offered to bear the sins of many; and unto them that look for him shall he appear the second time without sin [offering] unto salvation." Thus this whole dispensation is ante-typically the day of atonement, and its last emphasis will be the coming of Christ.

You might just as well take the auricle and ventricle out of the heart and expect that it would not affect the circulation of the blood, as to imagine for a moment that the doctrine of the second coming can be neglected without affecting and deranging the whole body of truth.

In the face of such testimony and demonstration, to neglect the preaching of the second coming seems well nigh criminal. And he who willfully does it with the light of an open Bible before him is arranging for himself at the judgment seat of Christ a moment of shame and sorrow, the shame and sorrow of a workman who has not studied to show himself approved unto God and who, in the hour of his chosen responsibility, failed to rightly divide His Word.

IV. CHRIST TO COME ONE DEFINITE SECOND TIME

From the scriptural point of view, the coming of Christ is a second coming.

It has been presented in such fashion that it might well be described as a many-times coming.

It is said that Christ came at the destruction of Jerusalem under the Romans; that He comes in pestilence and plague, whenever the clouds gather, the winds sweep or the tidal waves rush upon the shore as they did at Galveston; that He comes each time a godly man dies or a saintly woman goes home to God. And in all reverence, it may be said that only God Himself knows or can keep account of the different ways and times in which the Lord is to come as taught by those who have neglected the scriptural declaration, "He shall appear the second time."

The statement that the destruction of Jerusalem was the coming of Christ is one of those statements which has been repeated so often that it has all the sacredness of Holy Writ to a certain class of minds.

The statement, however, is so entirely and excuselessly absurd that it seems scarcely worth the while even to reply to its repetition.

The simple facts concerning the destruction of Jerusalem and its relation to the coming of Christ are these: In the 21st of Luke, our Lord says three things: (1) Jerusalem will be beseiged and taken; (2) Jerusalem will be trodden down by the Gentiles; (3) When the treading down by the Gentiles is fulfilled, "Then shall they see the Son of man coming." The order given by the Lord therefore is: (1) Jerusalem taken; (2) Jerusalem trodden down; (3) The appearing of Christ.

Thus a **whole period,** called the **treading down of the Gentiles,** occurs between the destruction of Jerusalem and the appearing of Christ a second time.

In the 24th of Matthew, the Lord declares that there shall be a Tribulation coming upon Jerusalem and Judaea such as the world has never known nor shall ever know again. This terrific Tribulation He declares will be followed immediately **by His appearing in glory,** as it is written:

"Immediately after the tribulation of those days shall the sun be darkened, and the moon shall not give her light, and the stars shall fall from heaven, and the powers of the heavens shall be shaken; And then shall appear the sign of the Son of man in heaven: and then shall all the tribes of the earth [of Judaea, according to the context—vs. 16: *Then let them which be in Judaea flee into the mountains*] *mourn, and they shall SEE the Son of man coming in the clouds of heaven with power and great glory."*

No such event took place immediately after the destruction of Jerusalem by Titus. It never has taken place. Therefore the Tribulation cannot refer to any destruction of Jerusalem in the past; it is a Tribulation in connection with Jerusalem in the future. And as the appearing of Christ is to take place immediately after the Tribulation, then the second appearing of Christ is still future. Whatever else may be involved in the Tribulation, it does not, cannot teach that the destruction of Jerusalem centuries ago was the coming of Christ. To assume that the agony of Jerusalem in that great siege and the providential visitation of judgment on the guilty people are equivalent to the appearing of Christ; or, to assume that Christ came at all, even invisibly, are gratuitous suggestions and not exposition.

To say that He who is health and strength, and who is promised to us in the glory of the Father comes in the bubonic plague, in pestilence and famine, are contradictions of terms.

To say that the wild lawless storm is the coming of Christ is to contradict the scene yonder in Galilee, when, arising from the pillow in the hinder part of the ship where He had been asleep, He looked out upon the black, raging tempest and said, "Peace, be still." And thus became the end instead of beginning of the storm.

But of all mistaken expositions is that which seeks to make death figure forth as the second coming of Christ. If it were not so grave a violation of the Word of God and every legitimate principle of exegesis, it might well provoke the keenest and most merciless satire.

But to the Word and the Testimony, what saith it? The answer is that so far from Christ coming to the believer at death, the believer at death GOES TO BE WITH CHRIST, even as it is written: "Having a desire to depart, and be with Christ."

Yonder we have a scenic demonstration of it. Stephen has been condemned to death by the Jewish Sanhedrin. In the Council he looks up and sees the heavens open and Jesus standing at the right hand of God. He sees Him standing there just as one might stand at the threshold of his home, if he desired to act the part of a cultured host in receiving his invited guests.

Thus Jesus, seeing the tragedy approaching and the hour of the martyr's death and departure for Heaven at hand, rises up in all the courtly love of the perfect host to receive His invited guest.

Now they have their victim down upon his knees outside the gate, the stones raining upon him, marring his face as his Master's face was marred. And knowing the end is near, Stephen lifts up his voice beseechingly—for what? That the Lord may come to him? Nay, he lifts up his voice and says: "Lord Jesus, RECEIVE my spirit."

Thus at death Stephen departs to be with his Lord. Wherefore speaking by inspiration, the apostle declares that at death we are "absent from the body and present with the Lord."

But yonder on the shore of the lake after His resurrection, the Lord Himself brings the truth to view in open demonstration. He had just told Peter how he might die; and Peter, filled with that unconquerable spirit of the unfitness of things which had so often betrayed him, turned to the Lord and demanded of Him what John should do. The Lord rebuked him, declaring that it was a matter that did not concern him, saying, "If I will that he tarry till I come, what is that to thee? Follow thou me." And we are told significantly, "Then went this saying abroad among the brethren that that disciple SHOULD NOT DIE."

Now if the coming of Christ meant death, then the disciples ought to have said, "This man will surely die, seeing that the Lord comes at death and has fixed the term of this man's service till He come." But just because they knew that the Lord was life, and therefore the enemy of death, they said, **"Since John is to wait till the Lord comes back, he will never die."**

It is true that the Lord had not said that John should positively wait until His return. It is true He had only raised the question and drawn Peter's attention to the fact that this issue of waiting was a matter entirely dependent on His will and that this was a domain into which Peter had no right to intrude. Yet, nevertheless, the possibility that John might remain till the second coming was *prima facie* evidence to the disciples that John would not die. No more living demonstration could be given of the utter fallacy of the doctrine that the coming of the Lord of life means death.

All this is in evidence that the coming of Christ is not the thousand and one things applied to it as such; but that it is indeed, and in very truth, what the apostle declares it to be—"a second appearing."

According to Scripture the coming of Christ is a personal coming. It is written: "The Lord HIMSELF shall descend from heaven."

Concerning this selfhood, we are in no doubt. No sooner had He ascended into Heaven than the angels descended to comfort the hearts of the sorrowing disciples with the sublime assurance: "Ye men of Galilee, why stand ye gazing up into heaven? this SAME Jesus . . . shall so come in like manner. . . ."

The same Jesus, He who walked by blue Galilee, who sat on the well-curb of Sychar with the shadows of noon under His feet, the dust of earth on His garments, the love of God in His heart, the grace of salvation on His lips and the touch of healing in His hands!

He is coming with the stigmata of the cross, so coming that every eye may see Him, and all they who pierced Him; coming so that repentant Israel may ask, "Whence are these wounds in thy hands?" and hear Him answer that these are the wounds which He received in the house of His friends; coming so that we may look at Him not only as He is, but as He was, looking upon Him with our eyes, hearing Him with our ears, handling Him with our hands; coming in the body which His mother Mary gave Him, the dust of earth crystallized with immortality.

V. CHRIST'S SECOND COMING IS IMMINENT

The doctrine of Scripture is that the second personal coming of Christ is imminent.

The apostles believed that the Lord might come in their day. They believed He might come at any moment, that at any turn of the road He might lay His hand upon them and with the sound of the trumpet shout them up into Glory.

So far from telling Christians to prepare for death and Heaven, the apostles exhorted them to be on the constant guard for the Lord's return, assuring them that "we shall not all sleep" [that is to say, die] and that there would be thus a possibility of belonging to that generation to whom the coming of the Lord could not mean death. They took up the exhortation of the Lord Himself, "What I say unto you, I say unto all, Watch."

As already shown, they based their exhortations to every precept of Christian living on the imminency of this coming and couched these exhortations in such precision of language that there is no other alternative if this coming is not imminent, but that these apostles were either deceived or ignorant men or wholly a set of shameless deceivers.

Either dilemma, whether of ignorance or willful deception, is destructive to New Testament authority, vitiates every other doctrine and rings the knell of their inspiration.

Assuming, however, that the New Testament is the inspired Word of God, it follows inevitably that there is no warrant for the interposition of times and seasons between us and the coming of our Lord. Certainly there is no warrant for that colossal heresy, that invented theory of a thousand years of gospel triumph, no warrant for that rhetorical sophistry that we are to have the "purple and gold of millennial glory" before He comes.

Those who have the courage to proclaim the postmillennial coming of the Son of God are forced to do so with the assumption that they possess a knowledge as to the date of that supreme event not only greater than that of any other set of men, greater even than that of the angels of God, but greater than that of the Son of God Himself. For He who is supposed to be the final authority in the matter has said, "Of that day and that hour knoweth no man, no, not the angels which are in heaven, *neither the Son.*"

There is no doubt that in the present state of the church, it would be easy in any address to start the issue and the controversy as to the inspiration and infallibility of the Bible.

There is a school of preaching which teaches that the Bible is true only in spots and that those who would read it must do so by a hop, skip and jump method, hopping clear over to the other side of the Hexateuch, skipping Joshua and the Judges, skipping the Synoptics, jumping over a large part of the Johannic Gospel, quietly but skillfully leaping over the book of Acts as a gymnast will leap over a patchwork quilt spread beneath him, and at the book of Revelation not jumping at all, considering that book no more worthy of attention than a wild man's ravings.

No doubt battles can be fought over the question as to whether the Bible is true or false. But there is one fact about which no intelligent, well-read man has any right to have a single second's issue, and that is: The New Testament does say in language which it is impossible to mistake, that the coming of Christ is imminent, that it may take place at any moment.

He, therefore, who places ten days or a thousand years between us and the coming of the Lord contradicts Him, falsifies Him, charges Him with fallibility within the sound of His own words: "Watch, therefore; for ye know *neither the day nor the hour* wherein the Son of man cometh."

The coming of Christ is the one event which in Scripture is always on the horizon and, like the sunlight, illuminates all the theologic landscape with its glow and color. So emphasized is this imminency that he who should read the New Testament for the first time would close the book with the involuntary impression that the next thing was the coming of Christ.

VI. ONE EVENT WITH TWO STAGES

The coming of Christ, while one grand event, has two distinct stages or parts—a secret and an open or public part.

In the first, He comes into the air; in the second, to the Mount of Olives. In the first, He comes to the church; in the second, to Israel.

In the first, He comes for His church; in the second, with His church. In the first, He comes to a marriage; in the second, to a judgment. In the first, as a Bridegroom; in the second, as the King. In the first, to gather the church and present it to Himself, a holy and acceptable church; in the second, to establish His kingdom and with the church in righteousness rule the earth.

The first part is symbolized by the morning star; the second, by the rising of the sun. The first, by a thief who comes in the night without warning; the second, by the lightning that flashes across the sky with accompanying thunder. In the first part, the church will be caught away into the air secretly as Enoch was caught away before the Flood; as Lot was snatched out of Sodom before the fire; as Elijah was swept up to Glory without dying; as Paul was caught up to the third Heaven alive; and as the Son of God Himself passed upward into and through the heavens to the throne of God without the knowledge of the world.

This first part in the Greek is called *parousia,* and means His bodily presence; the second in the same language is called the *epiphaniea,* and means the manifestation of His bodily presence. The first is called "Our gathering together unto him"; the second, "Our appearing with him in glory," or the glorious appearing. The first is commonly spoken of in Scripture as the "coming of the Lord"; the second is known as "The Day of the Lord."

Between these two parts of the second advent, there are at least seven prophetic years; and these seven years form the burden of the book of Daniel and the book of Revelation.

Between us and the secret coming of the Lord, the *parousia,* there is not a single predicted event. Between us and the second part of this second coming there are many predicted events: the universal European war, the restoration of Israel to their own land, the rise of Antichrist and the final union of all the eastern nations under Russia as the Gog and Magog of Ezekiel.

The attitude of the church is locally and practically in relation to the first or secret part of our Lord's coming, while the attitude of Israel is, and must always be, towards the open or glorious coming. Israel's attitude is that of waiting for a sign; the church's attitude is that of waiting for a sound. Just as Israel of old was waiting on the hither side of Jordan for the sound of a trump that they might go over and possess the land—so the church is waiting on the hither side of time for the sound of the trump of God that she may go over and possess in the glory of her promised immortality all the land that lieth beyond the shadow of death.

VII. CHRIST'S COMING OUR "BLESSED HOPE"

The coming of Christ is held out as the blessed hope of the church. Nowhere are Christians exhorted to prepare for death or hope for Heaven, but always, without a single break in the utterance, to watch, to wait, to hope for the coming of the Lord.

And well may the church so watch and wait and hope. That coming means the end of her long and weary pilgrimage.

It means the putting off the garments of the traveler and putting on the garments of home.

It means the triumph over sin, sickness, sorrow and death.

It means no longer the world's suppliant, but its ruler.

It means the presence of the King, the possession of His likeness, the share of His throne and the administration of His kingdom.

It means everything for which the church has hoped and prayed, all for which she has striven and endured.

It means the girding her with final power for the accomplishment of all the purpose for which God determined her from the unbeginning depths of eternity.

It means the accomplishment in certitude of that which is now sought with hesitation and uncertain success—the bringing of the whole world at last to the feet of the Crucified, where with unspeakable joy she may hear every tongue confess that Jesus Christ is Lord to the glory of God the Father.

It means the reaching of that moment when there will be no longer the need of intercession for erring saints, seeing that each saint shall be shining in all the glory of the Intercessor.

It means no longer the need of the written Word nor of teachers, seeing that "all shall know the Lord from the least to the greatest." As He says, "I will put my laws into their mind, and write them in their hearts," and shall Himself, *as the source of the written Word,* be the living, present and infallible revelation of God's mind to men.

Oh, this coming of Christ and the translation of the church mean the fulfillment as human minds have little dreamed of that immense promise that "the knowledge of the Lord shall cover the earth as the waters . . . the face of the deep."

Small wonder is it that the coming of Christ is called the blessed hope to the church when it means her exaltation, the triumph of her Lord and the salvation of the whole world. But wonder beyond measure it is that in the face of the fact that the beginning of these "days of Heaven on earth" is imminent in the imminent coming of our Lord and in the face of the fact that all Scripture proclaims it, that the church in any part of it, whether in pulpit or in pew, should turn her back upon it; or that any of her accredited ministers should neglect the story of it, seek to hide the beauty of its shining or rob the sorrowing of the blessedness of its comfort.

VIII. CHRIST'S COMING THE ONLY HOPE FOR ISRAEL

The coming of Christ, and in its last analysis, the appearing of Christ in glory, is the only hope for Israel. And this is concretely illustrated in the story of Paul's conversion. He was never converted by the preaching of the Gospel but by the appearing of Christ in glory above the Damascus gates.

He tells us that he is as one born out of due time and therefore set ahead of the time that he might be a prophecy and pledge of the way and manner in which his own nation should afterwards be saved.

Only when Israel shall see their Messiah coming in glory will they believe on Him. Then shall they be in mourning for Him as one mourneth for the dead. Then shall they take up the 53rd chapter of Isaiah and chant with lamentation and mingled hope before Him:

"We did esteem him stricken, smitten of God, and afflicted. But he was wounded for our transgressions, he was bruised for our iniquities: the chastisement of our peace was upon him; and with his stripes we are healed."—Vss. 4, 5.

Then shall a fountain be opened for uncleanness and sin in the city of David, and so "all Israel shall be saved" in fulfillment of that promise, 'The Deliverer shall come unto Zion and turn away ungodliness from Jacob.'

Only when Messiah the Lord shall come in glory can Israel become the 'head and no longer the tail of nations.' Only when Christ the Lord comes to take the throne of His father David will Israel and Judah fully enter into and possess the covenant land.

The coming of Christ, then, is that one event which holds out hope for this people "scattered and peeled."

IX. THE ONLY HOPE FOR GOOD WORLD GOVERNMENT

The coming of Christ taken in its completed sense is the only hope of the world governmentally.

Over all the vain endeavors at self-government, over all the uprise of human plans in governmental schemes, over monarchy and mob, may be heard the voice of God, saying, "I will overturn it, I will overturn it till he comes whose right it is to reign; and I will give it him." Only when the Lord's judgments are in the earth, so it is written, "will the people learn righteousness." Only when government is administered in the hands of a righteous man—God's Man, the Second and Eternal Man—will men beat their swords into plowshares and their spears into pruninghooks.

In short, only by the coming of Christ will the failure of the first man be undone, the subtlety of Satan be matched, sin be uprooted, death be abolished, redemption be completed, paradise be regained and the whole earth be filled with the glory of God.

X. BIBLE PREACHERS OUGHT TO PREACH CHRIST'S SECOND COMING

Such is this doctrine which in many quarters of the church has practically fallen out of the scheme of preaching.

All the more, then, because of the neglect of it, it ought to be preached. This is indeed apostolic principle. Just as soon as the apostle warns Timothy, the young preacher, that the time is coming when the church will no longer endure sound doctrine, he urges him by all means to preach it "in season and out of season."

This doctrine of the second coming, therefore, ought to be preached, insistently and fully preached.

It ought to be preached in order that the church might not get a false concept of her relation to the world in this age and that she might not continue to think that her only way to Heaven and Glory was through the darkness and gloom of the grave. It ought to be preached in order that she might always be on the alert to proclaim the Gospel committed to her charge, lest coming suddenly the Lord should find her asleep on the bosom of a dead world.

It ought to be preached in order that the elect remnant in Israel might, as in the days of Pentecost, believe and become a part of the church, thus attaining, even, unto more than natural blessing.

It ought to be preached that the men of the world might see that there is something more imminent than death and that at any moment the Master might rise up and shut to the door of grace.

It ought to be preached by the preacher for his own benefit, in order that he might see the stately march of all the doctrines of the Word of God as they move forward in serried rank and cast their trophies at the feet of the coming King, saluting Him as the inspiration and objective of them all.

The doctrine cannot be preached too much.

No more gratuitous libel was ever circulated than the assertion that the preaching of it has in it a tendency to lead the preacher to ride it as a hobby. Let any man try to ride it as a hobby and he will find instead that he is riding in the chariot car of God's glory and that every spoke in every wheel is flashing forth every other doctrine, testifying that every doctrine consummates itself in this doctrine of doctrines; and that this identical doctrine is being born swiftly and triumphantly forward because it rests on the revolution of all other doctrines.

No man can faithfully preach the second coming and neglect any doctrine of the Word. No man who believes in the imminent coming of the Lord and knows how to preach it will ever be guilty of denying the inspiration of that Word, the resurrection of the body or the glory and necessity of atonement. If any of the fundamental doctrines are neglected, as it is charged in "modern preaching," the neglect will not be found crouching at the door of him who preaches the coming of his Lord.

Nay, let anyone take up this doctrine and preach it.

It will make the risen and ascended Lord the most real thing in all the universe of God to him.

It will keep the door in Heaven open and let the light from the land of the living fall across the land of the dying.

It will keep the ear open and alert to hear the sound of His voice.

It will sweep through the soul like a purifying breath from the lips of the King, leading that soul to purify itself, as it is written, "He that hath this hope in him purifieth himself, even as he is pure."

It will make the written Word to shine as a burnished mirror, reflecting the glory of God.

It will gird him who believes and preaches it, in the face of any pain or disaster, with all the strength of one who sore beleaguered hears the sound of delivering footsteps or as of one who in the dark and black night feels the gleam of coming day upon his brow.

If today Jesus Christ is the supreme actuality of my life; if today this written Word is to me the symphony of Heaven and of earth; if today my faith is stronger and my hope brighter; if today in face of the world's deepening pessimism, its weakness, weariness and woe, I find myself filled with an unconquerable optimism, with an unhesitating faith in God's ultimate and infinite triumph, it is because I believe that at any moment I may hear a voice like the voice of a trumpet talking with me and saying, "Come up hither"; and that in an instant, in the twinkling of an eye, I may be in His presence, not to lay the armor down and be at rest, but to come forth clad in the Master's likeness and with Him descend as He goes forth to take His own world again, taking it as He will, by creation's undisputed right, by blood redemption and kingly conquest.

* * * * *

Let no man fear that in preaching the second coming he is committed to the minimizing of the cross. Nay, rather, let us hold up the cross till men shall see it as the very heartthrob of God, the mighty manifestation of His measureless love.

Let us hold it up till it shall be seen that all the claims of divine righteousness have been fully and finally met there.

Let us hold it up till men shall see that it is no longer the sin question but the Son question.

Let us hold it up till men shall see the crown of thorns stabbing His brow and marring His face as no face of man was ever marred. But let us hold it up so that men may see that this marred and crucified One is also the risen and glorified One. Yea, let us so hold it up that men may see that this risen and glorified One, this "Man in Glory," is coming back in the body in which He was crucified, "This same Jesus," yea and amen.

Let us hold it up for every eye like that of the serpent-bitten Israelite to see.

But let us hold it up in the light of that second coming, till as men cast their gaze upon it they shall behold the crown of thorns slowly but surely transforming into the crown of glory on the radiant head of your coming King and mine.

SAM MORRIS
1900-1988

ABOUT THE MAN:

Sam Morris was for many, many years best known as "J. Barleycorn's No. 1 Enemy." He was proclaimed by the liquor industry as "the most valuable man to have entered the service of the drys in several generations." For years he successfully fought liquor on the strongest stations in America and Mexico on his "Voice of Temperance" radio broadcast.

"HOWDY, NEIGHBOR!" Morris' listeners packed out great halls to hear his friendly greeting. One well-known writer described the mighty response that followed it: "I have been watching crowds closely all my life, but I never saw anything like this before. I have seen admiration, respect and veneration in the faces of people as they listened to Bryan or Billy Sunday. These people, packed tightly together in great auditoriums, had all that—but much more. It was massed, concerted, personal friendship and love. . . ."

Dr. Morris was not only a great temperance speaker; he was also a successful pastor in Weatherford and Stamford, Texas, before being offered time for his temperance talks on the world's most powerful radio station XERA, located across the border in old Mexico.

Dr. Morris also conducted great revival campaigns in some of America's largest churches.

No one can estimate the influence Morris had on the lives of individuals.

His 16 publications were very popular, among them: *Blessed Assurance, Mother's Bible, Voice of Temperance Scrapbooks, The Booze Buster,* and *Rats in the Brewery Vats.*

He taught Bible in Hardin-Simmons University; got his M.A. degree from Brown University in Providence, Rhode Island.

II.

Preparing for His Return

SAM MORRIS

**The Promise of His Coming
The Pollution of the World at the Time of His Coming
The Peril That We Face in the Light of His Coming
The Parting That Will Take Place When He Comes**

(Sermon preached in 1941 at Cedar Lake Conference Grounds, Cedar Lake, Indiana. Stenographically reported.)

I have made it a rule in my life to never hold a series of meetings without speaking on the second coming of Christ. The Bible does not tell us to be saved in order to be ready to die; it tells us to be ready for the return.

I invite your attention to the latter part of the 17th chapter of Luke:

"And he said unto the disciples, The days will come, when ye shall desire to see one of the days of the Son of man, and ye shall not see it. And they shall say to you, See here; or, see there; go not after them, nor follow them. For as the lightning, that lighteneth out of the one part under heaven, shineth unto the other part under heaven; so shall also the Son of man be in his day. But first must he suffer many things, and be rejected of this generation. And as it was in the days of Noe, so shall it be also in the days of the Son of man. They did eat, they drank, they married wives, they were given in marriage, until the day that Noe entered into the ark, and the flood came, and destroyed them all. Likewise also as it was in the days of Lot; they did eat, they drank, they bought, they sold, they planted, they builded; But the same day that Lot went out of Sodom it rained fire and brimstone from heaven, and destroyed them all."—Vss. 22-29.

I pause long enough to say I believe fire and brimstone fell out of

Heaven on Sodom and Gomorrah, set it afire and burned it up just like the Bible said it did. There is great blessing in that to us when we get to the book of Revelation.

Some people try to tell us that the book of Revelation is a lot of symbols and figures, that we cannot tell its meaning. On the other hand, some try to explain it away instead of accepting it. When Revelation speaks of fire and brimstone which will have such a terrible part in God's wrath upon the world, we have a historical incident in the Old Testament to demonstrate on a small scale what that is going to be on a large scale. When in this book we read that the final abode of the damned is a lake which burns with fire and brimstone which is the second death, that will be literal. It will be just as literal as the fire and brimstone which fell on Sodom and destroyed it.

"Even thus shall it be in the day when the Son of man is revealed. In that day, he which shall be upon the housetop, and his stuff in the house, let him not come down to take it away: and he that is in the field, let him likewise not return back. Remember Lot's wife. Whosoever shall seek to save his life shall lose it; and whosoever shall lose his life shall preserve it. I tell you, in that night there shall be two men in one bed; the one shall be taken, and the other shall be left. Two women shall be grinding together; the one shall be taken, and the other left. Two men shall be in the field; the one shall be taken, and the other left. And they answered and said unto him, Where, Lord? And he said unto them, Wheresoever the body is, thither will the eagles be gathered together."—Vss. 30-37.

There are four simple thoughts I give you about the second coming as revealed in this passage. First, The Promise of His Coming; second, The Pollution of the World at the Time of His Coming; third, The Peril That We Face in the Light of His Coming; fourth, The Parting That Will Take Place When He Comes. The promise, pollution, peril and parting.

The Promise of His Coming

A preacher stood in the town where I used to be pastor and arrogantly boasted that he never had preached on the second coming of Christ and never expected to.

That means that he had never spoken on the 14th chapter of John, that blessed promise, "Let not your heart be troubled: ye believe in God;

believe also in me. In my Father's house are many mansions: if it were not so, I would have told you. I go to prepare a place for you. And if I go and prepare a place for you, I will come again, and receive you unto myself; that where I am, there ye may be also."

That means he had never preached on Matthew, chapters 24 and 25.

That means he had never preached on the statement of those two celestial visitors at the time of Jesus' ascension, when the disciples, looking up into the clouds for a glimpse of the departing Lord, heard the angels say:

"Ye men of Galilee, why stand ye gazing up into heaven? this same Jesus [same eyes, same ears, same hands, same voice], *which is taken up from you into heaven, shall so come in like manner as ye have seen him go into heaven."*

That means he had never preached in all its fullness that great 15th chapter of the first book of Corinthians, that resurrection chapter where we have the statement, "Christ the firstfruits; afterward they that are Christ's at his coming."

That means, my friends, that he had never preached on the 4th chapter of I Thessalonians, where Paul comforted the Thessalonians with this wonderful statement:

"I would not have you to be ignorant, brethren, concerning them which are asleep, that ye sorrow not, even as others which have no hope. For if we believe that Jesus died and rose again, even so them also which sleep in Jesus will God bring with him. For this we say unto you by the word of the Lord, that we which are alive and remain unto the coming of the Lord shall not prevent them which are asleep. For the Lord himself [not a fire, not a flood, not death, not some calamity, not the Holy Ghost on the day of Pentecost—the Lord himself—] *shall descend from heaven with a shout, with the voice of the archangel, and with the trump of God: and the dead in Christ shall rise first: then we which are alive and remain shall be caught up together with them in the clouds, to meet the Lord in the air: and so shall we ever be with the Lord."*

That means he had never preached on the passage of Scripture in the book of Hebrews where they were admonished, "Not forsaking the assembling of ourselves together, as the manner of some is; but exhorting one another: and so much the more, as ye see the day approaching."

That means he had never preached on that blessed passage of Scripture in I Peter where he says,

"Blessed be the God and Father of our Lord Jesus Christ, which according to his abundant mercy hath begotten us again unto a lively hope by the resurrection of Jesus Christ from the dead, to an inheritance incorruptible, and undefiled, and that fadeth not away, reserved in heaven for you, who are kept by the power of God through faith unto salvation ready to be revealed in the last time."

That means he had never preached on that marvelous passage of Scripture in I John which says, "Beloved, now are we the sons of God, and it doth not yet appear what we shall be: but we know that, when he shall appear, we shall be like him; for we shall see him as he is."

That means he had never preached on II Thessalonians, because every chapter opens about His coming and closes about His coming.

It means he had never spoken on II Peter where it says, "For we have not followed cunningly devised fables, when we made known unto you the power and coming of our Lord Jesus Christ, but were eyewitnesses of his majesty."

That means he had never preached on the book of James where it said, "The judge standeth before the door," and, "The coming of the Lord draweth nigh."

That means he had never preached from the book of Jude, "Behold, the Lord cometh with ten thousands of his saints."

That means he had never preached on the first chapter of the book of Revelation where it says, "Behold, he cometh with clouds; and every eye shall see him, and they also which pierced him: and all kindreds of the earth shall wail because of him. Even so, Amen."

That means he had never preached on the last promise in the Bible. Do you know what it is? "He which testifieth these things saith, Surely I come quickly."

That means he had never preached on the last prayer in the Bible. Do you know what it is? "Amen. Even so, come, Lord Jesus."

When Paul wanted to urge a young preacher to be true to God, he said, "I charge thee before God, and the Lord Jesus Christ, who shall judge the quick and the dead at his appearing and his kingdom; Preach the word"—linking it up with the second coming.

That means he had never preached on the marvelous passage of Scripture over in Titus, "The grace of God that bringeth salvation hath appeared to all men, Teaching us that, denying ungodliness and worldly lusts, we should live soberly, righteously, and godly, in this present world; Looking for that blessed hope, and the glorious appearing of the great God and our Saviour Jesus Christ."

My, my, my! How much of the Bible he had left out of his ministry! I had known him as a minister for fourteen years when he made that statement. Brother, the Bible tells us all through the New Testament that Jesus Christ is coming again.

Why, that means that preacher never had preached on Genesis 3:15, "I will put enmity between thy seed and her seed; it shall bruise thy head, and thou shalt bruise his heel," because the serpent bruised Christ on the cross; Christ did not bruise the serpent. Doesn't Isaiah tell us, "He was wounded for our transgressions, he was bruised for our iniquities: the chastisement of our peace was upon him"? Doesn't Paul say, "The God of peace shall bruise Satan under your feet shortly"? Christ has not triumphed over Satan in that fullness of bruising yet, but it will happen at the second coming.

That means he had never preached on the threefold character of Christ's works as Prophet, Priest and King. He came and was a Prophet among us; He is now our High Priest in Heaven; He is coming back to be our King and reign upon this earth.

That is the promise of His coming. How precious it is! It makes us want to live clean after John has said,

"Behold, what manner of love the Father hath bestowed upon us, that we should be called the sons of God. . . it doth not yet appear what we shall be: but we know that, when he shall appear, we shall be like him; for we shall see him as he is. Every man that hath this hope in him purifieth himself, even as he is pure."

And here in this passage in Luke, Jesus said to His disciples that, as the lightning flashes from one part of the sky to another, one day the Son of Man is going to flash upon this darkened world. And if His second coming is not visible, not audible, not tangible, the second coming would not fulfill the Scripture, would not justify the faith of the saints and would not produce the results the Bible promises to be produced in this world. Just as literal as He was when He walked along the dusty road of Palestine, just as literal will He someday come back for us to see Him and look at Him. Now that is the promise of His coming.

The Pollution of the World at the Time of His Coming

Another question comes up. What kind of a condition is the world going to be in when He comes? And here is where there are a lot of divisions of opinion. I take the position that the world will be just about as rotten as it is possible for it to be.

Some of my preacher brethren rather amuse me. They preach over the radio and in the pulpit, "Jesus is soon coming. All signs point to His coming. Let's pray for a great revival just before Jesus Christ comes."

As I see it, the Bible does not teach there is going to be a great revival just in front of the Lord's return. Rather, it will be exactly the opposite.

Jesus, wanting to set before His disciples the condition of the world at the time of His second coming, reached back across the pages of history, picked out the story of the Flood and declared, "As it was in the days of Noe, so shall it be also in the days of the Son of man." Noah did not live in the time of a great revival. He preached one hundred and twenty years and never saw a soul saved, as far as we know. Noah did not live in the time of a great spiritual awakening. It was exactly the opposite. He lived in a world filled with lust, in a world dominated by violence, in a world which had gone astray after the things of the flesh and satanic leadership; and Jesus said, "Do you want to know how it is going to be when I come back? I will give you a picture"—and He flashes on the screen the story of Noah. Then thinking somebody might say, "That is just one picture; I know something is wrong about that," He said, "I will show you another picture"—and He reaches back over and gets the book of Genesis and flashes on the screen a backslidden, worldly Lot, living in a worldly Sodom.

Lot had traveled with Uncle Abraham; and when the hour of parting came, was given a choice where he would dwell. Lot beheld all the plain of Jordan, that it was well watered everywhere, so he pitched his tent toward Sodom, then dwelt in Sodom. Later when Abraham was told an angelic messenger was going to destroy the city of the plains, including Sodom, he began to think of his nephew. So he said, "O Lord, You won't destroy it if You find fifty righteous, will You?" The Lord said, "No." "Well, forty?" "No." "Well, thirty?" "No." "Twenty?" "No." "Will You destroy it if You find ten righteous?" The Lord answered, "Not if there are even ten righteous in the city."

But ten righteous people could not be found in Sodom. There was Lot, Mrs. Lot, the two single daughters that we know of and the two married daughters—six in all.

Abraham had Lot in mind when he was praying; he was just leading down to him and his family. "O Lord, here is my nephew. He knew me, knew how I knelt around the old family altar, knew how I lived." But you will find that Lot was backslidden, even willing to stoop to unlawful deeds with his single daughters. Then when he went out into the city and knocked on the door to wake up the married daughters to warn them, "Hurry! Get out!" he was to his sons-in-law as one that mocked. Then they left Sodom; and as they walked off down the trail, his wife looked back and turned into a pillar of salt.

Yonder in the cave the two single daughters, the only surviving members of the family, made their father drunk and lay down in adultery with him.

It is a backslidden picture which we see—a backslidden man and a backslidden city, a city of lust, violence, greed and business. The inhabitants married, gave in marriage, they bought and sold; but they did not have time for God.

That is not a picture of a spiritual revival, of a great spiritual awakening. It is not a picture of a world of goodness but a world of vileness. And Jesus said that this would be the condition of the world at the time of His return.

I do not know how the present age could be any nearer like that age than it is. Divorces abound, marriage vows are but slips of paper, meaning nothing. The popular hero on the screen is the man who has the largest number of supposed-to-be wives but who still runs around and off with other women. Yet church people relish such trash and let their children wallow in such mire. I hope God will wake you up. The damnable pictures and television are doing more to rob supposed-to-be Christians of their faith and consecration than any other thing I know of.

"Oh, but Brother Sam, there are some good pictures." I heard a story one time. A fellow working on the sewer pipe had his lunch in his coat pocket. He dropped his coat into the sewer. He dug out a great big hole in the sewer pipe, and there was a great piling up of stuff. He got a pole and was stirring around in it. One fellow said, "You don't want your coat now, do you?" And the man replied, "My lunch—I want my lunch out of the pocket."

God have mercy on men and women who are willing to stir around in all the rotten filth for a little trifling of a picture the Devil has put in as bait to catch you with.

Beloved, I ask you this question: How many would like to be found in a movie picture theater when Jesus comes? Not a man or woman in this building would. Let's love our Lord. Let's work for Christ in a wicked world. Let's say to the world, "We want none of your filth." The appeal of the industry is to the flesh, not to the brain. You can sit through picture after picture and never have a mental function. It is geared to lust.

Pick up a daily newspaper. What do you see spread out all over the front page? Lust, crime, murder, divorce. Why does the newspaper publish that kind of stuff on the front page? It is what the public wants. They are not out to reform anybody, not out to preach any sermons. They are out to sell newspapers; and whatever it takes to sell them, that is what they publish.

If a president of a college dies, a holy man who has lived for God, they may publish the day he died, the day he was buried, how many survivors. But let a Raymond Hamilton or John Dillinger be shot, and the newspaper will play that up with pictures and a front-page headline. Why? The public wants it. The newspaper and the TV and the movie picture industry bow to the wants and wishes of the American people, and these are making America rotten at the core.

This is the condition we will find when Christ comes. Not a revival, not a spiritual awakening, not a longing for God, but the exact opposite. When the antediluvian world turned against God, then He said, "I am going to destroy it." Sodom, with its lust, sensuality, sins, and even old Lot and family were so backslidden—not a picture of a revival in it. That is the way it is going to be when Jesus comes.

Someone says, "I would like to be a Christian, but there is so much hypocrisy in the churches," or, "It is so hard to live right in these days." It is easier tonight than it will be tomorrow night. It is easier this week than it will be next week. It is easier this year than it will be next year. If that is pulling you back, you had better fall on the overtures of the mercy of God and get right. It will get harder as you travel on.

The Peril That We Face in the Light of His Coming

Those are the promise and pollution of the world. There are two other thoughts. We look now at the peril that you and I face in connection with the second coming.

"Remember Lot's wife." We look at that and wonder why He put that in. What has that got to do with the second coming? Then He goes on to say: "In that day, let him that is on the housetop not come down to take any thing out of the house. And let him that is in the field not turn back to take up his garment." What is that pointing to? To the peril of getting our hearts set on natural things in this life instead of upon His coming.

Lot and Mrs. Lot and their two daughters walked out of Sodom; and as they walked down the road, Mrs. Lot got to thinking about the things she was leaving behind; thinking about the city, her home, what she had in Sodom; thinking about those two married daughters staying behind. So as she turned for one last look, she became a pillar of salt—a testimony of God's miraculous, supernatural power.

What Jesus is telling us here is to keep our eyes on His coming and not get too busy building our little homes, accumulating an old-age pension, laying by money in the bank for a rainy day. He wants us to obey Him, look for Him, walk with Him and let not our hearts become saturated with things of this world. "And take heed to yourselves, lest at any time your hearts be overcharged with surfeiting, and drunkenness, and cares of this life, and so that day come upon you unawares" (Luke 21:34).

Gipsy Smith was holding meetings in Tremont Temple in Boston. Great crowds were coming. The city was stirred in a great way. One night after he had preached, up the aisle came a woman, pulling her little boy by the hand. She walked up to Gipsy Smith and said, "I want my little boy to shake hands with you so that when he grows up he can say that he shook hands with a preacher that stirred the city of Boston."

As Gipsy Smith reached down to shake his hand, the little fellow just stood there looking up at him with both hands behind his back. "Come on, Sonny; let's shake hands." He just stood there. He kept resisting. Finally the little boy reached out with his left hand. Gipsy Smith chided him and said, "No! No! I don't want to shake your left hand. Give me your right one." The little fellow reached out his right hand with his fist all doubled up. Gipsy Smith said, "I don't want to fight you; I just want to shake your hand. I am your friend." The little boy put his left hand under his right hand, took something out of his right hand and shook hands with him.

Gipsy Smith asked, "What do you have in your hand?" The little boy wouldn't tell him. The Gipsy took hold of his hand and began to pull the fingers apart. Finally when he pried them open, guess what he had in his hand. Three little dirty pee-wee marbles! **He was more interested in the playthings of life than in shaking the hand of a great man.**

O men and women, I want to ask you: Have you been more interested in holding to the playthings of life than you have been in gripping the nail-scarred hand and looking up? "I would like to be a Christian, but I would have to stay away from such and such a place," you say. "I would like to give my heart to Christ, but I like to do this and I like to do that which a Christian ought not to do. Yes, I would like to be a Christian but—" and with a childlike grip, you hold to the playthings of life.

Turn loose! Reach up and hold the nail-scarred hand, a scar that you can feel that tells of Calvary, which tells of nails, of blood, of suffering and of His coming again.

The Parting That Will Take Place When He Comes

The final thought I want you to take with you tonight is the parting that will prevail when Jesus Christ comes. Two will be in the bed; one shall be taken, the other left. Two will be out in the field plowing; one will be taken, the other left. Two will be grinding at the mill; one will be taken, the other left.

The first parting is going to come out in the graveyard at the secret coming of Christ for His saints.

"I would not have you to be ignorant, brethren, concerning them which are asleep, that ye sorrow not, even as others which have no hope. For if we believe that Jesus died and rose again, even so them also which sleep in Jesus will God bring with him. For this we say unto you by the word of the Lord, that we which are alive and remain unto the coming of the Lord shall not prevent them which are asleep: For the Lord himself shall descend [Is He coming all the way down?] *from heaven with a shout, with the voice of the archangel, and with the trump of God: and the dead in Christ shall rise first: Then we which are alive and remain shall be caught up* [He will descend and we will be caught up to meet, not His body, but] *to meet the Lord in the air."*

There are reasons why the Scripture in one place speaks of Jesus coming like a thief and in another place where it says *every eye shall* see Him. How can He come like a thief and every eye see Him? Every eye doesn't see a thief when he breaks in. That is the reason why it speaks of Him descending into the air. Yet Zechariah says, "His feet shall stand on the mount of Olives." Why? Because that secret coming, the thief coming, is not the same thing He is speaking of here. They are two separate aspects of the one event of His coming. Remember how much time His first coming covered—thirty-three years. The Bible could speak of Him as a babe in the manger, then as being crucified on the cross. Separate those two events from each other, for they are two different things, two different aspects of His first coming. They were related events of His coming.

That secret coming and His public manifestation are two separate aspects of the one event of His second coming. He comes for His saints. And in that secret coming, husband and wife who have loved each other and walked together, one a Christian who loves the Lord and is looking for God, the other is not—in that secret coming down into the clouds, the believing one will be caught up while the unsaved one will be left.

It will be just like old Enoch who "was not; for God took him." Why was he not found? While Enoch walked with God one day, God took him up with Himself. Mrs. Enoch got up and put the coffee pot on, fried the bacon and eggs, toasted the bread. *Enoch is down about the barn. He will come in after awhile,* but he didn't. She went to the telephone: "Have you seen Enoch this morning?" The voice on the other end replied, "No, I haven't seen him anywhere." Then the daily newspapers flashed a big headline—MR. ENOCH MISSING—and a searching party went looking.

It is amazing how anxious people get over one who gets lost in a physical world, but never have that much love, never have that much compassion for those spiritually lost. If one of these children on the front row were to get lost tonight and we couldn't find him, this whole encampment wouldn't sleep a wink. We would fan out all over this place, hunt beside every camp, drag the lake. Yet people all over this encampment grounds are lost without Christ, and we show no anxiety about them.

A searching party was out looking for Enoch, and he was nowhere to be found. God had called him out.

That is exactly what He is going to do. That secret coming may take place before I finish this message. It may take place before the sun comes up in the morning or before nighttime tomorrow. Or it may not take place for a thousand years. But be it ever so long, it is coming.

You read the story of Elisha. He would go around with Elijah. Elisha wanted to be sure he saw Elijah when the Lord took him up so that he could get the mantle. And as Elijah went along, a chariot swooped down and he stepped up on the running board and went home to Glory. Elisha went back to the school of prophets. They didn't believe in a supernatural translation, so they put on a searching party. They went out over the hills to find the body of Elijah.

No one will need to put on a searching party when Jesus comes. Every true believer will suddenly be snatched out just like Elijah and just like Enoch. And the world will miss us. Two will be in a bed; one will be taken, the other left. Two will be in the field; one will be taken, the other will be left. Two will be out yonder at the mill; one will be taken, the other left.

One question for you tonight: If He were to come tonight, would you be taken, or would you be left? That is the issue, the basis of my appeal. You say, "I feel good. I had a physical examination the other day, and the doctor said I was one hundred percent. I am not afraid to die. I am not worried about dying." But how about the second coming? That is the big thing.

A preacher friend of mine preached one morning at eleven o'clock on this text. In his congregation was a wife, some children, and one little child about four years of age. The husband never went to church or Sunday school.

That day at the noon meal the little four-year-old spoke up. "Mama, if Jesus came today, would we have to leave Papa behind?"

The mother kind of turned the little boy off without making any reply, but he was not going to be put off—.

"Mama, if Jesus came today, would we have to leave Papa behind?"

Her husband spoke up. "What is this he is talking about?"

"The pastor spoke today on the second coming and pointed out that when Jesus comes there will be a separation, a parting between believers and unbelievers. He wants to know, if Jesus were to come today, would we have to leave you behind or could we take you with us?"

The man flew in a rage. "Is that what they are teaching up there to my children? If so, they can't go back." He was very much provoked about it. The wife called the pastor and told him that she wanted him to pray for her husband, that he had forbidden the children to come back to church.

At bedtime the little child was put in his bed; but he got up in the darkness of the night, after the lights had been turned out, and said, "Mama, if Jesus comes tonight, will we have to leave our daddy behind?" Hearing him, his father said, "Lie down there!" and scolded the little one. He fell back down on his little bed but said again, "Mama, if Jesus comes, will we have to leave Papa behind?"

The next morning he had to make a trip to San Antonio, Texas. This traveling salesman went out that day but couldn't do any work. One thought kept ringing in his mind: *If Jesus comes tonight, will we have to leave our papa behind?* He came back that night to his hotel but couldn't sleep. He rolled and tossed and tumbled. Still ringing through his mind was that question of his little child. It was Tuesday. He went out that day but couldn't do any business. He came back to the hotel, but still he couldn't sleep. So he caught a train back home. He told his wife how restless he had been. She called the pastor and asked if she could bring her husband to see him. They went.

He said to the pastor, "I'm going crazy!" The pastor said, "Thank God! You are under conviction. God is trying to save you," and he led him to the Lord.

On Wednesday night the baptismal water was ready. This man was going to be baptized. This fellow's little four-year-old son got up by the baptistry. When the usher tried to take the little boy away, the father said, "Let him stay. He won't bother anything." The pastor took the man who had given his heart to the Lord and lowered him down in the baptismal water, picturing the death, burial and resurrection of Jesus. As he raised him up, the building was dark except the baptistry light. The little boy turned and looked back into the congregation and said, "Now when Jesus comes, we can take our daddy with us!"

I close my message tonight with that question. If Jesus were to come tonight, would we take you with us, or would we have to leave you behind?

ROBERT REYNOLDS JONES, SR.
1883-1968

ABOUT THE MAN:

Called the greatest evangelist of all time by Billy Sunday, Robert Reynolds Jones, better known as Dr. Bob Jones, Sr., was born October 30, 1883, in Shipperville, Alabama, the eleventh of twelve children. He was converted at age 11, a Sunday school superintendent at 12 and ordained at 15 by a Methodist church.

"Dr. Bob" was a Christ-exalting, sin-condemning preacher who preached in the cotton fields, in country churches and in brush arbors. Later he held huge campaigns in American cities large and small, and preached around the world.

Billy Sunday once said of him: "He has the wit of Sam Jones, the homely philosophy of George Stuart, the eloquence of Sam Small, and the spiritual fervency of Dwight L. Moody."

He saw crowds up to 10,000 in his meetings, with many thousands finding Christ in one single campaign.

But Dr. Bob was more than an evangelist. He was also an educator—a pioneer in the field of Christian education, founding Bob Jones University some 62 years ago.

Behind every man's ministry is a philosophy. Dr. Bob's was spelled out in the sentence sermons to his "preacher boys" in BJU chapels. Who has not heard or read some of these: "Duties never conflict!" "It is a sin to do less than your best." "The greatest ability is dependability." "The test of your character is what it takes to stop you." "It is never right to do wrong in order to get a chance to do right."

"DO RIGHT!" That was the philosophy that motivated his ministry, saturated his sermons, and spearheaded his school.

His voice was silenced by death January 16, 1968, but his influence will forever live on and Christians will be challenged to "DO RIGHT IF THE STARS FALL!"

III.

Aspects of His Appearing

BOB JONES, SR.

(Preached at Arena in Chicago on May 6, 1946, during citywide Life Begins revival campaign. Mechanically recorded for THE SWORD OF THE LORD.)

"For Christ is not entered into the holy places made with hands, which are the figures of the true; but into heaven itself, now to appear in the presence of God for us: Nor yet that he should offer himself often, as the high priest entereth into the holy place every year with blood of others; For then [that is, if He had done that] *must he often have suffered since the foundation of the world: but now once in the end of the world* [the end of the age] *hath he appeared to put away sin by the sacrifice of himself. And as it is appointed unto men once to die, but after this the judgment* [It does not say that it is appointed unto ALL men once to die]*: So Christ was once offered to bear the sins of many; and unto them that look for him shall he appear the second time without sin unto salvation."*—Heb. 9:24-28.

In these verses we have three wonderful statements: Christ has appeared, Christ does appear, Christ is going to appear.

We have Christ appearing on the cross, Christ appearing in Heaven, and Christ appearing again to earth in glory.

In these verses we have Christ bearing our sins on the cross. We have Christ up in Heaven interceding for us. We have Christ coming back again to receive us.

In these verses we have Christ who has been here, Christ who has gone away, and Christ who is coming back.

Get it clear: He was here one time, He went away one time, He is coming back sometime. Just as certain as He was here, just as certain as He went away, just that certain is He coming back again.

The Devil hates those three things. He hates the atonement. We hear people in this day and time say, "The Sermon on the Mount is my religion." Brother, the Sermon on the Mount cannot save you. It is the Preacher who preached that sermon who can save you. People talk about living up to the Sermon on the Mount. You cannot live up to the Sermon on the Mount unless you go to the cross of Calvary and get your sins washed away in the blood and get a new heart. It is not Christ preaching on the mountain; it is Christ dying on the cross to which the Bible gives special emphasis.

All through the Bible the emphasis is on the cross, the cross, the cross. Christ died for us. Christ bore our sins in His body on the tree. Christ was wounded for our transgressions, He was bruised for our iniquities. Modernism puts the emphasis on the Sermon on the Mount, but the Bible puts the emphasis on Christ's dying on the cross.

Some religious systems in this country attempt to do away with the blood of Christ. I do not wish to enter into any controversial discussion tonight. Some do not agree with me about this—for instance, our Christian Science friends. Mrs. Eddy has a chapter in one of her books on the atonement, but it is a meaningless chapter from the conservative, orthodox, Christian standpoint. What becomes of the atonement if Jesus bore our sins, which were not sins, in a body, which was not a body, on a cross, which was not a cross? According to Christian Science, sin is not a fact, not a reality.

If there is no such thing as sin, then Jesus Christ had no sin to bear in His body on the cross. If there is nothing material, He had no body with which to bear my sin. If there is nothing material, there is no such thing as a real cross on which He died. All down through the years the Devil has tried to take people's eyes off Calvary.

> **I saw One hanging on a tree,**
> **In agony and blood,**
> **He fixed His languid eyes on me**
> **As near His cross I stood.**
>
> **At the cross, at the cross**
> **Where I first saw the light,**
> **And the burden of my heart rolled away.**

It is to Calvary that we must go. "Life begins at Calvary," as we have been singing in this campaign. The Devil does not want you to see this.

So Christ was here. He was born of a virgin. That is wonderful. He was a little babe in a manger. That is wonderful. But, bless God, the glorious thing is that the Baby who was virgin-born in a manger, one day hung on a cross for me. He died for me! Somebody has said: *That is all the gems of all people in one diadem. That is all the flowers of all springtimes in one bouquet. That is all daydawns of all mornings breaking forth into a glorious spring day.*

Take Christ as our Intercessor. He is at the right hand of the Father saying a good word for us. You do not need anybody else to intercede for you. You do not need a bishop or a priest or a preacher. The humblest Christian in this house has as much access to God the Father through Jesus Christ His Son as has a bishop or a priest or the Virgin Mary or anybody on this earth or in Heaven. We are a kingdom of priests, blessed be God! And we Christians can walk up to God in the name of Jesus Christ and do our own talking. Oh, how the Devil wants to veil Jesus so we will not see Him up yonder interceding for us!

Take the second coming of Christ. Oh, how the Devil tries to discredit this glorious doctrine! First, the Devil hitches all the fanatics up with this doctrine. Strange, weird people, good people, some of them, but peculiarly fanatical people, go around talking about the Lord's coming. Don't forget that He is really coming again. The Devil tries to laugh out of court every doctrine in the Bible. He wants to discredit these glorious doctrines. He wants to get preachers where they will not say anything about them.

Take the doctrine of holiness. There is a Bible doctrine of holiness, but some people are afraid to mention the word *holiness*. They are afraid to mention the word *sanctification*—afraid of those words because they have been discredited by certain extremists and a certain radical type of people. But our business is to go right on and not hesitate to tell people that we ought to live victorious, sanctified lives; that we ought to be set apart for His service.

I only heard one sermon on the second coming of Christ before I was almost a grown man. The first time I heard people talk about His coming again, I thought they were crazy—exactly what the Devil wanted me to think. But that doctrine is a Bible doctrine. It is there as clear as daylight. Jesus Christ came down from Heaven's noonday to earth's midnight. He died on the cross to save us. He was buried. The third day He rose again. Then after awhile He went back up on High and is up yonder at the Father's right hand. And someday He is coming again.

One day an old preacher friend of mine was walking down a street in Philadelphia with a modernistic preacher. The modernist said, "You are looking for Jesus to come, aren't you?"

The preacher answered, "Yes, I am."

"Well, do you know the difference between you and me?"

"What's the difference?" asked my old friend.

"Well, you are looking for Jesus and you will be disappointed. I am not looking for Him and I will not be disappointed," the modernist replied.

As quick as a flash the old-time preacher said, "There is another difference between you and me. I am doing what Jesus said to do, and you are not doing what Jesus told you to do. He told us to look for Him, and I am looking for Him."

I. MUST BE A LITERAL COMING

Some people think of the second coming of Jesus as a sort of mystical, spiritual something. It is not. His coming is to be a literal coming. He came literally the first time. He literally went back to Heaven. He is literally coming again.

A friend says he can count in the Bible 152 prophecies that have been literally fulfilled. Somebody else has said there are over 300. Let's notice just a few of them.

The prophet said Jesus would be born of a virgin. That was fulfilled literally.

The prophet said He would be betrayed by a friend. That was fulfilled literally.

The prophet said He would be sold for thirty pieces of silver. That was fulfilled literally.

The prophet said a potter's field would be bought with the price of His blood. That was literally fulfilled.

If I had time I could mention many more prophecies in the Bible that have been fulfilled, not figuratively but literally.

Now if these prophecies about the first coming of our Lord and other prophecies have been fulfilled literally, why should we say that the prophecies having to do with the second coming are figurative? He was born into this world literally. He literally lived among men. He walked around among men, ate with men, traveled with men, talked with men. With His own blessed hands He touched human bodies. He was here literally. Then literally He went away. And literally He is coming back.

II. IS NOT DEATH

The coming of Jesus is not death. He is personally coming. "For the Lord *himself*. . . ." Put the emphasis where God puts it. "The Lord *himself* shall descend from heaven."

(This is not the Holy Ghost. The Holy Ghost has already come. The power of God is here. People are preaching under the power of the Holy Ghost. Men and women are being convicted. The body of Christ is being made up. The church is being gathered in. Yet the inspired writer says, "The Lord himself shall descend from heaven.")

The second coming of Christ is not death. I used to think that it was when I was a boy. I somehow picked up the idea that when a man died, that was the second coming of Christ. But death is not the second coming of Christ. When Jesus rose from the dead, He said to one of His disciples, "If I will that he tarry till I come, what is that to thee? follow thou me" (John 21:22). He did not say he would tarry. He said, "If I will that he tarry. . . ." They went around saying that John will never die, John will be alive when Jesus comes. Now Jesus did not say he would. Rather He said, "If I will that he tarry. . . ." He was saying, 'That is none of your business; you follow Me.'

Take this passage: "Our conversation [our citizenship] is in heaven" (Phil. 3:20). O Christians, we do not belong in this world. We are pilgrims and strangers here.

Do you ever get homesick? Do you have a sort of feeling that you do not belong here? I get lonesome sometimes. I have traveled in foreign lands where I did not understand the language. Their customs were not my customs. You and I are traveling in a foreign country. Our citizenship is in Heaven. We do not belong here. Just wait until someday when we get Home!

Some people do not know who we are yet. They do not know how wonderful, how prominent we are. They do not know that we are joint heirs with Jesus Christ and will reign with Him one day.

"Our conversation is in heaven; from whence also we look for the Saviour, the Lord Jesus Christ: who shall change our vile body, that it may be fashioned like unto his glorious body."

Now that word *vile* is not the best translation. A better translation would be: "the body of our humiliation." The curse of sin is on your body. The curse of sin is on all creation. Paul says, 'All creation groans and travails in pain, waiting for deliverance.' The curse of sin is everywhere. The roses bloom, but they have thorns—signs of the curse. All chords of nature are in the minor key. The wind sighs. The sea moans. There is a curse on creation. And your body is under the curse. We have aches and pains, loss of hair. Old Father Time comes up and pinches wrinkles under our eyes. We get where we have to help our legs up the steps. Our shoulders begin to stoop under the weight of the years.

I saw a man and woman going down a street not long ago. He was about sixty and she, about fifty-five. The man looked as if he had given up a little. She was holding up her shoulders, looking nervously out of her eyes. She touched her husband on the shoulder and said, "Stand up straight. Everybody will think you are old!"

We are getting old. We can fight and fight, but we will surrender someday. Our body is under a curse, under its humiliation. We work, but we get tired. We run, but we get weary. We are under the curse, under the humiliation; and after awhile we die.

I do not like the thought of dying. I never saw a day in my life when I wanted to die. I want Jesus to come. I have been active all my life. Here I am a little over six feet tall, weighing over two hundred pounds. I have been burning up my energy through the years.

After awhile I am helpless. I stop breathing. The doctor says, "He is gone." Then somebody comes in, opens up my veins, drains out all the blood and pumps something artificial in there. Then they dress me up. They say, "Get that tie over there, and that collar." They do not ask me anything about it. Then they comb my hair like they want it combed. Then they put a little something red on my cheeks so I will not look as if I am dead. But I am dead! After they dress me as they want me dressed, one man says to another, "Take hold over there." They place me in a coffin, screw the lid down, and soon they will carry me off to the graveyard and cover me up with dirt.

I want to wait on myself! I do not like to be waited on! I do not want to die. I do not want to be buried. I do not want people pitching dirt in on me. I do not want to be cremated either. When you bury a fellow, you do know where you left him. I do not want to die! I want Jesus Christ to come. Don't tell me the second coming of Jesus Christ is death. When He comes, He will break up funerals! He will take the dead out of coffins!

III. A PHYSICAL, BODILY COMING

The second coming of Christ is to be a bodily coming. Now follow me rapidly. Jesus Christ is upon the mountain, and He stretches His hand out to bless those with Him. While His hands are stretched out, He begins to climb up into space. That is the most dramatic picture in all literature. There He is—going up. He has been on a cross, has been buried in a tomb; now standing on a mountain talking to some friends, suddenly He stretches out His hands to bless them and then He goes up through space.

We read those things and just pass on. Can you conceive it! Let's try to imagine we are talking to somebody who has been dead and is now alive again, and as we talk, he goes up through space. As Jesus went up, the clouds parted and let Him pass. The sun, moon and stars stood to one side and saluted. He went up and up. I suppose those with Him on the mountain stood on tiptoe trying to go up with Him. As they watched, two men stood by in white apparel and said, "Ye men of Galilee, why stand ye gazing up into heaven? This SAME Jesus, which is taken up from you into heaven, shall so come in like manner as ye have seen him go into heaven" (Acts 1:11).

Oh, the emphasis God gives to it! He did not say, "Why are you looking up? He will come back." He said, "This same Jesus, which is taken up from you into heaven, shall so come in like manner as ye have seen him go into heaven."

Now, if I can find how He went up, I will know exactly how He is coming back. Is there any way to find out how He went up? Yes.

When He rose from the dead, some disciples came to touch Him and He said, "Touch me not; for I am not yet ascended to my Father: but go to my brethren, and say unto them, I ascend [present tense] unto my Father, and your Father; and to my God, and your God" (John 20:17).

Jesus Christ went on up to Heaven then. The Jews should have understood that. In the old dispensation, if anyone touched a Jewish priest going into the holy place to present the blood, the blood was of no avail. Jesus Christ has shed His blood on the cross, but now He is on His way to present that blood on the altar of the sky, His blood that was shed on Calvary. He is going within the veil to present it, and He says, "Go to my brethren, and say unto them, I ascend."

Now later He was up in a room and said in substance, "Thomas, you see this hand? This is the hand that wiped tears of sorrow from human faces. Thomas, this is the same hand that touched blind eyes and flooded them with light; touched deaf ears and made them to hear; touched the leper and chased his leprosy away. Thomas, this is the hand I took to the tomb with Me. Thomas, this is the hand that washed your feet. Thomas, touch Me. Put your hand right here. Come on. I am not a ghost. A spirit hasn't flesh and bones."

On Calvary's cross He shed His blood. We read in Leviticus 17:11, "For the life of the flesh is in the blood." And, by the way, that is a scientific statement. You hear people talk about the Bible not being scientific! Possibly those men in those days knew nothing about the circulation of the blood. Men were studying astronomy before they understood the circulation of the blood. But back in Leviticus we read: "For the life of the flesh is in the blood: and I have given it to you upon the altar to make an atonement for your souls: for it is the blood that maketh an atonement for the soul."

Now when Jesus hung on Calvary's cross, He gave His blood. "Without shedding of blood is no remission" (Heb. 9:22). He gave His blood, His life on the cross. So do not lightly talk about a "bloody gospel." Don't ridicule a "slaughterhouse religion."

"In the cross of Christ we glory." "There is a fountain filled with blood." On the cross He shed, poured out His blood. When He rose from the dead, He had a risen life, a literal body, a body so real He could actually sit down and eat breakfast with people.

Jesus Christ went to Heaven in that body. I shall never forget when it dawned on me as a young preacher: Jesus has never been a ghost. It dawned on me one day that up in Heaven at the Father's right hand is Jesus Christ, a man who came back from the dead, a man with a body of flesh and bones.

Listen, the same feet that were nailed to Calvary's cross are standing tonight on streets of gold. Listen! The same hand that fondled the cheek of a mother is lifted up in the presence of the Father in Heaven. He has a body of flesh and bones. He is coming back someday in that same body. We are going to see Him someday. We are going to see the same eyes, the same face that men saw when He was here. It was the same body that came out of the tomb that entered the tomb—a literal, risen body of flesh and bones. This same Jesus who came from the dead like that and went back to the skies like that shall so come in like manner as they saw Him go.

IV. MUST BE VISIBLE

The coming of Jesus will be a visible coming. "Behold, he cometh with clouds; and every eye shall see him, and they also which pierced him: and all kindreds of the earth shall wail because of him. Even so, Amen" (Rev. 1:7). I used to read that Scripture, ". . . and all kindreds of the earth shall wail because of him. Even so, Amen," and say, *John, I wouldn't say "Amen" when people are wailing.* But one day I saw these words: "Beloved, now are we the sons of God, and it doth not yet appear what we shall be: but we know that, when he shall appear, we shall be like him; for we shall see him as he is" (I John 3:2). Now I say, "Even so, Amen."

I am going to see Jesus someday. Every eye will see Him. Some are going to wail, but the saved are not. We are going to be like Him when we see Him.

Oh, how I would love to see Jesus! If He were in the heart of China I would cross the Pacific Ocean and go there to look into His face for one second. But one day with undimmed eyes I am going to look into His holy face. I am going to see Him as He is.

Say! I see Him as a Saviour now with the eyes of my soul. I see Him with the eyes of my soul as my Lord and Master. But we have never seen Jesus Christ as He really is. His glory! His glory! No wonder the angels veil their faces and say, "Holy! Holy! HOLY!" No wonder in Heaven clouds never gather in the sky! No wonder there is no night there! He shines in that city. We who are saved will see Him as He is and be like Him!

Years ago somebody told this story; I believe it was A. B. Simpson.

A steamboat with a pleasure party on board was going down the Mississippi River. A woman on deck fell overboard. As quick as a flash a man leaped into the water and rescued her. She stood shivering in the wind, dripping wet when somebody rushed up and said, "Take this wrap." She said, "Take that wrap away! I want to look into the face of that man who saved me!"

I want to see Jesus, the One who found me when I was a little country boy at the age of eleven, the One whom I have never seen but loved all these years. I want to see Him!

I wish I could have seen Him when He was a baby. He must have been beautiful.

I wish I could have seen Him in the manger.

I wish I could have seen a star leading the Wise Men to His cradle.

I wish I could have seen Him when His mother and His foster father Joseph took Him down to Egypt.

I wish I could have seen Him at the age of twelve as He talked to the doctors of the Law in the Temple. I would have enjoyed watching those old wise men as they sat under the spell of His personality.

I wish I could have seen Him at Jordan when He was baptized.

I wish I could have seen Him on the mountaintop in the wilderness or on the pinnacle of the Temple when He was tempted.

I wish I could have been at the marriage supper that night and seen the look of astonishment on their faces when He changed the water to wine.

I wish I could have seen Him perform some of His miracles. I should like to have been with Him at the tomb of Lazarus when He said, "Lazarus, come forth," and there walked out of that grave that man who had been dead.

I wish I could have seen Him on the cross. I think it would have broken my heart if I had stood there that day and seen Him hanging in agony and blood. But, oh, how I would have loved Him!

I wish I could have seen Him when He pulled off His graveclothes and walked out of the tomb.

I wish I could have seen Him down there that day at the shore when they saw Him this side of the grave.

I wish I could have seen the astonished look on the face of Thomas when he saw the nailprints.

I wish I could have watched with that crowd when He climbed back up to His Father's house.

BUT I WOULD RATHER SEE HIM WHEN HE COMES AGAIN! The humblest Christian in this building tonight will have the glorious privilege of seeing Him come in glory someday. We shall see Him! And if He takes His nail-pierced hand and puts a crown on my head, I will let it stay there for just a minute because He put it there. Then I want to lift that crown from my head and put it at His feet and ask the redeemed hosts to sing

All hail the pow'r of Jesus' name!
Let angels prostrate fall:
Bring forth the royal diadem,
And crown Him Lord of all.

I shall see Him! He is coming again. "This same Jesus, which is taken up from you into heaven, shall so come in like manner as ye have seen him go into heaven."

V. WILL BE SUDDEN, UNEXPECTED

He is coming suddenly, in a moment, in the twinkling of an eye. It will not be the permeating of human society with the Gospel, not the spreading of Christian influence in the world. That is not the second coming of Christ. It will be in a moment, in the twinkling of an eye. Like a flash of lightning He is coming. Oh, what a startled world it will be! What a startled Chicago and New York and London and Paris when He comes like that!

Listen! People are going to find out some of these days that we Christians were not the fools after all. Do not let them get you down. Do not let this wicked world oppress you. Keep lifting up your heads and keep looking up to the sky. He is coming one day, suddenly.

He is coming unexpectedly. A thing may be sudden and unexpected. I may expect a gun to shoot, and it shoots suddenly; but I expected it. The second coming of Jesus is to be both sudden and unexpected. He says, "Therefore be ye also ready: for in such an hour as ye think not the Son of man cometh" (Matt. 24:44).

"For when they shall say, Peace and safety; then sudden destruction cometh upon them, as travail upon a woman with child; and they shall not escape. But ye, brethren, are not in darkness, that that day should overtake you as a thief. Ye are all the children of light, and the children of the day: we are not of the night, nor of darkness. Therefore let us not sleep, as do others; but let us watch and be sober. For they that sleep sleep in the night; and they that be drunken are drunken in the night. But let us, who are of the day, be sober."—I Thess. 5:3-8.

Let us be looking. Some of us are not going to be surprised. Every night for years I have gone to sleep saying to Jesus, "O hasten Thy coming!"

You folks who are back of this revival—every time you bring a soul to Christ you are hastening His coming. After awhile the last member of the bride will come in; then He will come. Our business is to work with the Holy Ghost in this dispensation to get a bride for Jesus. He is coming suddenly and unexpectedly, but not unexpected to us who know Him and love His coming.

Years ago a prominent church official in New York City said to another prominent church official in the same city, "John, let's go to this theater tonight and see the play."

John said, "No, Bill. I do not want to see that show. I understand it is rather dirty, vile and sensational."

"Oh, come on; let's go," urged Bill.

"No, I do not want to go," John kept saying.

"Why don't you want to go?"

John said, "I'm looking for Jesus. He is coming someday, and since He might come while I am in that show, I would not want Him to catch me there."

Listen! "Every man that hath this hope in him purifieth himself, even as he is pure" (I John 3:3). There is nothing that weans Christians from the world like the assurance of His coming. Sometime when you are inclined to love money, position, fame, worldly honors, just sit down for a few minutes and contemplate His coming.

I went through a crisis in my life. We have a large enrollment in our school. We must turn away many students next year whom we cannot take care of. There is no strain on us financially. Oh, the mortar in the buildings is almost made up of my blood! There I was. What should I do: turn away students? No. Put up buildings! Make more room for young people who desire training for Christian leadership! Shall I take it easy? What shall I do? It is so easy to take it easy. Well, I cannot, I dare not. I would not want Jesus to catch me sitting down. I want to be out on the battlefield fighting for God. I do not want, when He comes, to hear Him say I was too lazy to work for Him.

When I was young I used to think I would take it easy someday. I have never taken it easy. All my life I have staggered under burdens that I could not have carried without God. This strain while I am here is just a little part of it. If I had nothing but this campaign—that used to be all I had—it would seem very light. However, this is only part of the load. But I would not want Him to come and find me sitting in an easy chair.

One day a woman in a meeting got up and gave this testimony: "God saved me from a life of drunkenness and debauchery. He has been better to me than anybody else." Then she sat down. Another woman, prominent socially, a woman of wealth, got up and said, "Jesus has done more for me than He did for her. He saved me from the love of an easy chair."

Christian, how can you take it easy? Your Lord is away, but He is coming back someday. Is He going to find you busy when He comes?

VI. CHRIST IS COMING FOR HIS SAINTS

One last point. He is coming for the saints.

"But I would not have you to be ignorant, brethren, concerning them which are asleep, that ye sorrow not, even as others which have no hope. [He did not say for you not to sorrow. He did not say for you not to weep when loved ones die. But you do not weep as those weep who have no hope.] *For if we believe that Jesus died and rose again, even so them also which sleep in Jesus will God bring with him. For this we say unto you by the word of the Lord, that we which are alive and remain unto the coming of the Lord shall not prevent them which are asleep. For the Lord himself shall descend from heaven with a shout, with the voice of the archangel, and with the trump of God: and the dead in Christ shall rise first: Then we which are alive and remain shall be caught up together with them in the clouds, to meet the Lord in the air: and so shall we ever be with the Lord. Wherefore comfort one another with these words."*—I Thess. 4:13-18.

He is coming back someday. I do not think He is going to raise all at the same time; but He is going to raise all the dead. Everybody who ever lived and died will some time be raised up. Indian maidens will leap from the dust of city streets, and city skyscrapers will overturn to let Indian chiefs to judgment. Wanderers will push aside winding sheets of sand in the desert and get up. The ocean will swell and heave, and out of its watery depths multiplied thousands who were buried there will come back to life. All the mummies of Egypt will come from the dead. All the dead! The battlefields of the earth will reproduce their dead. All the dead!

But there will be this difference: He is going to watch over especially the tombs of His own. The dust of the saints is sacred dust. Jesus Christ died not only to redeem your soul but also to redeem your body. Somebody says, "It makes no difference to me about my body." Well, it matters to me. I have lived in this house sixty-two years. I have suffered pain. I have been restricted. I have been tied down to the earth by the law of gravitation when I wanted to be up in the stars finding out what was there. It matters to me! My body is the temple of the Holy Ghost. It matters to me whether my body is raised or not.

My mother sleeps in a lonely graveyard. How many times have I felt her hand on my brow and her loving lips kissing mine. Do not tell me it does not matter whether Jesus raises the dead. It matters to me whether I ever see my mother again! I used to sit in her lap, put my arms around her and kiss her over and over. That is precious dust to me. Do not tell me it does not matter whether God raises my mother from the dead!

There is a woman here tonight whose son sleeps somewhere in the Pacific or over in Europe. She gave him to die for his country. Do not tell that mother that it makes no difference whether Jesus will raise the dead.

There is a woman here tonight—one day God reached out of Heaven and put a little baby in your arms. You held him a little while. You saw him smile one night and thought angels were making him dream. You saw tears on his cheeks and heard him cry. A little later he died. A little coffin was brought into the home, and the baby was put into it; then it was taken out yonder and put in the tomb. In the coffin was not only the baby but with the baby was buried the heart of the mother. Some nights now you wake up and imagine you feel the little velvety, chubby hand on your cheek. You wake up startled to find it is all a dream. One day you will feel that hand. Someday that little baby's coffin will be opened in the cemetery, and God will give back your precious baby.

Christians, what a wonderful thing it is to be saved! We sorrow not as those who have no hope. He is coming! Someday David will get up and ask for his harp with which to praise God. Abraham will shake the dust off his shroud and say to Sarah, "Get up, Sarah." Someday it will look like a camp meeting around some of these old country churches. But instead of the risen dead going into the churches, they will be going up into the sky.

God is going to raise the dead and translate the living. All the Christians who are alive at the coming of Jesus will not die. We shall not precede those who are dead. You know, it seems to be God's way of compensating those who had to die. "Now all of you living—wait just a minute. These folks had to die, and I want to get them up first; then you can join them. They had to fall at the end of the journey. They went through the valley. They struggled for breath. I will not let you get ahead of them." He will translate the living into the air. Somebody says, "How?"

Well, He has already done it. Elijah and Elisha were walking along one day, talking things over. I can imagine this. Elisha said, "I do not know what we will do when you go. You've been the head of this School of Prophets a long time. Elijah, I would like to wear your robe."

Elijah said one of the most significant things in all the Bible: "If thou see me when I am taken from thee, it shall be so unto thee." He was saying, "I am going to be supernaturally translated. If you can apprehend the supernatural, you can wear a prophet's robe." No man is fit to wear a prophet's robe who cannot apprehend the supernatural.

Suddenly there was a strange noise like chariot wheels and a strange breath like air from the wings of angels, and Elijah stepped into the chariot. Up the shining highway to Heaven he rode! He threw his mantle back, and it fell on Elisha.

Elijah did not die. He is up in Heaven tonight.

There was Enoch. A little girl said it this way. Enoch and God had a long walk. After awhile Enoch said, "It is getting a little late. I suppose I had better go home. Won't You go and spend the night with me?"

God said, "Enoch, since we are so much nearer My home than yours, I believe I'll take you home with Me."

God took Enoch by the hand and led him up to the gate. The gates opened. There was an angelic host there, and God said to the angels, "Show Enoch to his room. He has been My friend. He walked with Me in a wicked day when the lights were dim. Show him his room!" And God said to Enoch, "Enoch, if you want anything, just ring for the angels. They are the bellboys up here."

Enoch did not die.

And when Jesus gets ready, He is going to take us all up. I wish He would come now. I am ready. I am under the blood. But wait a minute, just a minute, Jesus; there might be somebody else who is not.

Are you saved tonight? Are you under the blood? Are you a child of God?

MARTIN R. DEHAAN
1891 - 1965

ABOUT THE MAN:

Martin R. DeHaan was born in Zeeland, Michigan, the son of a cobbler who had emigrated from the Netherlands. He graduated from Hope College in Holland, Michigan and the University of Illinois College of Medicine. In 1914 he married and soon became a successful physician in Western Michigan.

When DeHaan got the call to preach the Gospel, he gave up his medical practice and completed training at Western Theological Seminary in Holland, Michigan.

He pastored two churches in Grand Rapids which grew quickly under his forceful preaching and his ability to make Bible truth simple and easily understood. Then he began large Bible classes, and in 1938, as an outgrowth of one of these classes in Detroit, the Lord led in the expansion of this teaching by means of radio.

The Radio Bible Class grew rapidly and was soon on two national networks. In more than a quarter of a century, DeHaan saw the broadcast grow from a local venture on a fifty-watt station to a ministry of more than 600 selected stations around the world.

During those years he spoke at many Bible conferences and wrote 25 books and numerous booklets. He also edited and published a monthly devotional guide, *Our Daily Bread*.

Dr. DeHaan died on December 13, 1965. Having sustained serious injuries in an automobile collision in July, his recovery had been slow because of complications of heart trouble. His strength gradually waned and his death came as he rested at home.

IV.

Return of the King

M. R. DE HAAN

A Bible Study Concerning the Certainty and Results of That Blessed Hope of Christ's Return

(Preached over the Coast to Coast Networks of Mutual Broadcasting System and the American Broadcasting Radio Network and by short wave in foreign lands.)

"When they therefore were come together, they asked of him saying, Lord, wilt thou at this time restore again the kingdom to Israel?"— Acts 1:6.

PART ONE

This was the last question which the disciples of our Lord were privileged to ask our Saviour while He was here on the earth. It was a question born of eager expectation and shattered hopes.

"Wilt thou at THIS TIME restore the kingdom again to Israel?"

This was the most important question, uppermost in the minds of the disciples at this particular moment. They had expected, as all the devout Jews of that day had, that when the Messiah would come, He would set up the long-awaited Messianic, but surely promised, kingdom upon this earth. All the prophecies had foretold that when the Messiah came, Israel would be delivered from the Roman yoke, the kingdom would be established, and earth's millennial peace would be ushered in.

They as yet, of course, knew nothing about the intervening church age between the first and second comings of this Messiah. They did not look for a rejected, crucified Saviour, but a victorious, conquering One who would deliver Israel from the cruel yoke of bondage and oppression and restore the glory of the kingdom of Israel, foreshadowed in the reigns of David and of King Solomon.

It was this faith that Jesus was the Messiah which had prompted them to leave all and to follow Him. Even John the Baptist believed this; and when he was cast into prison and Jesus did not set up the kingdom as he expected, he began to doubt and sent his disciples with the question, "Art thou he [the Messiah] that should come, or look we for another?"

But the disciples were in for a very severe shock, for instead of delivering Israel from bondage, instead of sitting upon the throne of David, as all the prophets had foretold, He goes instead to the cross of Calvary and dies as a criminal upon the cruel tree. All their hopes of the kingdom were shattered and dashed into pieces in a moment.

But we can hardly blame the disciples for leaving Him and fleeing in terror at that critical moment, for they as yet knew not the meaning of Calvary.

And then their hopes were revived when He arose. For a little while they again took courage. Surely now He would set up the kingdom, after His resurrection, but no—again they must be disappointed, and forty days Jesus spent with them talking about the kingdom but doing absolutely nothing about it. And so we read in Acts 1:3:

"To whom [the disciples] also he [Jesus] shewed himself alive after his passion by many infallible proofs, being seen of them forty days, and speaking of the things pertaining to the KINGDOM OF GOD."

The topic of conversation with the disciples during the last forty days of the Lord here upon the earth was the KINGDOM. And now forty days afterwards, their hopes soared to the very highest pitch. Jesus leads them to the Mount of Olives, the very place where the prophets had foretold that the Messiah would come when He came to set up the KINGDOM upon the earth (Zech. 14:4). The same mountain where Peter, James and John had seen a vision of the glory of His kingdom in the transfiguration (Matt. 17). Surely the Lord was now at last about to set up the Throne of David, and so the question in verse 6:

"Lord, wilt thou at THIS TIME restore again the kingdom to Israel?"

Three words arrest our attention in this verse: "AT THIS TIME." They knew, if God's Word were true, that someday Messiah would set up the kingdom. Was THIS then the time of which they had been instructed? "Lord, wilt thou at THIS TIME restore again the kingdom to Israel?"

But instead of a definite answer to this question which Jesus might have given, He merely assures them that it is not for them to know WHEN this should occur and so He says:

"It is not for you to know the times or the seasons, which the Father hath put in his own power."—Acts 1:7.

Now this is a tremendously important verse. If, as the majority of professing Christendom teaches today, the church is the kingdom, and all the prophecies concerning the Messianic, earthly kingdom of our Lord must be spiritualized and applied to the church, and, therefore, God is all through with national Israel, then here certainly was the one opportunity for Jesus to set His disciples, and all of us, straight on this subject. If God is all through with Israel and the church is now spiritual Israel, then here was the opportunity of our Saviour to state that fact clearly, so that there would be no question or confusion about it. He could have said, for instance: "Forget about the millennial kingdom. The church is the kingdom; God is all through with the nation of Israel, and they will never return literally to the land." This would have cleared up all the confusion which is dividing Christendom today.

But instead Jesus says, "The time is not for you to know. Just wait until Pentecost, and the Holy Spirit will give you instructions and further information on what you are to do in the interim before I set up the kingdom, for the promises will still come true."

And then came the shock of their lives. Jesus, after assuring them in this way that the kingdom would be set up ultimately, suddenly leaves them, and we read:

"And when he had spoken these things, while they beheld, he was taken up; and a cloud received him out of their sight."—Acts 1:9.

Their Lord is gone. The King has departed. And their hopes are shattered once more and come tumbling down like a house of paper about their heads. Just after He had them all keyed up to a high pitch with the assurance that the kingdom was not forgotten, He suddenly disappears from their midst, and they are struck dumb. No one utters a single word; their grief is too great for expression. All they could do was stand and gaze in despair and wonder, and we read that they:

". . . looked stedfastly toward heaven as he went up. . . ."

And then follows the climax of the entire scene, for while they looked stedfastly toward Heaven as He went up,

Behold

". . . Behold, two men stood by them in white apparel."—Acts 1:10.

The Lord was gone. Jesus had departed, but He had immediately dispatched two men with a message from Heaven for them. Jesus knew that loneliness of despair must have gripped the hearts of those disciples as He disappears into the blue, and so without delay, He sends back His very first message from Heaven.

And what a message it was—a message that dispelled their fears, assured their doubting hearts, rekindled all their hopes and caused them to return to Jerusalem, the city of the King, to await the next heavenly messenger, the Holy Spirit at Pentecost.

Jesus' First Message

Now will you notice the content of this first message, the very first message our ascended Lord ever sent back from Heaven to His disciples? Here it is:

"Two men stood by them in white apparel; Which also said, Ye men of Galilee, why stand ye gazing up into heaven? this same Jesus, which is taken up from you into heaven, shall so come in like manner as ye have seen him go into heaven."—Acts 1:10,11.

This then was our Lord's first message from Heaven after His ascension. "I AM COMING BACK AGAIN! I WILL RETURN, and when I do, then the kingdom promises still will all be fulfilled without a single exception." Now a number of things are important in this verse which we have quoted.

1. It will be the very same Jesus, the very same One who was born of a virgin, taught among men, died on the cross, arose from the grave. Yes, THIS SAME JESUS in a human body with the prints of the nails in His hands and feet—this same Jesus is coming back again.

2. He will come in the same manner as He went away. He went away visibly. He will return visibly. He left them from the Mount of Olives; He will return to the Mount of Olives (Zech. 14:4). He went away leaving the promise of the kingdom as His last message before He ascended, and His first message after He ascended was the assurance of His return to set up this kingdom.

3. When He ascended, He lifted up His hands to bless His disciples (Luke 24:50,51). When He returns, it will be to bring in the full and

complete blessing upon Israel and the nations and the entire earth.

The Certainty

Yes, indeed, Jesus Christ is coming again. He is coming literally, visibly, bodily, in like manner as He has gone away. The fact is absolutely certain, while the time has not yet been revealed. If Jesus had told His disciples and us the date, the exact moment of His return, He would have robbed the truth of Christ's second coming of all of its power, its incentive and its blessing. It is the imminency of His return which gives to the second coming of Christ the power and comfort which it contains. Jesus will return someday, and He MAY return today.

The early disciples expected our Lord's return momentarily, and we today have a perfect right to look for Him to come at any moment. To delay our Lord's return by asserting that this or that event must first take place is severely condemned by Jesus Himself.

To say that we must first have a great world revival before the Lord can come back again is delaying His coming. It implies that Christ cannot come today, and it robs the coming of Christ of its imminency. To teach that we must see another world war or that Russia must first invade Palestine before the Lord's return is to be guilty of delaying the coming of the Lord, for we then imply that Jesus cannot come until AFTER that event has taken place and, therefore, He could not come today. This is delaying the Lord's coming.

To teach that the church must pass through all or part of the Tribulation is delaying the Lord's coming, for if the church must pass through only one day of the Tribulation, then we cannot look for Him until after that day and, therefore, Jesus cannot come today.

Oh, let us beware of delaying the Lord's return, of putting it off. Our Lord said, "It is not for you to know the times or the seasons," and He certainly implied by this that we are to look for Him ALL the time and at ANY time.

Dire Warnings

In view of the many, many strange teachings and deceptions so prevalent today concerning the time of our Lord's return, a warning needs to be sounded. To place anything, any event before our Lord's return is a terrible sin, which will be severely judged. To state that anything must still happen before our Lord comes back is to destroy the imminency and the power of the second coming and to take away the incentive for holiness for service and for patience which the imminent, any-moment expectation of our Lord promotes.

To all who would, therefore, have us believe that something, no matter what it may be, must still occur before we can look for our Lord's return, I would like to quote the words of our Lord in Luke 12, without comment.

"But and if that servant say in his heart, My lord delayeth his coming; and shall begin to beat the menservants and maidens, and to eat and drink, and to be drunken, The lord of that servant will come in a day when he looketh not for him, and at an hour when he is not aware, and will cut him in sunder, and will appoint him his portion with the unbelievers."—Luke 12:45,46.

We want to sound the warning, that if we give up the expectation of the Lord's imminent return, we make the entire truth sterile, fruitless and helpless.

Jesus MAY come today. If we really believe that He might come before tomorrow morning, it would stir us to the very depths of our souls, I am sure. There would be some things that we have left undone, that we would want to do before we meet Him. There are some things that we have done, that we would want to make right before the Lord's return to call us before the judgment seat of Christ. We would live such lives that not a finger could be laid upon us because we would be found working for Him.

Surely if we believe with all our hearts that the Lord Jesus Christ might come back again before another day passes, it would stir us to action. It would cause holiness of walk and conduct and conversation. We would make this last day really count for our Lord and Saviour Jesus Christ. And so we ask the question in closing, "How real is this blessed hope of our Lord's return?" The Apostle John tells us very definitely concerning this:

"And every man that hath this hope in him purifieth himself, even as he is pure."—I John 3:3.

"Watch therefore: for ye know not what hour your Lord doth come."—Matt. 24:42.

PART TWO

"He which testifieth these things saith, Surely I come quickly. Amen. Even so, come, Lord Jesus."—Rev. 22:20.

In this verse, the very next to the last verse in the entire Bible, we find two last things spoken of. First, we have the last promise, and then we have the last prayer in the Bible. The last promise is from our risen, ascended Lord; the last prayer is by His waiting, redeemed people on the earth; and both of these—the last promise and the last prayer— have to do with just one single thing—the coming again of our Lord Jesus Christ, the only answer to the world's problems, the only hope of a groaning creation, the blessed hope of the waiting bride. The promise is, "Surely I come quickly." And the prayer is, "Even so, come, Lord Jesus."

Important Doctrine

The unique way, therefore, in which the Bible closes is in itself an indication of the tremendous importance of the doctrine of the second coming of the Lord Jesus Christ. I hope that you will see this.

Last words are always very precious words, important words, meaningful words. If you, for instance, knew that you had only a few more minutes to spend with your loved ones here on earth, you certainly would not spend those minutes in idle conversation or inconsequential chatter. You would weigh every word, you would speak of the thing that is nearest and dearest and heaviest upon your heart.

The same certainly must have been true of our Lord Jesus Christ. For when He spoke these last words, He knew that this was the end of His revelation to us in the Bible; and in these last few words He speaks again of the thing which is closest to His own heart, His second coming, the climax of His redemptive program.

Let those who tell us that the doctrine of the second coming of Christ is not an important doctrine, a vital doctrine, a fundamental doctrine, consider this fact, that our Lord in His very last closing words to the waiting church chose to speak only of His coming again.

In our message last week, you will remember, we called your attention to the first words which Jesus ever sent back from Heaven AFTER He ascended. It was, "I am coming again." This was the promise of Acts 1:11; and just as His FIRST word AFTER He went to Heaven was, "I am coming back again," so the very LAST words which He sent down from Heaven before the canon of Scriptures was closed, are again, "I am coming back again."

And between these two verses, the first and the last words of our ascended Lord from Heaven, there are some three hundred references to this blessed, glorious hope in the New Testament from the first chapter of Acts to the end of the book of the Revelation.

Must Be Preached

Considering, therefore, the importance attached by the Holy Spirit and the Lord Jesus Christ to this great truth, as indicated by the volume of space and the prominence given to it in the writings of Paul, John, James, Peter and Jude, we wonder, yes, I say, we wonder why it is preached on so seldom in many, many quarters.

A preacher friend said to me, "I never preach on the second coming, for I do not consider it a fundamental or important doctrine."

What a serious indictment, what a charge to hurl against the blessed person of the Holy Spirit, who devotes so much space to it in the Bible and gives it such an important place. What an accusation against the apostles who constantly preached it and the writers of the Bible who ceaselessly proclaimed it.

Do you realize that far more is said concerning the glorious second coming of Christ in the Old Testament than about His first coming in humiliation? For without His second coming, the first coming is sterile, abortive, barren and incomplete.

Read the Old Testament, and you will find many, many times more references to the Lord's glorious second coming and the setting up of His kingdom than to His first coming and humiliation at Calvary. No wonder that the people of Israel lost sight of the first coming in the mass of revelation concerning His second coming. As a result, almost everyone, including the disciples and even John the Baptist, expected that, when the Messiah would come, He would set up His kingdom in Glory.

And so when He came nineteen hundred years ago and the revelation of the cross was given, it was to them a great, a tremendous shock and a terrible disappointment. And just as Israel was at that time so occupied with the glory of Messiah's kingdom that they failed to consider and lost sight of the cross, which must precede it, so today I fear that there are many so occupied with the cross and His first coming that they have lost sight of the value and the necessity and the meaning of His second coming to set up the kingdom.

It is not that we would in any way minimize the importance of the cross, but without the second coming the entire plan remains incomplete. And so the Jews of Jesus' day knew only kingdom truth and knew nothing about the church; and today the very opposite is true, and the mass of Christendom sees only the church and knows nothing about the kingdom truth of our Lord's return.

Consider Its Prominence

Do you realize that the very first promise God ever gave to man after he fell was the promise of the second coming of the Messiah? In Genesis 3:15 God, in pronouncing judgment upon the serpent, immediately after Adam's fall, says:

"And I will put enmity between thee and the woman, and between thy seed and her seed; it shall bruise thy head, and thou shalt bruise his heel."

Now everyone knows, everyone agrees that this promise refers to the coming of the Redeemer, the Seed of the woman; but have you ever seen the two comings of the Redeemer in this verse? They are both very clearly there. Here is the first coming:

"Thou [the seed of the serpent] *shall bruise his* [the Seed of the woman] *heel."*

Now this, everyone agrees, is already history. It was literally fulfilled nineteen hundred years ago when Jesus hung upon the cross with His feet nailed to a literal tree and His heel literally bruised by the emissaries of the serpent, Satan.

But this verse (Gen. 3:15) contains more than the bruising of the Saviour's heel; it also speaks of the crushing of the serpent's head, which, of course, means his final end; for when the head is crushed, that means the end of his existence. It refers, therefore, to the ultimate, complete and final victory of our Lord Jesus Christ over Satan. To say that Jesus crushed the serpent's head at Calvary is to ignore the plain teaching of the Word of God. At our Lord's first coming, His heel was bruised; but it will only be at His second coming that Satan's head will be finally crushed and bruised and complete victory for the Saviour be assured.

I repeat, to say that this prophecy of the crushing of Satan's head was fulfilled at Calvary is to ignore the plain teaching of the Word of God. Paul gives us the answer in Romans 16:20. Listen to Paul:

"And the God of peace shall bruise Satan under your feet shortly."

Now this was written by the Apostle Paul some thirty years after Calvary, and Paul tells us the bruising of Satan is still in the future. Certainly if Jesus is not coming back again, then Calvary was a victory for Satan instead of for the Lord Jesus Christ. How significant, therefore, that the very first promise in the Old Testament includes both the first coming when the Saviour's heel will be bruised, and also the second coming when He will crush the serpent's head.

Close of the Old Testament

But even more astonishing is the fact that the very last promise in the Old Testament was also the promise—not of our Lord's first coming, but of His second. We, of course, do not underestimate the importance of our Lord's first advent, to suffer, to die and to rise again. We would not make His second coming more important than His first, for they are inseparable and of equal importance. The first coming is incomplete without His second, and the second is impossible without the first. We merely want you to see how equally important our Lord's return is, and absolutely essential in the final consummation of the redemption which He began at Calvary, and will be completed when He comes again.

And so consider the last promise in the Old Testament. You will find it in Malachi chapter 4, verse 1, where we read:

"For, behold, the day cometh, that shall burn as an oven; and all the proud, yea, and all that do wickedly, shall be stubble: and the day that cometh shall burn them up, saith the Lord of hosts, that it shall leave them neither root nor branch."

Now the teaching of this passage is unmistakable. Malachi, of course, is referring to the "day of the Lord," an expression occurring hundreds of times in the Scriptures and without exception invariably refers to that awful day of earth's judgment which will be ushered in at the coming again of Christ. It is called not only the "day of the Lord," but also the "Great Tribulation," the "day of vengeance of our God," the "time of Jacob's trouble," and many other equally descriptive titles. And then will you notice verse 2 of Malachi 4:

"But unto you that fear my name shall the Sun of righteousness arise with healing in his wings."

This is a clear, definite reference to the return of our Lord Jesus Christ as the "Sun of righteousness" to dispel the darkness and the gloom of this present age. To the nation of Israel, the Messiah, Jesus will come as the Sun of righteousness to dispel the darkness of the time of Jacob's trouble in particular during the Tribulation. Malachi describes this day in chapter 3, verses 1-4:

"Behold, I will send my messenger, and he shall prepare the way before me: and the Lord, whom ye seek, shall suddenly come to his temple, even the messenger of the covenant, whom ye delight in: behold, he shall come, saith the Lord of hosts. But who may abide the day of his coming? and who shall stand when he appeareth? for he is like a refiner's fire, and like fullers' soap: And he shall sit as a refiner and purifier of silver: and he shall purify the sons of Levi, and purge them as gold and silver, that they may offer unto the Lord an offering in righteousness. Then shall the offering of Judah and Jerusalem be pleasant unto the Lord, as in the days of old, and as in former years."

When the earth's darkest moment arrives, it will only be by the coming of the Lord that its problems will be solved and peace and righteousness will be ushered in.

The Morning Star

But just as Christ will come AFTER the Tribulation to the nation of Israel as the Sun of righteousness to deliver them, just so He will FIRST come as the Morning Star to catch away His church. In Revelation 2:26-28 we read:

"And he that overcometh, and keepeth my works unto the end, to him will I give power over the nations: And he shall rule them with a rod of iron; as the vessels of a potter shall they be broken to shivers: even as I received of my Father. AND I WILL GIVE HIM THE MORNING STAR."

Now you will notice in this passage, which of course refers to the church, that our Lord here is referred to as the "morning star" for His waiting bride. But to Israel He is presented as the "Sun of righteousness." Now the figure is most suggestive and instructive. The morning star is one of the brightest stars in the heavens. It always rises shortly before dawn and is followed by the darkest hour of the entire night, the hour just before the dawn. The morning star heralds the night's darkest hour but also proclaims the promise of the soon coming sunrise. And then after this darkest period of the night, after the morning star rises, the sun shows itself, dispelling the darkness, awaking all nature and bringing in a new day.

This is the Bible revelation concerning our Lord's return also. The next event is the rising of the morning star for the church when Jesus comes from

". . . heaven with a shout, with the voice of the archangel, and with the trump of God: and the dead in Christ shall rise first: Then we which are alive and remain shall be caught up together with them in the clouds, to meet the Lord in the air: and so shall we ever be with the Lord."—I Thess. 4:16,17.

And then after this event of the rapture of the church will come the Tribulation, the day of the Lord, the time of Jacob's trouble and earth's bath of blood, the blackest period in human history, a time of suffering so intense that Jesus said:

"Except those days were shortened there should no flesh be saved."

And then after this period of seven years, when everything seems to be lost, the Sun of righteousness, the Lord Jesus Christ, will suddenly return with His glorified bride, the church, and usher in the glad millennial day of earth's redemption, Israel's restoration and universal blessing upon all nations of the earth, when:

> **Christ shall have dominion,**
> **Over land and sea;**
> **Earth's remotest regions,**
> **Shall His empires be.**

This, beloved, is the program of God. This is the only hope of the world, for the nations and for creation. The next event on the program, then, in the schedule of God is that glorious event called also "that blessed hope" when the Lord Jesus Himself shall return according to the promise of His Book:

"He which testifieth these things saith, Surely I come quickly. Amen."—Rev. 22:20.

May our hearts respond, "Even so, come, Lord Jesus."

HARRY A. IRONSIDE
1876-1951

ABOUT THE MAN:

Few preachers had more varied ministries than this man. He was a captain in the Salvation Army, an itinerant preacher with the Plymouth Brethren, pastor of the renowned Moody Memorial Church in Chicago, and he conducted Bible conferences throughout the world. Sandwiched between those major ministries, Ironside preached the Gospel on street corners, in missions, in taverns, on Indian reservations, etc.

Never formally ordained and with no experience whatever as a pastor, Ironside took over the 4,000-seat Moody Memorial Church in Chicago and often filled it to capacity for 18½ years. A seminary president once said of him, *"He has the most unique ministry of any man living."* Although he had little formal education, his tremendous mental capacity and photographic memory caused him to be called the "Archbishop of Fundamentalism."

Preaching—warm, soul-saving preaching—was his forte. Special speakers in his great church often meant nothing; the crowds came when he was there. He traveled constantly; at his prime, he averaged 40 weeks in the year on the road—always returning to Moody Memorial for Sunday services.

His pen moved, too; he contributed regularly to various religious periodicals and journals in addition to publishing 80 books and pamphlets. His writings included addresses or commentaries on the entire New Testament, all of the prophetic books of the Old Testament, and a great many volumes on specific Bible themes and subjects.

In 1951, Dr. Ironside died in Cambridge, New Zealand, and was buried there at his own request.

V.

Relation of the Church to the Second Coming of Christ

H. A. IRONSIDE

"Let not your heart be troubled: ye believe in God, believe also in me. In my Father's house are many mansions: if it were not so, I would have told you. I go to prepare a place for you. And if I go and prepare a place for you, I will come again, and receive you unto myself; that where I am, there ye may be also. And whither I go ye know, and the way ye know. Thomas saith unto him, Lord, we know not whither thou goest; and how can we know the way? Jesus saith unto him, I am the way, the truth, and the life: no man cometh unto the Father, but by me. If ye had known me, ye should have known my Father also: and from henceforth ye know him, and have seen him."—John 14:1-7.

I need not read further, for these verses give us that which I have particularly upon my heart: What we may call the heavenly side of the truth of the second coming of our Lord Jesus Christ—that is, His return for the church, which is His body and His bride, an event which is clearly distinguished in Scripture from the actual second coming of the Lord to this world.

In the so-called Synoptic Gospels—Matthew, Mark and Luke—our Lord speaks again and again of the coming of the Son of Man, a term which always refers to His coming back again to establish the long promised kingdom of righteousness on the earth. If you bear this in mind when you are reading the warnings in the Synoptics as a preparation for that coming, you will not read the church position into them.

To understand them aright, you must put yourself in spirit where the disciples were when Jesus was speaking to them, remembering that at that time nothing had yet been revealed concerning

The Mystical Body of Christ

or the heavenly bride of the Lamb. Of Israel as the wife of Jehovah now divorced but by and by to be brought back into the nuptial relationship with Him, they knew something from the Old Testament; and the teaching of the Lord fitted into that. But they knew nothing whatever of the precious truth which means so much to us today—*the relationship of the indwelling Spirit of God to a glorified Man in Heaven.* That was never revealed in Old Testament times nor yet during our Saviour's ministry on the earth. Therefore, when He, for instance, says to His disciples, "Pray that ye may be counted worthy to escape these things that are coming upon the earth, and to stand before the Son of man," He speaks to them of that which they could understand. In other words, He addresses them as the remnant of Israel, the people of whom we read in Isaiah and elsewhere, who will be preserved and kept by the grace and power of God in that day of awful judgment upon the earth, in order that they may enter into the displayed kingdom, which will have its capital on Mount Zion, in the land of Palestine.

The Great Tribulation of which He speaks is the precursor of His second coming in this sense. We are told that "immediately after the tribulation of those days, they shall see the Son of man coming in the clouds with power and great glory." But the promise to the church is, "Because thou hast kept the word of my patience, I also will keep thee *from the hour* of temptation, which shall come upon all the world, to try them that dwell upon the earth."

Again, take such a passage as

"He That Endureth Unto the End

the same shall be saved." What is the end here referred to? Surely the end of the *age;* this is the close of the Great Tribulation, and the Lord's reference is to the awful experiences so many of the Jewish remnant will be exposed to and the efforts that will be made by Satan and his minions to turn them away from the path of devotion to the coming Messiah. In that day, by divine power, they may be kept to the end, no matter what the enmity of the evil agencies here on earth may bring forth. So with all other Scriptures that seem to cast a doubt, perhaps, on the church's being kept out of the Great Tribulation.

When we turn to the second part of John's Gospel and come as here to the Upper Room, it is as though Israel's day for the time being was

looked upon as already ended. To that little group of believers...
our Lord

Reveals Certain Things

which had never been made known before.

Not a word is said about the Holy Spirit as Comforter in Matthew, Mark and Luke. We never read about the Spirit of God as a divine Person, dwelling in believers, until in this section we hear the Lord Jesus say, 'He hath been with you, he shall be in you.' There you have a great dispensational change intimated.

The Holy Spirit Ever Active

All through Old Testament times and during the days of our Lord's ministry on earth, the Holy Spirit was with all who believed. He was with the antediluvian saints, for Noah, by the Spirit, bore testimony in the days before the Flood. He it was who guided the patriarchs and was with Moses empowering for testimony. We read that God gave His good Spirit to be with Israel and to guide them through the wilderness.

From the depths of a broken and penitent heart David cried, "Take not thy holy spirit from me." The Spirit of God fell upon men in the days of the judges and of the kingdom afterwards. He filled certain individuals for particular service. The prophets predicted the glorious outpouring of the Spirit in the days of the Messianic kingdom. But nowhere in the Old Testament or in the Synoptics or in the first part of John's Gospel is there set forth the truth of a divine personal Holy Spirit coming from Heaven to dwell in believers, baptizing them into one body and linking them to their glorified Head above. This is just barely intimated in John 7:37-39.

But these truths are first introduced here to prepare the disciples for the new administration so soon to begin. It is in this connection He speaks for the

First Time Clearly of His Return

for His own in an altogether different way than that of His coming to Israel. Instead of speaking of the Son of Man coming in the glory of the Father with the holy angels like a lightning flash; instead of His glorious apocalyptic manifestation; and instead of His coming to earth and sending forth His angels to gather together the elect of Israel and bring them back to the city of the Great King, you find the Lord giving them a wonderful revelation, though in few words, that He has something else in view for them.

Of this they will learn more fully in due time, for He says, "I have yet many things to say unto you, but ye cannot bear them now." That might be rendered, "You cannot apprehend them now." It was as though He said, "You are not now ready for them; you have not been cut loose from Israel's dispensational hopes. After the Holy Spirit is come and the new economy has been ushered in, you will be prepared to comprehend these things; then you will understand."

But He tells them, 'I am going away, and where I am your heart should be. I am going to the Father's house; there are many resting places there, but none are suitable for you. I am going to prepare a place for you.' I think we have a revelation of that later on. That is the place in the immediate presence of God, in the holiest of all inside the rent veil; that never could be until after an accomplished redemption.

It was better than the wildest dreams of the Old Testament saints— that redeemed men should actually dwell with the glorified Christ in the immediate presence of God in Heaven.

Jesus, by going to the cross, opened up a new and living way "through the veil, that is to say, his flesh." So today in spirit, we already enter into what shall be our portion for eternity. The veil is already rent, and our souls draw near with boldness to a throne of grace. That is the prepared place, and that will be our portion forever.

How Are We Going to Reach All This

actually? Well, He says, "If I go and prepare a place for you, I WILL COME AGAIN"—and do what? Set up My kingdom on earth? No, that is not what He is speaking of here. Execute judgment on the wicked? No, it is not that which He has in view.

What then?—Redeem Israel as a nation? Now now—but "I will come again, and *receive you unto myself;* that where I am, there ye may be also."

How their hearts must have thrilled as they heard this first mention of what we now speak of as the rapture! He does not unfold the nature of it. He simply declares the truth. He *is coming again to receive His own unto Himself.*

I know you might get a beautiful picture of this in the parable of the ten virgins; and, of course, that parable sets forth the proper attitude that His people should have during all the time of His absence and the joy that will be theirs when He returns, if they are ready to meet Him. But strictly speaking, here in John 14, we have the first clear definite instruction concerning the rapture.

We have to turn to the writings of the Apostle Paul to get a fuller unfolding of this glorious event. How will the Lord receive us to Himself? How will He fulfill this promise? We return to the great resurrection chapter, I Corinthians 15, and we read from verse 51, "Behold,

I Shew You a Mystery"

MYSTERY! I hardly need remind you that this word, as used in Scripture, does not refer to something difficult to understand. It is not something that is in itself mysterious. But it means something that has been *kept secret until the time for its revelation* had come. The word was commonly used among the Greeks in the day the New Testament was written, for the secrets of the various oath-bound religious organizations that were revealed to the initiates after they had passed through certain ceremonial rites. And people use it today in exactly the same way. You hear a lot of the mysteries of various secret oath-bound lodges.

Here I may turn aside to say a word as to these. Possibly many of you are members of such societies. Three Scriptures have kept me out of anything of the kind, though I have often been urged to apply for membership in some of them. Many come up to me at the close of meetings and shake hands with me in peculiar ways and look to see if I respond. But the only handshake I know anything about is a good, straightforward Christian greeting. I belong to the G.A.R—the

Grand Army of the Redeemed

and to no worldly society of any kind! The three Scriptures I refer to are these: First, "Jesus said, In secret have I said nothing." Second, "He left us an example that we should follow his steps." Third, "Be ye not unequally yoked together with unbelievers." These Scriptures leave no place in an esoteric hidden cult for saved and unsaved alike to participate. The precious mysteries of the Word of God are now made known to all who will believe.

Just as those who are on the inside know the secrets of the lodges and religious cults, so believers should be familiar with the mysteries of God. All through Old Testament times He had precious and wonderful secrets of which Moses spoke, when he said, "The secret things belong to the Lord our God, but the things that are revealed are for us, and for our children for ever."

Now in this glorious dispensation of the Holy Spirit, many hitherto concealed mysteries have been made known. The complete revelation of the will of God comes later. We read in Revelation 10:7, "But in the days of the voice of the seventh angel, when he shall begin to sound, the mystery of God should be finished, as he hath declared to his servants the prophets." This will be at the close of the Great Tribulation, whereas the mystery of which Paul speaks in I Corinthians 15 will *precede* that time of trouble.

So, if you have any unsolved problems as to

God's Agelong Toleration of Evil

or other difficulties, you will have the explanation then. Everything will be perfectly clear in that day. But God has already opened up to us some very wonderful mysteries, and this is one of them. "Behold, I shew you a mystery; we shall not all sleep, but we shall all be changed" (I Cor. 15:51). Paul is speaking of believers; but, of course, when he uses the term "sleep," he means "death."

Do not make the mistake of thinking that Paul was a soul sleeper. He has made it very clear elsewhere that, for the believer, death means "absent from the body, present with the Lord." But when he speaks of sleep, he refers to *physical death*. All down through the ages death has claimed the bodies of believers, but there are some here, perhaps, who will not taste of death until you see the blessed Lord coming to call His own to be with Himself.

"WE SHALL NOT ALL SLEEP, BUT WE SHALL ALL BE CHANGED."

Changed! Transformed!

"Flesh and blood cannot inherit the kingdom of God." We cannot enter upon the full enjoyment of the heavenly side of that kingdom in these bodies and under present conditions. We must be transformed. Our bodies of humiliation must be made like unto the body of His glory. And when will it take place? "In a moment, in the twinkling of an eye, at the last trump." Just as quickly as the flash of light appears in the eye, this change will take place when our Lord returns.

"FOR THE TRUMPET SHALL SOUND, AND THE DEAD SHALL BE RAISED INCORRUPTIBLE, AND WE SHALL BE CHANGED. For this corruptible must put on incorruption, and this mortal must put on immortality."

Notice again the two classes of believers. This corruptible—those who have died, whose bodies have all been seized upon by corruption. This mortal—those who are living when the Lord returns, living on the earth in their mortal bodies—shall immediately become immortal. So when these two changes take place—when "this corruptible shall have put on incorruption, and this mortal shall have put on immortality, then shall be brought to pass the saying that is written, Death is swallowed up in victory."

Therefore, in the light of this hope, the apostle can

Challenge Our Great Enemy:

"O death, where is thy sting? O grave [Hades], where is thy victory? The sting of death is sin; and the strength of sin is the law." Sin was settled for at Calvary's cross, and the believer is no longer under the law.

"THE STRENGTH OF SIN IS THE LAW." What an astounding expression! Is not the law the strength of holiness? If you want to live a holy life, must you not put yourself under the law and strive with all the energy of your being to keep its commandments? No, the Word of God declares, "The strength of sin is the law," because the law stirs up everything that is evil in the heart of unregenerate man, and he finds himself hopeless to obey its commandments.

You say, "Yes, that was true of us in our unconverted state, but when we were born of God, everything changed, and now the law has become the strength of holiness." But, no; the strength of holiness is the indwelling Spirit of God, He who is spoken of characteristically as the Holy Spirit. He fulfills the righteousness of the law in us, "who walk not after the flesh, but after the Spirit." And so we can say, "Thanks be to God which giveth us the victory through our Lord Jesus Christ."

Observe, then,

The Rapture Takes Place in a Moment

and at the last trump. There are those who think of this as the last of the seven trumpets, the judgments in the book of Revelation, but there is no connection whatever between the two. They are trumpets of doom; this is a trumpet of blessing. But the last trump, I understand, is that which winds up the church's history in the earth.

Some think, possibly rightly, that it is really a military term, which was used of old in connection with the Roman army. There were three trumps. Suppose the camp is wrapped in darkness and the legionaries are all sound asleep. An enemy is approaching; the warning word comes to the commander who calls the trumpeter to sound an alarm. At the first trump everyone is aroused. At the second trump all fall into line. At the last trump they march away.

So you and I who are saved heard the first trump when we were sound asleep in our sins. That was the gospel trump; it awakened us from our sleep, and we sprang to our feet as new creatures in Christ Jesus. I trust that we have also heard the trump which calls us to take our place in the ranks of yielding ourselves in ready obedience to the Lord Jesus Christ. Now what wait we for? For the last trump—not to march away, but to be caught up to meet the Lord in the air.

Turn to the corresponding passage in I Thessalonians 4:14. You notice this trump is spoken of there as "THE TRUMP OF GOD"; not, therefore, to be confounded with

The Trumpets of Angels

in the book of Revelation. It is God Himself summoning His own to meet His blessed Son in the air. Let us read the passage: "For if we believe that Jesus died and rose again"—and we do, if we do not we are not Christians, according to Romans 10:9. On the authority of that Scripture, we dare to say without any unkindness, that *no man is what the Bible calls a Christian if he denies the physical resurrection of the Lord Jesus.* Everything for us depends upon that blessed fact that "He was delivered for our offences, and *raised again* for our justification," and so we read, "If we believe that Jesus *died* and *rose again, even* so them also which sleep in Jesus will God bring with him."

Now this is most striking. Bring with Him where? When He comes in the glory of His Father with the holy angels. You see, this event links up with the revelation given concerning the coming of the Son of Man in the Synoptics and the Old Testament prophecies concerning the same event. We read in Zechariah 14 that in the darkest hour of Palestine's distress the Lord God shall come and all the saints with Him. Some might think of those saints as simply angels, but the New Testament shows us that there will also be redeemed men and women in association with Christ in Glory. True, He will come with the holy angels, but also with the saints, once poor sinners, but saved by grace. These will shine forth with Him. But how can that be? Their bodies throughout the centuries have been corrupting in the grave, and those who come with Him will not merely be unclothed, but resurrected, or changed believers.

How Will This Be Brought About?

The next verse tells us. "FOR THIS WE SAY UNTO YOU BY THE WORD OF THE LORD, THAT WE WHICH ARE ALIVE AND REMAIN"—meditate on that expression. How blessed to realize that these words may refer to some who are now living on the earth. Throughout this dispensation this event is ever treated as imminent, though never declared to be immediate. "We which are alive and remain unto the coming of the Lord, shall not prevent them which are asleep." The old English word *prevent* means "precede." We shall not enter into Christ's train before the saints who have died. "For the Lord himself shall descend from heaven with a shout, with the voice of the archangel, and with the trump of God, and the dead in Christ shall rise first."

In other words, if we are living on the earth when the Lord returns, we will not go into the kingdom one moment ahead of anybody else, for "the Lord himself" is first to descend to the air, and His voice will raise the righteous dead. We read of the shout of the Lord, the voice of the archangel; and in the book of Daniel He is particularly linked with the destinies of Israel, "the great Prince which standeth for the children of thy people." So in the same instant the thousands of the Israel of God who have died in faith all over the world and the redeemed of the Lord of all other dispensations will be raised.

"Stand Up" and "Caught Up"

"The dead in Christ"—no one else—"shall rise first"; literally, *stand up first*. The word for resurrection throughout the New Testament has this meaning. They will stand up from the graves in their resurrection bodies, an exceeding great army. "Then we which are alive and remain shall be caught up together with them in clouds to meet the Lord in the air, and so shall we ever be with the Lord." In this way the church and Old Testament saints will all be with the Lord in their resurrection or changed bodies, prior to His descent to take the kingdom. So at God's appointed time He will bring these with Christ when He returns to earth again.

Others have pointed out that that word *meet* does not merely mean "casually running into someone," as, for instance, on the side of the roadway, as we say, "I met So-and-so." But rather, as we say, "So-and-so is coming, and I am going out to meet him." When you meet him, possibly you go immediately home; or perhaps there is something else to occupy you before you take him to the house.

Now the word used here has that meaning. We will be caught up to meet the Lord, not in order to return with Him immediately; for certain events must take place on earth before His manifestation, when we shall come back with Him. There are others that take place in Heaven: the judgment seat of Christ and the marriage supper of the Lamb. It will be after this that He will descend to take the kingdom and all His saints with Him.

Just one other passage, the first chapter of Thessalonians, verse 9. Speaking of the conversion of these Thessalonians, Paul writes, "For they themselves shew of us what manner of entering in we had unto you, and how ye turned to God from idols to serve the living and true God; and to wait for his Son from heaven." This certainly suggests the imminent coming of the Lord. There are no events that must necessarily take place first.

The Spirit of God was not pleased to reveal at that time the course of the last nineteen hundred years. Every believer living before, and all through the centuries since, was entitled to look up in

Daily Expectation of the Lord's Return,

an expectation which has a sanctifying effect upon our hearts and lives as we read in I John 3:3, "And every man that hath this hope in him [Christ] purifieth himself even as he is pure."

It is important, however, to note that, while Scripture clearly teaches the imminency of the Lord's return, it never insists on the immediateness of that event. We cannot say when it will take place, but we should always be looking for it.

But now let us finish the passage. "To wait for his Son from heaven, whom he raised from the dead, even Jesus, which delivered us from

the Wrath to Come."

The past tense is used here, but scholars tell us it hardly conveys the full thought. It is rather "which shall deliver us from the wrath to come." What is that? Eternal judgment? No, we have been saved from that already. We shall never come into judgment. "The wrath to come" is that which is yet to fall upon this world when the wrath of the Lamb and the wrath of God will be visited upon the dwellers of the earth and when Satan shall be cast down from Heaven, "having great wrath because he knoweth that his time is short."

At that time the church will no longer be here. We shall be delivered from that wrath to come. How? Snatched away when our blessed Lord descends from Heaven with a shout. This is the believer's hope. God grant it may be yours and that you may ever live in view of this glorious event.

> **Midst the darkness, storm and sorrow,**
> **One bright gleam I see;**
> **Well I know the blessed morrow,**
> **Christ will come for me.**
>
> **Oh, the blessed joy of meeting!**
> **All the desert past!**
> **Oh, the wondrous words of greeting**
> **He shall speak at last!**
>
> **Meet companion then for Jesus,**
> **From Him, for Him made;**
> **Glory of God's grace forever**
> **There in me displayed.**
>
> **He who in His hour of sorrow**
> **Bore the curse alone;**
> **I who through the lonely desert**
> **Trod where He had gone.**
>
> **He and I in that bright glory**
> **One deep joy shall share—**
> **Mine, to be forever with Him!**
> **His, that I am there!**

(Reprinted with grateful acknowledgment to Loizeaux Brothers, Publishers)

LEE ROBERSON
1909-

ABOUT THE MAN:

When one considers the far-reaching ministries of the Highland Park Baptist Church and pauses to reflect upon its total outreach, he has cause to believe that it is close to the New Testament pattern.

In the more than forty-one years—from 1942 when Roberson first came to Highland Park until his retirement in April 1983—the ministry expanded to include Camp Joy, reaching some 3,000 children annually; World Wide Faith Missions, contributing to the support of over 350 missionaries; 50 branch churches in the greater Chattanooga area; Union Gospel Mission, which feeds and sleeps an average of 50 transient men daily; a Sunday school bus ministry, which covers 45 bus routes; a deaf ministry; "Gospel Dynamite," a live broadcast held daily, now in its 47th year; a church paper, THE EVANGELIST, being mailed free twice monthly to over 73,000 readers; and Tennessee Temple University, Temple Baptist Theological Seminary, and Tennessee Temple Academy.

He is an author of many books.

Preaching to thousands, training preachers, supporting the mission cause, Dr. John R. Rice called him "the Spurgeon of our generation."

VI.

The Imminency of His Coming

LEE ROBERSON

"Watch therefore: for ye know not what hour your Lord doth come."—Matt. 24:42.

"Watch ye therefore: for ye know not when the master of the house cometh, at even, or at midnight, or at the cockcrowing, or in the morning."—Mark 13:35.

"Be ye therefore ready also: for the Son of man cometh at an hour when ye think not."—Luke 12:40.

"For the earnest expectation of the creature waiteth for the manifestation of the sons of God."—Rom. 8:19.

"And not only they, but ourselves also, which have the firstfruits of the Spirit, even we ourselves groan within ourselves, waiting for the adoption, to wit, the redemption of our body."—Rom. 8:23.

"So that ye come behind in no gift; waiting for the coming of our Lord Jesus Christ."—I Cor. 1:7.

"For our conversation is in heaven; from whence also we look for the Saviour, the Lord Jesus Christ."—Phil. 3:20.

"And to wait for his Son from heaven, whom he raised from the dead, even Jesus, which delivered us from the wrath to come."—I Thess. 1:10.

"Looking for that blessed hope, and the glorious appearing of the great God and our Saviour Jesus Christ."—Titus 2:13.

"Be ye also patient; stablish your hearts: for the coming of the Lord draweth nigh."—James 5:8.

"Behold, I come as a thief. Blessed is he that watcheth, and keepeth his garments, lest he walk naked, and they see his shame."—Rev. 16:15.

I want to press one great truth in this message: the imminency of His coming. This is emphasized in many portions of the Word of God; and the Lord Jesus tells us that we should be ready, "for in such an hour as ye think not, the Son of man cometh."

At any hour—at any moment—He may come!

What exhortation does the Bible give through this teaching? The Bible says, "Be ye also ready."

This means the Christian must be ready for the coming of the Saviour.

This means that the sinner should come to Christ for salvation and be ready for the return of his Lord.

When we say that His coming is imminent, we mean that Christ may come at any moment.

Webster tells us in the *New World Dictionary* that *imminent* means

"likely to happen without delay; impending; threatening."

The *New English Dictionary* gives about the same definition:

"hanging over one's head," "ready to befall or overtake one," "close at hand in its incidence," "coming on shortly."

The coming of the Lord Jesus is an imminent second coming: it may happen at any moment.

I cannot think of any person who would not be benefited by an understanding of the second coming. This is for the young as well as for the aged; for the businessman as well as for the housewife; for the wealthy as well as for the poor; for the sick as well as for the healthy.

I have tried to think of all the people who would be benefited by a message on the second coming of Christ.

This doctrine is for the man who is a failure; this should spur him on. If a man is failing in his Christian activities, this truth should spur him on to do still more for the Saviour.

This is the doctrine for the money-mad Christian. Christ is coming. What you have will be left. The accumulation of much goods will not benefit in the day when Jesus comes to catch us up into His presence. (If you don't like this doctrine, then you had better check on your salvation.)

Here is the doctrine for the worldly Christian—the carnally minded one. My friend, you will have to face Him! You must give an account of yourself unto the Lord. This is the doctrine for the careless and the unconcerned. Here is the teaching that should send us out to do still more for our Lord. This truth should take away the unconcerned attitude.

This is the doctrine for the sick. When He comes, the dead in Christ shall be raised and the living changed, and we shall be caught up into the presence of our Lord.

I mentioned Philippians 3:20, which speaks of our citizenship being in Heaven and that we are looking for the Lord Jesus. Then Paul says, "Who shall change our vile body, that it may be fashioned like unto his glorious body, according to the working whereby he is able even to subdue all things unto himself."

This is the doctrine for the discouraged. "Your redemption draweth nigh." Have faith in God and look up.

Here is the doctrine for the sorrowing. How many blessed verses are given to comfort those in sorrow! In John 14 Jesus tells us about the Father's house of many mansions. He told His disciples that He was going to make ready a place for them; then He said, "I will come again, and receive you unto myself; that where I am, there ye may be also."

This is the doctrine for the dying. Paul in the last hours of his life stated that he was "now ready to be offered, and the time of my departure is at hand." He says, "I have fought a good fight, I have finished my course, I have kept the faith."

Then the apostle gives us a special word that tells us of his anticipation of the coming of the Lord Jesus: "Henceforth there is laid up for me a crown of righteousness, which the Lord, the righteous judge, shall give me at that day: and not to me only, but unto all them also that love his appearing" (II Tim. 4:8).

Yes, Christ is coming again; and His coming is imminent.

I. THE IMMINENCY OF HIS COMING CALLS FOR ALERTNESS

"And that, knowing the time, that now it is high time to awake out of sleep: for now is our salvation nearer than when we believed.

"The night is far spent, the day is at hand: let us therefore cast off the works of darkness, and let us put on the armour of light.

"Let us walk honestly, as in the day; not in rioting and drunkenness, not in chambering and wantonness, not in strife and envying.

"But put ye on the Lord Jesus Christ, and make not provision for the flesh, to fulfil the lusts thereof."—Rom. 13:11-14.

"But of the times and the seasons, brethren, ye have no need that I write unto you.

"For yourselves know perfectly that the day of the Lord so cometh as a thief in the night.

"For when they shall say, Peace and safety; then sudden destruction cometh upon them, as travail upon a woman with child; and they shall not escape.

"But ye, brethren, are not in darkness, that that day should overtake you as a thief.

"Ye are all children of light, and the children of the day: we are not of the night, nor of darkness.

"Therefore let us not sleep, as do others; but let us watch and be sober.

"For they that sleep sleep in the night; and they that be drunken are drunken in the night.

"But let us, who are of the day, be sober, putting on the breastplate of faith and love; and for an helmet, the hope of salvation."—I Thess. 5:1-8.

In these portions of the Word of God, Paul is calling for alertness of the people of God. We are faced with three lamentable conditions in this day and time.

First, we are faced with the dullness of man to spiritual truth. We are well aware that "the natural man receiveth not the things of the Spirit of God." Quite often the spiritual man—the Christian man—is dull to spiritual truth. Too often he is carnally minded. He does not read the Bible, does not pray believingly, does not engage in the work of Christ aggressively. This dullness to spiritual truth is dangerous. Because of this dullness, many will turn away into evils of the world. Too many will fail to follow Christ in the service that He wants them to render.

Second, we are faced with the dullness of man to spiritual dangers. He does not see the pitfalls of life. Sin has been in the world since the Garden of Eden. There is no change in sin. It has ever been the same. Some have a foolish idea that the sin of this present day is quite different from what it used to be. Some even suggest that young people are discovering certain things today that were unknown in the past.

I have news for you: The sin of this day is the same as the sin of Sodom and Gomorrah hundreds of years ago.

A reporter tells of taking a tour in what is called "Sin City," which happens to be several hundred apartment units next to the University of Florida. The reporter made his visit to some of the apartments. They were filled with boys and girls. Off-color records were played. Wicked dances were being performed. The reporter said, "Against one wall, empty beer cans had been stacked in a grocery store pyramid. The structure was higher than my head. The pop art on the walls spelled out the brands of beers one may purchase in Gainesville environs. A bar had been installed under the stairway that led to the second-floor sleeping quarters."

The reporter went on to make his tour of Sin City. He saw the things that were happening between college young people. Then the reporter in these few words tried to justify the actions of the young people: "They are still groping for a way to cope with the present day. They are trying to hide honest sensitivity. They wear outlandish clothes and long hair." And the reporter says that many of them are bright young people and will doubtless come out of all this on the right side.

First of all, the wickedness of Sin City is the same as it has ever been. Men are men, and sin is sin. Men and women engage in sin and go away from God. There is nothing new, nothing revolutionary about it. It is the same old wickedness. Man is dull to his spiritual danger.

Third, we are faced with the dullness of man to prophesied events. If you tell people of this world that Christ is coming, in many cases they laugh at you, thinking you are a foolish fanatic. But the truth is, man is simply dull to that which has been promised us in the Word of God. The exhortation of the Scriptures is to watch, be alert and be on your toes and ready for His coming.

II. THE IMMINENCY OF HIS RETURN
CALLS FOR AWARENESS

First, be aware of all that Christ has done for you. He has saved your soul through faith in His name. He shed His blood that you might have the forgiveness of sin.

Second, be aware of the greatness of the event of the future — the coming of Christ. Who can measure the import of His coming? Men try to minimize the first coming of Christ, and now they are trying to do the same thing regarding the second coming. This is not new. It has ever been so. It was true in the first century, for Peter said, "Knowing this first, that there shall come in the last days scoffers, walking after their own lusts." It is indicated that there were scoffers in that day, and there are scoffers in this day.

We must be aware of the events that will take place when He comes.

Our Saviour is coming. The dead in Christ shall be raised from the graves. The living shall be changed. There will be a great reunion. (Read I Thess. 4:13-18.)

His coming will bring us to the judgment seat. We are going to be judged, not for salvation but for our works and service. "There is therefore now no condemnation to them which are in Christ Jesus." By faith in the Lord Jesus, our salvation is secure, as secure as God Himself; but when we come to the judgment seat, we shall give account of ourselves and our works will be judged.

Be aware, my friend, that one day you will face the Son of God. We anticipate seeing certain people, certain faces. I read about the Statue of Liberty before I ever saw it. I had heard about Niagara Falls a long time before I saw the beauty and power of the falls. We think about the day when we shall see our Lord face to face. Is there any way for us to comprehend how great it will be to stand before the Lord? Yet there may be some shame when you stand there because you have not given Him your best. You will see Him, yes, but the judgment seat will bring sorrow because you have not given Him your best.

Then after we see our Saviour, there will follow the events as prophesied in the Book. There will be the marriage supper of the Lamb. We shall come with Him in the revelation. We shall be with Him at the battle of Armageddon and the judgment of the living nations. We shall reign with our Lord for a thousand years upon this earth. Then with our Saviour we shall enter into the new heavens and the new earth.

Yes, the imminency of His coming calls for awareness.

III. THE IMMINENCY OF HIS COMING
CALLS FOR ACTIVITY

We must engage in the work that He has left us to do. This is aptly covered by the Great Commission. We are told to "go into all the world, and preach the gospel to every creature." We must be busy; we must be active in doing the task that He has given unto us.

When I pastored the First Baptist Church in Fairfield, Alabama, I gave a series of sermons on the second coming of Jesus Christ. In the course of my messages, I emphasized the fact that He might come at any moment and that we should be ready to meet Him. A lady of the church wrote to one of the outstanding Southern Baptist leaders, asking him his opinion of the second coming. She stated in the letter that I had been preaching that Christ would come at any moment and that we must be watching for His coming. She told the fine doctor that I was a premillennialist and believed in the imminency of the return of Christ.

In a few days a letter came back from this leader. In the first paragraph he told the lady, "I do believe in the premillennial, imminent return of Jesus Christ." He went on to give a few statements about his faith in the return of Christ. Then in the second paragraph he said, "Though I believe in the second coming, I do not preach it, for I feel that it destroys the interest of people in the work of missions and soul winning."

What a gross misunderstanding of the whole doctrine was in the mind of this leader! Yes, Christ is coming, and He may come at any moment. This simply means that we must be busy and doing the tasks that He has assigned to us.

First, be active, for one day your works will be brought before the judgment seat.

"Every man's work shall be made manifest: for the day shall declare it, because it shall be revealed by fire; and the fire shall try every man's work of what sort it is.

"If any man's work abide which he hath built thereupon, he shall receive a reward.

"If any man's work shall be burned, he shall suffer loss: but he himself shall be saved; yet so as by fire."—I Cor. 3:13-15.

Every man's work will be tested. If we have built of lasting materials as gold, silver and precious stones, our works will abide, and we will receive a reward. But if our works are of wood, hay and stubble, they will vanish. We will be saved "yet so as by fire."

Second, be active in service that you might glorify Him. This should mean more to us than we could ever express in words. Christ is our Saviour, our Lord, our Master, our King. By every means we should try to glorify His name. Jesus tells us in John 17 that when He walked upon the earth He glorified the Father. He said, "I have glorified thee on the earth: I have finished the work which thou gavest me to do." The entire portion indicates that we must be busy in bringing glory to our heavenly Father and to our Saviour by the activity of our lives.

Third, be active that you might bring souls to the Lord Jesus. This is our main task. We must not fail.

We have been discussing for these moments the imminency of the coming of Jesus Christ. Are you ready for His coming? Are you prepared to stand before Him? Is your life counting for Him?

In the time that we have, let us be busy. We may have hours. We may have days. We may have weeks. We may have years. We know not; but in the time that we have, we must be busy. Christ is coming!

It is an easy thing to make our plans and announce what we will do. My wife and I were sitting in a restaurant. Just back of us were two couples. They were talking about their vacation and what they were going to do. One said, "We will spend tonight in Fort Lauderdale." The others went on to comment on plans for the future. But you see, the plans that they were making may never take place. There may be car trouble, a wreck, a heart attack. A thousand things could hinder their arrival at Fort Lauderdale.

But when Jesus says, "I will come again"—He is coming. Nothing will hinder. He may come at any moment.

I always announce my topics for Sunday. I plan to speak at 10:50 a.m. and 7:35 p.m. on certain subjects. But many things may happen. I may become ill. I may be killed in a plane crash. Something might happen to my family. Someone else might preach in my pulpit. My plans do not amount to very much.

But God's plans do not change. He tells us that certain things will take place, and they will. He has given His announcement of the coming of the Saviour, and Christ is coming. Are you ready for His coming? His coming is imminent. He may come at any moment.

DWIGHT LYMAN MOODY
1837-1899

ABOUT THE MAN:

D. L. Moody may well have been the greatest evangelist of all time.

In a 40-year period, he won a million souls, founded three Christian schools, launched a great Christian publishing business, established a world-renowned Christian conference center, and inspired literally thousands of preachers to win souls and conduct revivals.

A shoe clerk at 17, his ambition was to make $100,000. Converted at 18, he uncovered hidden gospel gold in the hearts of millions for the next half century. He preached to 20,000 a day in Brooklyn and admitted only non-church members by ticket!

He met a young songleader in Indianapolis, said bluntly, "You're the man I've been looking for for eight years. Throw up your job and come with me." Ira D. Sankey did just that; thereafter it was "Moody will preach; Sankey will sing."

He traveled across the American continent and through Great Britain in some of the greatest and most successful evangelistic meetings communities have ever known. His tour of the world with Sankey was considered the greatest evangelistic enterprise of the century.

It was Henry Varley who said, "It remains to be seen what God will do with a man who gives himself up wholly to Him." And Moody endeavored to be, under God, that man; and the world did marvel to see how wonderfully God used him.

Two great monuments stand to the indefatigable work and ministry of this gospel warrior—Moody Bible Institute and the famous Moody Church in Chicago.

Moody went to be with the Lord in 1899.

VII.

Our Lord's Return

D. L. MOODY

Some people tell us when we take up prophecy, there is no use trying to understand it. But Paul says: "All scripture is. . . profitable for doctrine" (II Tim. 3:16). If God doesn't mean to have us study the prophecies, He wouldn't have put them into the Bible. Some are fulfilled, and He is at work fulfilling the rest.

We are told how He is going to come. When those disciples stood looking up into Heaven at the time of His ascension, there appeared two angels who said unto them:

"Ye men of Galilee, why stand ye gazing up into heaven? This same Jesus, which is taken up from you into heaven shall so come in like manner as ye have seen him go into heaven."—Acts 1:11.

Some have tried to tell the very day He would come. Perhaps that is one of the reasons why people do not believe this doctrine. He is coming, we know that, but just when He is coming we do not know. Matthew 24:36 settles that. Christ tells us to watch. "Therefore be ye also ready, for in such an hour as ye think not, the Son of man cometh."

Some people say that this means death; but the Word of God does not say this means death. John 21:23 seems to settle the matter.

There is another mistake, as you will find if you read your Bibles carefully. Some people think that at the coming of Christ everything is to be done up in a few minutes; but I do not so understand it. The first thing He is to do is to take His church out of the world. He calls the church His bride, and He says He is going to prepare a place for her.

In the closing verses of the fourth chapter of I Thessalonians, Paul says:

"If we believe that Jesus died and rose again, even so them also which sleep in Jesus will God bring with him. . . . We which are alive and

remain unto the coming of the Lord shall not prevent them which are asleep. For the Lord himself shall descend from heaven with a shout, with the voice of the archangel, and with the trump of God: and the dead in Christ shall rise first: Then we which are alive and remain shall be caught up together with them in the clouds, to meet the Lord in the air: and so shall we ever be with the Lord. Wherefore comfort one another with these words."

That is the comfort of the church. Dean Alford says that he must insist that this coming of Christ to take His church to Himself in the clouds is not the same event as His coming to judge the world at the last day. The deliverance of the church is one thing; judgment is another. *The trump of God may be sounded, for anything we know, before I finish this sermon*—at any rate, we are told that He will come as a thief in the night, and at an hour when many look not for Him.

In the first chapter of I Thessalonians, Paul says:

"Ye turned to God from idols to serve the living and true God; and to wait for his Son from heaven, whom he raised from the dead, even Jesus, which delivered us from the wrath to come."

To wait for His Son; that is the true attitude of every child of God. Then over in the next chapter (I Thess. 2:19) he says:

"For what is our hope, or joy, or crown of rejoicing? Are not even ye in the presence of our Lord Jesus Christ at his coming?"

And again, in the third chapter, at the thirteenth verse:

"To the end he may stablish your hearts unblamable in holiness before God, even our Father, at the coming of our Lord Jesus Christ with all his saints."

Still again, in the fifth chapter:

"For yourselves know perfectly that the day of the Lord so cometh as a thief in the night."

He has something to say about this same thing in every chapter. Indeed, I have thought that this epistle to the Thessalonians might be called the Gospel of Christ's coming again.

There are three great facts foretold in the Word of God. First, that Christ should come; that has been fulfilled. Second, that the Holy Ghost should come; that was fulfilled at Pentecost. Third, the return of our

Lord from Heaven—for this we are told to watch and wait till He come.

Take the account of the words of Christ at the *communion table*. It seems to me that the Devil has covered up the most precious thing about it, *"For as often as ye eat this bread, and drink this cup, ye do shew the Lord's death till he come."*

Some people say: "I believe Christ will come on the other side of the millennium." Where do you get it? I cannot find it. I do not find any place where the Lord says the world is to grow better and better. I find that the earth is to grow worse and worse, and at length there is going to be a separation. 'Two women grinding at a mill—one taken and the other left; two men in one bed—one taken and the other left.' The church is to be translated out of the world, and we have two examples already in Christ's kingdom of what is to be done for all believers: Enoch and Elijah. And we have the Saviour Himself, who became the first fruits of them that slept.

Now some of you think this is a new and strange doctrine and that they who preach it are speckled birds. But let me tell you that most of the spiritual men in the pulpits of Great Britain are firm in this faith. I have heard Newman Hall say that he knew no reason why Christ might not come before he got through with his sermon. But in certain wealthy and fashionable churches where they have the form of godliness but deny the power thereof, this doctrine is not preached or believed. We live in the day of shams in religion. The church is cold and formal; may God wake us up! And I know of no better way to do it than to get the church to looking for the return of our Lord.

I have felt like working three times as hard ever since I came to understand that my Lord is coming again. I look upon this world as a wrecked vessel. God has given me a lifeboat and said to me, "Moody, save all you can." God will come in judgment and burn up this world, but the children of God do not belong to this world; they are in it, but not of it. This world is getting darker and darker; its ruin is coming nearer and nearer. If you have any friends on this wreck unsaved, you had better lose no time in getting them off.

But someone will say, "Do you, then, make the grace of God a failure?" No, grace is not a failure, but man is. Man has been a failure everywhere when he has had his own way and been left to himself. Christ will save His church, but He will save them finally by taking them out of the world.

"Behold I come quickly," said Christ to John, and the last prayer in the Bible is, "Even so, come quickly." Were the early Christians disappointed then? No, no man is disappointed who obeys God. The world waited for the first coming of the Lord 4,000 years, and then He came. He was here only thirty-three years, and then He went away; but He left us a promise that He would come again; and as the world watched and waited for His first coming and did not watch in vain, so now to them WHO WAIT for His appearing shall He appear a second time unto salvation.

W. B. RILEY
1861-1947

ABOUT THE MAN:

Dr. W. B. Riley was for 45 years pastor of First Baptist Church, Minneapolis, and pastor emeritus three years. His ministry there built this church to the largest membership in the Northern Baptist Convention.

But all over America Dr. Riley moved and swayed audiences. Thousands were won to Christ in great campaigns.

Riley's ministry was one of preaching the Gospel as well as fighting foes of the Gospel. He sometimes prefaced what he wrote with: *"As one who has given his life to the defense and propagation of fundamentalism."*

William Jennings Bryan once called him *"the greatest Christian statesman in the American pulpit."*

The teaching of evolution was a hot issue in his day, so his debates became another phase of his ministry. Bryan had died in 1925, so the mantle for fighting evolution passed to Riley.

One can well compare Dr. Riley with Charles Spurgeon in the largeness of his work: 1. Like that prince of preachers in London, the Minneapolis pastor-evangelist-crusader carried on for several decades an effective ministry; his church grew about as large as Spurgeon's. 2. Like Spurgeon, he turned out many books, including a 40-volume sermon-commentary. 3. Even as Spurgeon, he was a prophet to a whole nation of moral decline and infidelity in the church. 4. As Spurgeon withdrew from the Baptist Union, so Riley withdrew from the Northern Baptist Convention. 5. Like Spurgeon, he founded a growing training college and seminary. 6. Like Spurgeon, he was an editor, editing *The Christian Fundamentalist* and *The Northwestern Pilot*.

Truly, in the days of his strength, Dr. Riley was one of America's greatest preachers.

VIII.

Return, Resurrection and Rapture

W. B. RILEY

These three great words deserve each a separate and extended discussion. The only reasons, therefore, for trying to bring them within the limits of a single chapter exist in two circumstances. First, the discussion of the kingdom, through which we have just passed, has involved very many of the features of both the return and the resurrection; and second, Paul, by the pen of inspiration, links these all together in both logical and doctrinal order. With that marvelous brevity which is the soul of inspiration, he presents them in five short verses:

"But I would not have you to be ignorant, brethren, concerning them which are asleep, that ye sorrow not, even as others which have no hope.

"For if we believe that Jesus died and rose again, even so them also which sleep in Jesus will God bring with him.

"For this we say unto you by the word of the Lord, that we which are alive and remain unto the coming of the Lord shall not prevent them which are asleep.

"For the Lord himself shall descend from heaven with a shout, with the voice of the archangel, and with the trump of God: and the dead in Christ shall rise first:

"Then we which are alive and remain shall be caught up together with them in the clouds, to meet the Lord in the air: and so shall we ever be with the Lord."—I Thess. 4:13-17.

This inspired statement is to the whole subject of the return, the resurrection and the rapture, what the architect's preliminary sketch is to the finished structure. In each instance it remains for the workers to fill in and to fill up.

A good student will, in a Spirit-led research of the Word, find material at hand for the completion of the great doctrines that Paul here briefly, yet boldly, outlines. As the stones wrought into the Temple of God were each ready for its place, requiring not the touch of the hammer but rather a perfect knowledge of the plans and careful placing, so the man who works on these great doctrines, with Paul's plan before him, will find no need to change, carve or unnaturally constrain the sacred sentences of Scripture. When properly put together, they give perfect proof of the divine plan and provide an unanswerable argument for pre-millennialism.

Men have sometimes sought to set Peter or Paul or John against Jesus, but on this subject it will be seen that inspired servants and divine Lord speak together.

In the presentation of these great themes to the Thessalonians, Paul speaks of the second coming, the first resurrection and the supreme rapture.

I. THE SECOND COMING

It Is to Be Both Literal and Personal. To speak of the Lord's return as a mere figure of speech that is to know no literal fulfillment is little less sacrilegious than the total denial of inspiration. To identify that return with the coming of the Holy Spirit or with the experience of death is to despise the Master's own differentiations.

He was extremely careful to distinguish between the office of the Son and that of the Spirit. The Son was manifested in the flesh—"The Word was made flesh, and dwelt among us" (John 1:14); the Spirit was contrasted with the flesh—"That which is born of the flesh is flesh; and that which is born of the Spirit is spirit" (John 3:6). The Son's office was that of sacrifice and substitution—"The good shepherd giveth his life for the sheep" (John 10:11); the Spirit's office was that of illumination, instruction—"But the Comforter, which is the Holy Ghost, whom the Father will send in my name, he shall teach you all things, and bring all things to your remembrance, whatsoever I have said unto you" (John 14:26).

The Son's personal absence from the earth He declared to be a necessity to the Spirit's appearance in the church—"It is expedient for you that I go away: for if I go not away, the Comforter will not come unto you; but if I depart, I will send him unto you" (John 16:7).

If the plain references to the return of the Lord do not involve a personal coming, language has lost its meaning. For the comfort of His disciples, sorrowing over His approaching departure, He said, "If I go and prepare a place for you, I will come again." In the same discourse He said, "I will not leave you comfortless: I will come to you."

The men in white who stood by at the ascension said to the anxious onlookers, "Ye men of Galilee, why stand ye gazing up into heaven? this same Jesus, which is taken up from you into heaven, shall so come in like manner as ye have seen him go into heaven" (Acts 1:11).

It is little wonder, then, that Paul, writing to the Thessalonians, employs the phrase, "The Lord himself shall descend from heaven with a shout, with the voice of the archangel, and with the trump of God." There is not a hint in Scripture that the Lord is ever to be identified with death—which the Bible denominates an "enemy" to be eventually "destroyed" (I Cor. 15:26). This attempt is, as Ottman suggests, a shift by which some have sought to blunt the keen edge of Scripture.

That Christ is representatively present in the world by the Spirit, no man disputes; but that there is another coming "for which we look," a revelation of His presence, which "every eye shall see," is the contention of the Book.

Our hymnology—than which no truer theology has ever been written—sets that hope to sweetest harmony; and yet to tear the expectation of a personal return out of your best hymnbook would not leave it in such tatters as would be that more blessed Book—the Bible— when you had torn the same from its sacred pages.

The Time Is Indefinite; the Event, Imminent. 'Of that day and hour knoweth no one, no, not even the angels of heaven, but the Father only.' But, "Be ye also ready: for in such an hour as ye think not the Son of man cometh."

It is little wonder that Paul—perfectly familiar with his Lord's speech— should have written to Titus concerning the grace of God which had appeared, bringing salvation to all: "Teaching us that, denying ungodliness and worldly lusts, we should live soberly, righteously, and godly, in this present world; Looking for that blessed hope, and the glorious appearing of the great God and our Saviour Jesus Christ" (Titus 2:12,13).

The wisdom of making this great event imminent and the date of it indefinite exists in the fact suggested by Baines, namely, that disciples were to be so living in the hope of it that they would not be surprised if it occurred, while not so confidently dating it as to suffer disappointment in its delay. The argument that this event could not be "at hand" nearly two thousand years ago and yet, so remote as time has proven it to have been, ignores alike the difference between man's and God's computation of time and the transcendency of the event. If with God "a thousand years are as a watch in the night" when it is passed, we see no difficulty in the Spirit's expression, "the time is at hand."

Again, the proportions of this event are such as to make that language not only permissible but accurate. In the far West a carload of passengers were excited by the announcement, "We are coming to Mt. Shasta. Look!" Windows were pushed up, men and women put out their heads to behold that snowcapped peak, full before them. Yet as one put it, "I rode on and on, from a little after break of day until high noon, and still we had not reached its base; and when the Western sun had dipped far toward the horizon, glancing backward, we beheld its bold, beautiful peak, glorious with the vesture of the sun."

You could not have said that of a hill. A hill a mile away is not at hand; but 150 miles away, and Mt. Shasta is "at hand."

The second appearance of Jesus, as compared with the most important of human events, is so splendidly transcendent that no wonder those seers, realizing something of its mighty significance, should have lost the sense of distance and time and exclaimed, "The coming of the Lord draweth nigh!" or else, speaking for that Spirit who does not measure time by minutes and hours, but rather as it relates itself to eternity, say, "The Lord is at hand" (Phil. 4:5).

His Coming Will Perfectly Accord With Prophecy. For some time there has been a discussion in the premillenarian ranks as to whether the "any moment" theory of the second appearance could be retained; one school contending that it is a necessity of the interpretation of Scripture and another that we can certainly recognize the fulfillment of prophecy and that some portions of this, not having occurred already, must come to pass before we see in the heavens the "sign of the Son of man."

This problem finds its solution in the very fact that the last letter of prophecy, named as premillenary to the Lord's appearance, may have its perfect fulfillment; and yet the most of professed Christian men fail so to mark the movements of time as to clearly recognize the perfecting of the divine plan.

When Jesus appeared the first time, how few there were that saw in the Babe of Bethlehem the completion of prophecy! The visit of the star-led men from the East and the inquiry of the song-surprised shepherds seem to have found an answer in the faith of Simeon and Anna and in the fears of the criminal Herod, but to have left unmoved multitudes of men who were supposed to be the great Scripture students of the day.

Again, the certainty of a lapse of time between the coming of Christ for His people and His coming to the earth with them, cannot be disposed of by dubbing it "a theory to meet a difficulty of the premillenarian view." In the 24th chapter of Matthew there are two comings described that are so absolutely unlike as to demand an explanation. That explanation is found in the fact that Christ comes for His saints (I Thess. 4:16,17; II Thess. 2:1); an appearance which is apart from "the coming of our Lord Jesus Christ with all his saints" (I Thess. 3:13) to take His throne and "judge the world in righteousness"; and to this period the Tribulation seems unquestionably assigned. The conversion of the Jew is at its close; and the "wars and rumours of wars, earthquakes," convulsions of nature, etc., both naturally and scripturally belong to the same time!

Dr. Arthur Pierson tells us that in 1882, when the transit of Venus was occurring, some German scientists at Aiken, South Carolina, had drawn an elliptical circle upon a great stone, from which they made their observations. Later, they presented a request to the city that this stone might remain undisturbed until 120 years had passed and another transit of Venus had occurred, at which time the then-living scientists might make their observations and compare them with the work of 1884. Pierson reminds us that 120 years is a long time; every throne will have been emptied of occupant after occupant; and the map of the world will have been made over; for aught we know the march of the millennium may have begun; but prompt to the day, the hour, the minute, the transit of Venus will be on. Such is the accuracy of science.

But again and again the accuracy of prophecy has been put past dispute. Read Zechariah's description of the first appearance of Jesus in His triumphal entry into Jerusalem, "riding upon an ass, and upon a colt the foal of an ass," and remember this: over 700 years intervened between the declaration and the deed.

Generation after generation had passed; almost countless kings had been born to the various thrones of the earth; the little sentence, for the most part, was forgotten by even Bible students; yet in perfect accord with the Word of God, it came to pass. So it will be again when "his feet shall stand . . . upon the mount of Olives" and 'Out of Zion shall go forth the law, and the word of the Lord from Jerusalem,' and His scepter shall extend "from sea even to sea, and from the river even to the ends of the earth," "for the mouth of the Lord hath spoken it."

II. THE FIRST RESURRECTION

It Will Be Concurrent With the Saviour's Appearance. "The Lord himself shall descend from heaven with a shout, with the voice of the archangel, and with the trump of God: and the dead in Christ shall rise first." The word "first" here simply assigns the resurrection of the righteous dead—when "this corruptible must put on incorruption"—to precedence over the marvelous change of the living saints—when "this mortal must put on immortality."

The rest of the sentence, however, makes the return of the Lord and the resurrection of the saints concurrent events—the latter the instant resultant of the former. At the last trump that resurrection will occur "in a moment, in the twinkling of an eye" (I Cor. 15:52). "Afterward they that are Christ's at his coming" (I Cor. 15:23).

A. J. Gordon truthfully remarks, "Any doctrine of the resurrection dissociated from the Advent must be false . . . no atonement apart from the cross; no resurrection apart from the coming."

It is at "the coming of our Lord Jesus Christ" that there is to be a "gathering together unto him" (II Thess. 2:1).

A writer tells of the old slave, father of a numerous family, who lived in northern Georgia in 1833, when the notable meteoric display, known as "the falling of the stars," occurred. Being wakened by the noise and confusion in the street, he looked out from the window of his humble home and seeing, as he supposed, the stars of heaven falling like snowflakes, he thought the end had come and quickly roused his wife and children, saying, "The day of the Lord is at hand!" Hurrying them into the streets where the scene was indescribable, the old man turned to his companion and said, "Old woman, the Lord is coming; and just you take the children along up to the public square and stop there till I come. I am going down in the garden and see the master get up, and just as soon as he does, he and I will come along up to the square and we will all go up to meet the Lord together!" He knew that the Saviour's re-appearance would be the signal for the resurrection of every sleeping saint.

It Will Be Accomplished by the Saviour's Voice. "The Lord himself shall descend from heaven with a shout, with the voice of the archangel, and with the trump of God: and the dead in Christ shall rise first." It is doubtful if there be a great event of the future that has not already been enacted upon a small scale—an adumbration of that which is to come; it is equally to be questioned if there be a great truth that has not found its symbols in some circumstance of the past. The resurrection is no exception! The resuscitations of the New Testament—recorded to the credit of Christ—are the shadows of the resurrection. They were accomplished, every one, by the Saviour's voice.

To the widow's son He said, "Young man, I say unto thee, Arise. And he that was dead sat up, and began to speak" (Luke 7:14,15).

To Jairus' daughter, "I say unto thee, Arise. And straightway the damsel arose, and walked" (Mark 5:41, 42).

While to Lazarus, who had lain four days in the grave, "He cried with a loud voice, Lazarus, come forth. And he that was dead came forth" (John 11:43,44).

It is said that Calhoun was unwilling to die until they should bear him again to the Senate chamber that he might listen to Clay's voice once more—the voice he regarded as the most eloquent known to the tongue of man. But the voice of Christ will be so much more eloquent that by it the dying shall be revived and the dead quickened into life again. "The dead shall hear the voice of the Son of God: and they that hear shall live."

The Resurrection Will Concern Only the Sleeping Saints. "The dead in Christ" are all that are mentioned as having any part in this resurrection (I Thess. 4:16). The explanation is at hand. "But the rest of the dead lived not again until the thousand years were finished. This is the first resurrection. Blessed and holy is he that hath part in the first resurrection" (Rev. 20:5,6).

It will require a more ingenious man than has yet employed tongue or driven pen to disprove the two resurrections of Scripture. The number of instances in which the first and second resurrections are spoken of, the easy explanations of such passages as Daniel 12:2 and John 5:28, together with the meaningful phrase, "The resurrection from the dead," as employed in Luke 20:35; Philippians 3:11; Acts 4:2—making the first resurrection clearly elective—form the chain of argument which such men as Baines, Blackstone, Gordon, Brooks, West and others too numerous to mention have forged on the anvil of the Word.

The translation of Daniel 12:2 by Tregelles, "And many from among the sleepers of the dust of the earth shall awake. These [that awake] shall be unto everlasting life. But those [the rest of the sleepers who awake later] shall be unto shame and everlasting contempt," instead of being "a theory created by a premillenarian to carry his point and absolutely unknown to commentators," as one writer at least contends, is approved by such eminent rabbis as Saadia Haggion and Eben Ezra and employed by some of the best commentators; while the refusal to let the word "hour" in John 5:28,29 refer to at least as long a period as has already been covered by its use in John 4:23 and 5:25, reveals an indisposition to be convinced.

However, the utter absurdity of straining or spiritualizing Scripture is only reached when one opponent of two resurrections comes to treat Revelation 20:4-6 and contends that the first resurrection, there spoken of, is not that of persons at all but of "principles"; an interpretation which as one has already suggested, "would present the spectacles of 'principles' being beheaded 'for the witness of Jesus,' 'principles' refusing to worship the beast, 'principles' with foreheads and hands on which they decline to receive a mark, and 'principles' over 'such the second death hath no power,' but which shall be 'priests of God and of Christ.' Following this to its logical conclusion, 'the rest of the dead' must also be 'principles,' so that we could have no resurrection of persons at all."

It is no argument against two resurrections to remind us that for centuries "reverent students of the Bible" knew nothing of it, any more than it is against the Great Commission, which, for the same length of time, was overlooked, neglected and, when brought to light, ardently disputed.

But to accept this biblical doctrine is to receive an inspiration to holy living such as that which characterized Paul who, cutting loose from all things that bound him to the world, affirmed his willingness to count them all but loss, "if by any means [he] might attain unto the RESURRECTION OF THE DEAD."

III. THE SUPREME RAPTURE

Returning to our preliminary sketch, again we find the apostle describing it in these words: "The dead in Christ shall rise first: Then we which are alive and remain shall be caught up together with them in the clouds, to meet the Lord in the air: and so shall we ever be with the Lord."

Three features of the rapture are here clearly suggested. It will be signalized by the re-wedding of body and spirit; it will be characterized by the change of the mortal and the corruptible, and it will consummate the communion of the saints and the Saviour.

It Will Be Signalized by the Re-Wedding of the Body and Spirit. The clear significance of the phrase "even so them also which sleep in Jesus will God bring with him," is to the effect that "the spirits of just men made perfect" are now with God. But their bodies lie buried in sea and on land. Our coming Christ will bring the spirits down with Him, and at the sound of His voice the graves shall give up their dead. And when the body and the spirit, divorced by the last enemy, meet in the presence of our Master, He by His Word will so wed them together that neither man nor devil will ever again divide them asunder.

If one could conceive the glory that shall clothe these bodies of ours, when redeemed from humiliation, they are "conformed to the likeness" of our Lord, and the splendor that shall mark our "spirits"—"made perfect"—he would somewhat realize the meaning of the eternal marriage of the two.

This is the hour and the event of which the apostle wrote to the Romans:

"The earnest expectation of the creature waiteth for the manifestation of the sons of God. . . . For we know that the whole creation groaneth and travaileth in pain together until now. And not only they, but ourselves also, which have the firstfruits of the Spirit, even we ourselves groan within ourselves, waiting for the adoption, to wit, the redemption of our body."

It is little wonder, therefore, that an Old Testament prophet who was speaking to quicken Israel—"dead in trespasses and sins"—should have expressed the very thought that will characterize that glad hour when the voice of the Son shall proclaim the approaching rapture; and men shall know the more remote and more blessed meaning of Isaiah's words, "Awake and sing, ye that dwell in dust: for thy dew is as the dew of herbs, and the earth shall cast out the dead" (26:19).

We have read Ingraham's *Prince of the House of David,* and have tried to imagine the joy of that marriage occasion when Lazarus, whose recent decease had thrown every participant into pitiful sorrow, now resuscitated, lent by his living presence such surpassing happiness as no wedding party had ever before experienced; but we confess frankly that the joy of the hour when all perfected spirits and all glorified bodies shall be joined by the word of the Lord Jesus cannot be compassed by the imagination! Rapture is the word!

It Will Be Characterized by the Change of the Mortal and the Corruptible.

"The dead shall be raised incorruptible, and we shall be changed. For this corruptible must put on incorruption, and this mortal must put on immortality. So when this corruptible shall have put on incorruption, and this mortal shall have put on immortality, then shall be brought to pass the saying that is written, Death is swallowed up in victory."

What an hour! At that moment those that have come out of their graves in the full realization of their eternal conquest will almost tauntingly ask of their defeated foe, "O death, where is thy sting?" while those that have not slept, but, by the coming of Christ the Master, have put on their immortality, will voice their conscious triumph in the speech, "O grave, where is thy victory?" and sing their joy in the sentence, "Thanks be to God, which giveth us the victory through our Lord Jesus Christ."

Dr. Gordon's comparison—"the charcoal and the diamond are the same substance, only that one is carbon in its humiliation and the other carbon in its glory. So is this tabernacle in which we now dwell in comparison with our house which is from Heaven"—is not only full of beauty but biblically justified. When, however, one comes to speak of the saints perfected in spirit, soul and body, there are no objects of earth with which to liken them. Jesus said, "They are equal unto the angels; and are the children of God, being the children of the resurrection" (Luke 20:36).

It Will Consummate the Communion of the Saints and the Saviour. The phrase "shall be caught up together with them in the clouds, to meet the Lord in the air: and so shall we ever be with the Lord" involves a twofold communion—the communion of one with another and of all with their Lord. The closeness of that communion and the sweetness of that fellowship finds no expression sufficient, short of the marriage relation. "They that were ready went in with him to the marriage" (Matt. 25:10).

It is little wonder that on the consummation of this event there should be heard the voice of a great multitude as the voice of many waters and as the voice of mighty thunder, saying:

"Alleluia: for the Lord God omnipotent reigneth. Let us be glad and rejoice, and give honour to him: for the marriage of the Lamb is come, and his wife hath made herself ready."—Rev. 19:6,7.

We confess frankly that, when all of this imagery of prophetic promise passes before one's mind, he begins to understand the spirit and speech of Samuel Rutherford who, while he languished in prison at Aberdeen, divided his time between singing God's praises on the one side and pleading for the re-appearance of His Son on the other, and we marvel not at his speech: "O fairest among the sons of men; why stayest Thou so long away? Oh, heavens move fast! Oh, time, run, run, and hasten the marriage day, for love is tormented with delays!"

WILLIAM ASHLEY SUNDAY
1862-1935

ABOUT THE MAN:

William Ashley (Billy) Sunday was converted from pro baseball to Christ at twenty-three but carried his athletic ability into the pulpit.

Born in Ames, Iowa, he lost his father to the Civil War and lived with his grandparents until age nine when he was taken to live in an orphanage. A life of hard work paid off in athletic prowess that brought him a contract with the Chicago White Stockings in 1883. His early success in baseball was diluted by strong drink; however, in 1886 he was converted at the Pacific Garden Mission in Chicago and became actively involved in Christian work.

Sunday held some three hundred crusades in thirty-nine years. It is estimated that a hundred million heard him speak in great tabernacles, and more than a quarter million people made a profession of faith in Christ as Saviour under his preaching. His long-time associate, Dr. Homer Rodeheaver, called him "the greatest gospel preacher since the Apostle Paul."

Billy Sunday was one of the most unusual evangelists of his day. He walked, ran, or jumped across the platform as he preached, sometimes breaking chairs. His controversial style brought criticism but won the admiration of millions. He attacked public evils, particularly the liquor industry, and was considered the most influential person in bringing about the prohibition legislation after World War I.

Many long remembered his famous quote: "I'm against sin. I'll kick it as long as I've got a foot, and I'll fight it as long as I've got a fist. I'll butt it as long as I've got a head. I'll bite it as long as I've got a tooth. And when I'm old and fistless and footless and toothless, I'll gum it till I go home to Glory and it goes home to perdition!"

Those who heard him never forgot him or his blazing, barehanded evangelism.

The evangelist died November 6, 1935, at age 72. His funeral was held in Moody Church, Chicago, and the sermon was by H. A. Ironside.

IX

Implications of Christ's Imminent Coming

BILLY SUNDAY

"Then we which are alive and remain shall be caught up together with them in the clouds, to meet the Lord in the air: and so shall we ever be with the Lord. Wherefore comfort one another with these words."—I Thess. 4:17,18.

There have been some wonderful meetings, but never has there been one to compare with this one.

It was a wonderful meeting the children of Israel had on the shore of the Red Sea after Pharaoh's pursuing host had been destroyed in the angry waters and Miriam the prophetess, with her timbrel, led the people in singing, "Sing ye to the Lord, for he hath triumphed gloriously; the horse and his rider hath he thrown into the sea" (Exod. 15:21).

It was another great meeting they had at the foot of Mount Sinai when the law of God was given to them amid thunders and lightnings, fire and smoke.

That was a great meeting, too, on Mount Carmel when Elijah, the sturdy Tishbite, defied the prophets of Baal.

That was a great meeting where David danced before the ark of God as it was borne into Jerusalem.

It was a great meeting when Solomon dedicated the Temple and the glory of the Lord came upon the people.

Those were great meetings that were held on the banks of the Jordan, when Jerusalem and all Judaea went out to hear the man who dressed in camel's hair, wore a linen girdle and lived on locusts and wild honey.

It was a wonderful meeting when Jesus preached the Sermon on the Mount and another when He fed the multitude with five loaves and two fishes.

That was a great meeting on the day of Pentecost, when the Spirit came like a rushing mighty wind and, under Peter's preaching, about three thousand were converted.

All these were great meetings, and any number of others have been held, both in former times and in our own day.

Those were great meetings in the early days of Methodism, when Wesley and Whitefield preached to great multitudes in the fields.

Those were great meetings when multitudes were flocking to hear Finney and Moody; and great meetings have since been held by other great evangelists all around the world.

But no meeting has ever been held anywhere or in any time that could begin to compare in importance with the greatest of all meetings that is to be held in the air, when our Lord comes to make up His jewels. That meeting is the one for which all others have been preparing the way. It will be the crowning meeting of all history. The purpose of all that has been done in this world up to the present time has been to prepare for that great meeting in the air.

From Adam, mankind has been marching, step by step, up a grand stairway leading direct to that meeting in the air. The call of Abraham was one step toward it, and Jacob and his twelve sons were another. Joseph ruling in Egypt was another; the deliverance under Moses another; the conquest of Canaan under Joshua another, and so on with every event in sacred history.

It was for this Jesus suffered on the cross to make atonement for sin. It was for this He arose from the dead and ascended into Heaven, where He took His place at the right hand of the Father. It was for this the Holy Spirit came at Pentecost, and it was for this that churches have been organized and missionaries sent to the ends of the earth. These things have all been done to prepare the way and lead up to the meeting which is so graphically described in the text. It was for this meeting God made His plans before He laid the foundations of the earth, and it was of this meeting He was thinking before the morning stars sang together.

I. WE ARE COMMANDED TO WATCH FOR CHRIST'S COMING

We are not told when Jesus will come, but we are told that His coming is sure, and we are charged to watch for it. Yet the church today shows as little concern about His coming again as His disciples did about His going away. All of this is fully in accord with Peter:

"There shall come in the last days scoffers, walking after their own lusts, And saying, Where is the promise of his coming? for since the fathers fell asleep, all things continue as they were from the beginning of the creation."—I Pet. 3:3,4.

Jesus not only foretold His going away, but charged His followers to expect His return and be ready for it:

"Watch therefore: for ye know not what hour your Lord doth come. But know this, that if the goodman of the house had known in what watch the thief would come, he would have watched, and would not have suffered his house to be broken up. Therefore be ye also ready: for in such an hour as ye think not the Son of man cometh."—Matt. 24:42-44.

Every time we lift the communion cup to our lips we "do shew the Lord's death till he come." There is no prophecy needing to be fulfilled before Christ comes. Jesus said:

"And this gospel of the kingdom shall be preached in all the world for a witness unto all nations; and then shall the end come."—Matt. 24:14.

There is not a nation on the face of the earth that has not had the Gospel preached within its bounds.

The second coming of Christ is the emphatic doctrine of the New Testament. It is mentioned and referred to more than 350 times; yet the majority of church members never heard a sermon on the subject. That is the reason they think so little of looking into the matter themselves. The church makes much of baptism, but in all of Paul's epistles baptism is only mentioned or referred to thirteen times, while the return of the Lord is mentioned fifty times. This certainly shows which he considered the most important.

McCheyne, the great Scot preacher, once said to some of his friends, "Do you think Christ will come back tonight?" One after another answered, "I think not"; then he solemnly repeated,

"Watch therefore: for ye know not what hour your Lord doth come. . . . Therefore be ye also ready: for in such an hour as ye

think not the Son of man cometh."—Matt. 24:42,44.

With such admonitions, what right have we to be unconcerned about it and say, as many preachers do, "It is nothing to me; I take no interest in the subject whatever"? Who would care to travel on a train where the engineer would never read his orders? Who would ride on a ship where the captain never looked at the compass? You may call it rubbish, but the disciples called it the "blessed hope." "Why call ye me, Lord, Lord, and do not the things which I say?"

If Jesus had said, "I will not return for two thousand years," nobody would have begun to look for Him before the time was near; but He expects His followers to be always looking for His return. Just as Simeon and Anna watched and waited for His first coming, so we should be watching and waiting for His return. It is not enough to say, "Oh, I'm a Christian; I'm all right." We are not all right unless we obey the command to watch. Nothing else will do so much to keep us right where we should be in our religious experience. Knowing that the bank examiner may drop in at any moment keeps many a cashier from becoming dishonest.

Some years ago Mr. Moody called a convention of Christian workers to meet in Chicago, and that convention was in session there in Moody's Church for two months. Out of it came the great Moody Bible Institute. The daily program was to spend the forenoon at the church in prayer and Bible study, the afternoon and evening in doing practical Christian work.

My assistant attended that convention. He told me that one day Mr. Moody asked him to go down among the anarchists, in the hard part of Chicago, and hold a meeting there. "Do the best you can," said Mr. Moody, "and some night I'll come down and help you." My friend said that promise was a continual incentive to him to keep up his courage and do his very best. He didn't know when Mr. Moody would come, and so he looked for him every night, and the harder time he had, the harder he hoped and looked.

This shows how the constant expectation of the coming of Jesus will inspire and encourage us.

II. NO MILLENNIUM OF PEACE AND RIGHTEOUSNESS UNTIL JESUS COMES

A great many say, "I believe the millennium will come first, then Christ at the end of it." What people think has nothing to do with it, but what God says has everything to do with it. Many have missed railroad trains because they believed they would come at a time that did not correspond with the official time card. You will see God's time card if you carefully read the Bible. Not a word can be found there that gives the slightest hope for the millennium before the return of Christ; but we can find plenty of verses that tell us to look for the coming of the Lord first.

As we look back over the two thousand years since Christ, how far we seem to be away from the time when the will of God shall be done on earth as it is in Heaven. Every edition of the press seems to make it clear that the Devil is still having his way.

Look at the reign of wickedness in our great cities in both high life and low. No college has ever yet made a saint, or ever will. Education may improve conditions, but it can never change or cleanse the heart.

Look at the lukewarmness and indifference in the churches everywhere, and see what many of them are compelled to resort to in order to keep from going under. See to what schemes and dodges and foolishness some preachers have to resort to get anybody to go and hear them.

There can be no millennium until Jesus comes; it is His presence that makes the millennium. You might as well talk of daylight not coming until the sun goes down. The millennium cannot begin until Satan has been bound in the pit. Nothing is more certain than that the glory of God shall cover the earth, but it will be after Jesus comes.

Many have an idea the world will grow better and better until the coming of the millennium, and everybody will be converted. We hear that stuff preached, but the Bible does not teach any such trash.

On the day before the Flood, no doubt many people were sincere in thinking that the world was growing better, yet it was so hopelessly wicked that God had to destroy it. Some of the men who married into the family of Lot may have made the same claim for Sodom only a day or two before its destruction; no doubt Lot's wife was of the same opinion. On the day before the crucifixion there were men in Jerusalem who undoubtedly agreed with each other that the world was growing better.

The world will grow worse and worse. They did eat, they drank, they married wives, they were given in marriage until the day that Noah entered the ark and the Flood came and destroyed them all. Likewise also as it was in the days of Lot; they did eat, they drank, they bought, they sold, they planted, they builded. But the same day that Lot went out of Sodom it rained fire and brimstone from Heaven and destroyed them all. Even thus shall it be on the day when the Son of Man is revealed (Luke 17:27-30). Lawlessness, vice and crime will increase; communism, nihilism, anarchy, adultery, divorce, graft—all will continue to grow until they will finally ripen into the Antichrist.

Many think and preach that the millennium will be brought about by the increase of knowledge, culture, great discoveries, such as the gasoline engine, automobile, electricity, radium, liquified air, wireless telegraphy, airships, etc. These have nothing to do with bringing the millennium. It is the personal reign of Christ that brings the millennium. Those who have been the greatest blessing to the world were filled with this hope— and preached it.

III. HUMAN TRADITION SPIRITUALIZES AND EXPLAINS AWAY THE SCRIPTURES

The Word of God was vitiated and neutralized by the traditions of men when Jesus first came: that is very largely the trouble in present times. Instead of going to the Bible to find out what God says, the preacher is too apt to go to his books to see what the great men of his church have to say about it, and all their preaching and teaching takes its color from the glasses the rabbis wear, just as was the case in the time of Jesus.

The fact that Jesus was not recognized by the high-up authorities, but was rejected and crucified as an imposter, shows what a dangerous and deadly thing it is to accept the traditions of men rather than what God says about things. Too many who are now masters in Israel are as much in the dark as Nicodemus was. The truth is no harder to get at than corn on the cob, if we will first strip off the husk and shell it. We need to depend more upon the Holy Spirit and less upon our libraries if we would preach so that those who hear us will also hear the voice of God in our message.

It is not what Doctor This or Professor That has to say about it that settles the question, and settles it right, but how reads the Word? What does the Bible say about it? And what we need to do is to take the Bible as it reads, not as some big man says it means. Big men have been mistaken about vital things just as often as little ones. The safest pilot is not the one who wears the biggest hat, but the one who knows the channel the best. We should let the Bible speak to us just as God means it should, without distorting it by the prejudices and vagaries of those who are always trying to put their own camel into it and strain out somebody else's gnat.

It is high time for Christians to interpret unfulfilled prophecies by the light of prophecies already fulfilled. The curses on the Jews were brought to pass literally; so also will be the blessings. The scattering was literal; so also will be the gathering. The pulling down of Zion was literal; so also must be the building up. The rejection of Israel was literal; so also must be the restoration. The first coming of Christ was literal, visible and personal; and what right has anybody to conclude that His second coming will be altogether spiritual? If His first advent was with a real body, why not the same with His second coming?

When Jesus first came, the smallest predictions were fulfilled to the very letter; and should this not teach us to expect that the same will be true when He comes again? There are very many more prophecies concerning His second coming than His first: does this mean that God wants to give us the most favorable opportunity possible to prepare for it? If the humility and shame of Christ at His first coming was literal and visible, should not His coming in power and glory be also literal and visible?

What right have we to say that Judah, Zion, Israel and Jerusalem ever mean anything but literal Judah, Zion, Israel and Jerusalem? Someone has called attention to the fact that there are only two or three places in the whole New Testament where such names are used in what may be called a spiritual or figurative way. "Jerusalem" occurs eighty times, and in every case is unquestionably literal, except when the opposite is clearly indicated by such qualifying terms as "heavenly," "new," or "holy." "Jew" occurs a hundred times, and only four are even ambiguous. "Israel" and "Israelite" occur forty times—all literal. "Judah" and "Judaea," about twenty times—literal in every case.

John Bunyan was once studying the passages foretelling that the feet of the Lord should stand on the Mount of Olives, and he thus reasoned:

> Some commentators say that the Mount of Olives means the heart of the believer; that it is only a figurative expression and means that the Lord will reign in the heart of the believer, and the Holy

Spirit will dwell there. But I don't think it means that at all. I just
think it means the Mount of Olives, two miles from Jerusalem, on
the east.

That is why the Lord could use the poor tinker so marvelously, even
when shut up in Bedford jail.

While face to face with them, Jesus taught His disciples to be in constant expectation of His early return, and they so understood Him and
lived accordingly. They preached the doctrine and taught it in their
epistles, every one of them. Certainly, if anybody ever understood the
Lord correctly, it was the men whom He personally trained to do that
very thing, that they might hand the truth He gave them down to us.
If they failed to understand Him, what hope is there that anybody else
may do so?

IV. CHRIST WAITS THE COMPLETION OF HIS
MYSTICAL BODY BEFORE HE COMES

Jesus is going to come and reveal Himself to the members of His
body at the very moment when the last soul is saved necessary to complete that body—for the body of Christ must consist of a certain number
of souls, or it never could be completed. If it were an infinite number,
it would be an endless task, and Jesus would never return; for He can
no more come without His heavenly body than He could come the first
time without a human body. It is the completion of the body of Christ,
therefore, that will bring Him, and this shows how we may help and
hasten His coming.

*"Looking for and hasting unto the coming of the day of God, wherein
the heavens being on fire shall be dissolved, and the elements shall melt
with fervent heat?"*—II Pet. 3:12.

Every time we do personal work or try to get anybody saved, we
may be doing something that will bring the coming of the Lord. Instead
of being discouraged by looking about us and seeing what a small pros-
pect there is of the whole world being converted, it will set our bones
on fire to think that perhaps the last man needed to complete the Lord's
body and bring Jesus back to earth may be converted this very day.
That gives us something definite and tangible to work for and hope for,
don't you see?

Colonel Clark, the founder of the Pacific Garden Mission in Chicago, put in six nights out of every seven at the mission as long as he lived. One day somebody said to him, "Colonel, why don't you take some rest? You are killing yourself by sticking to that mission so close. Why don't you take a vacation and go away somewhere and rest?"

"I can't do it, brother," answered the Colonel. "I could never do that, for every time I start for the mission I think, *Maybe that last man may be saved in our little meeting tonight, and the Lord will come; and I wouldn't miss being at my post for anything in the world. When Jesus comes I want to be right where He expects me to be."*

The Bible very clearly makes known the great truth that God's purpose for this dispensation is the completing of the body of Christ. He is not trying to save the world now; that is to be the work of the next dispensation. Here is the Scripture for it:

"God at the first did visit the Gentiles, to take out of them a people for his name [the body of Christ]. *And to this agree the words of the prophets; as it is written, After this I will return, and will build again the tabernacle of David* [the Jewish nation], *which is fallen down* [scattered and no longer being used]; *and I will build again the ruins thereof, and I will set it up: That the residue of men might seek after the Lord"* (through their missionary efforts)—Acts 15:14-17.

That is the present dispensation, and that is what God is doing now. There is nothing said here about the conversion of the world, but it is made clear that a people is being chosen, and much Scripture might be quoted to show that the people so referred to will constitute the body of Christ. Throughout this dispensation the Lord has been working among the Gentiles (those not belonging to the Jewish nation), and the above shows the purpose for which He has been working. There is no thought expressed there of the millennium.

"And to this agree the words of the prophets [about God's purpose in gathering a chosen people from the Gentiles]; *as it is written* [and that means what God says], *After this* [after the number of people to be chosen from the Gentiles has been fully completed] *I will return* [to direct dealing with Israel], *and will build again the tabernacle of David, which is fallen down."*—Acts 15:15,16.

"Fallen down." What does that mean? What does it mean for a house to be fallen down? Certainly that it cannot longer be used as a house while in that condition. Read the prophecy of Amos, from which this is taken, and see why it is that God is through with Israel until He has taken from the Gentiles the people for His name (to bear His name, to glorify His name).

The mission of the church—the bride of Christ or body of Christ—is to get ready to meet the Bridegroom. When the body of Christ is completed, He will reveal Himself to the members who are alive and in this world at that time, and at the same moment they will be caught up to meet those who have gone on before in the air, and from that moment they are forever with the Lord.

There remains no prophecy to be fulfilled. There is not a nation where the Gospel has not been preached. So Christ must be waiting for the completion of the body of believers. When the rapture comes, it will come in the twinkling of an eye. Those who have died in the Lord will be resurrected; and they, with the believers who are alive, will be caught up to meet the Lord in the air.

V. RAPTURE FOR SAINTS: TRIBULATION FOR THOSE LEFT BEHIND

When the rapture comes, it will come in the twinkling of an eye and will be altogether unexpected except by those who have been searching the prophecies and are looking for it, just as Simeon and Anna and the Wise Men were looking for Jesus at His first coming.

The notion that people have about the second coming of Christ is that when He comes the judgment day will also come and that the world will come to an end. This idea is unscriptural and shows how little the Bible has been searched to find and make known the real truth by those who are leaders and teachers in the church.

Business and governments will go on as now. After Jesus comes and takes the believers out of the world, then takes place the Great Tribulation, a description of which you will find later on. At the close of the Tribulation, the Lord will return, bringing with Him saintly members of His body, to begin His millennium reign. Then He will reveal Himself to the Jews. They will accept Him as their long-rejected Messiah. Then the millennium will begin; the Devil will be cast into the bottomless pit for a thousand years; nations will be born in a day through the missionary efforts of the Jews.

The Jews have always been full of energy in business, as no other people, and when they become ambassadors for Christ there will be no lukewarmness or indifference. Either before or during the Tribulation the Jews will have been restored to the Holy Land, will rebuild their Temple and restore the Jewish worship. Also during the Tribulation, the Antichrist will come, most likely in the person of some great king. It is supposed that he will be a personal incarnation of the Devil, just as Jesus was an incarnation of God. He will go to Jerusalem and there do great signs and wonders by which he will so delude the chosen people that they will accept him as their Messiah and pay him divine honors as in the Temple. It will be during this that Jesus will return and destroy him by the brightness of His coming.

"And then shall that Wicked be revealed, whom the Lord shall consume with the spirit of his mouth, and shall destroy with the brightness of his coming: Even him, whose coming is after the working of Satan with all power and signs and lying wonders."—II Thess. 2:8,9.

In the Lord's coming there are to be two distinct phases: (1) His coming for the members of His body and revelation to them at the time of the rapture or taking up into the air; (2) His coming with the members of His body at the close of the Tribulation, when He is revealed to the Jews and destroys the Antichrist. Overlooking these two phases has put some people in confusion about the order of events, just as the failure to distinguish between the prophecies pertaining to the first and second coming confused the Jews who rejected Jesus, through what they supposed to be His failure to fulfill prophecy.

Let us consider something of what it may mean to have a part in that meeting in the air:

1. Well, the most glorious thing about it is that if we are there we shall be members of the body of Jesus Christ.

It will mean that we are members of the royal family of the universe; that we are kings and princes who are to sit on the throne and reign with Jesus, that we shall be with Him forevermore, never to be separated from Him again. And this will mean that we shall be the most exalted beings in all the universe, for who could be higher than the sons of God or the bride of our Lord?

In talking to men, God must use the language of men; but He can only put into our words just a little of what He would tell us. A very little looking into the matter, however, will show that He has used the most expressive words in our language to show how near and precious is to be our relationship to Him. In fact, He has used about all the words we have that could be used for that purpose, as "members of his body," His "bride" and "sons of God."

2. If we have a place in that meeting in the air, it will mean that we are like Christ, for "when he shall appear, we shall be like him; for we shall see him as he is."

The true child of God is always longing to be like His Master, and this heart-yearning is the sure prophecy of what we shall then be. It will also mean that we shall nevermore be separated from Him. The Devil will never again have power to separate us from Him for a single moment; and wherever He is, there shall we be also. The fact that Jesus is to be here during the millennium would be proof conclusive that we shall be here with Him; even if there were no other Scripture for it.

3. For some that meeting will mean that they reached it without having to pass through death, for it is to be composed of those who have gone on before and those who are still living at that time.

Some who are born into this world are never to die, and we may hope to be of that elect number. The Christian has no business looking for death. It is his right to hope to live forever; and instead of expecting to go to the grave, he should be looking for the coming of his Lord and the meeting in the air.

4. It will also mean that we shall then have bodies that will remain young forever.

Pains and aches, gray hair, wrinkles and feebleness will never again be known. Listen to this:

"Behold, I shew you a mystery; We shall not all sleep [die], *but we shall all be changed, In a moment, in the twinkling of an eye, at the last trump: for the trumpet shall sound, and the dead shall be raised incorruptible* [no longer subject to age or decay], *and we shall be changed* [into His likeness]."—I Cor. 15:51,52.

And it will come in the twinkling of an eye—in a moment—and that moment will be what all time was made for. In that moment some will give up old age to be young forever. Others will go from beds of pain upon which they may have lain prostrate for years. Others, from the most grinding poverty, will spring to eternal wealth. Some will go from burdens from which they expected no relief save death. From what tribulations and troubles and afflictions will not that moment be a deliverance, and how the angels will begin to crowd the battlements of Heaven upon that glad meeting when they know it is about to come! In a moment! In the twinkling of an eye!

"Come, Lord Jesus; come quickly," ought to be the daily prayer of every Christian. Yet as we look about us now and see how the Devil seems to be having his way as much as ever, it looks as if that great time will never come. But you can't tell by appearances. An hour before the tidal wave comes there is nothing to indicate that it will ever come. Nobody dreamed of an earthquake ten minutes before San Francisco began to rock and tumble.

The President touched a golden key in the White House; and in a moment, in the twinkling of an eye, the acres of machinery at the great Seattle Exposition, on the other side of the country, were in motion, and countless flags began to fly in the breeze. That's the way the Lord will come. Just that quick! Quicker than a clock can tick! Quicker than lightning can flash! Ten minutes before the President touched the golden key it looked as if the machinery would never start, but when the right moment arrived it was going. "Therefore be ye also ready: for in such an hour as ye think not the Son of man cometh." God's clock is never behind the smallest fraction of a second.

5. If we have a part in that meeting, it will mean that we shall be here in this world with the Lord during the millennium — a thousand years — with the Devil chained and cast out — not a saloon, gambling hell or brothel in the world and everything just as we want it.

Hear this:

"And cast him into the bottomless pit, and shut him up, and set a seal upon him, that he should deceive the nations no more, till the thousand years should be fulfilled: and after that he must be loosed a little season. And I saw thrones, and they sat upon them, and judgment was given unto them: and I saw the souls of them that were beheaded for the witness of Jesus, and for the word of God, and which had not worshipped the beast, neither his image, neither had received his mark upon their foreheads, or in their hands; and they lived and reigned with Christ a thousand years. But the rest of the dead lived not again until the thousand years were finished. This is the first resurrection. Blessed and holy is he that hath part in the first resurrection: on such the second death hath no power, but they shall be priests of God and of Christ, and shall reign with him a thousand years."—Rev. 20:3-6.

6. To have part in that meeting will be to meet those who have gone on before—fathers and mothers and other loved ones.

Think of how glorious and blessed that will be, and there will doubtless be infinite surprises that the Lord will have in store for us. "Eye hath not seen, nor ear heard, neither have entered into the heart of man, the things which God hath prepared for them that love him."

7. Think of the delight of meeting and continuing with the other members of the Lord's body, who will then be as dear to us as the apple of our own eye.

Think of being intimate with Peter, James and John, Andrew, Philip and the others, and of hearing from them again and again all the incidents they witnessed in the life of Jesus.

Think of being more intimate with Paul and Silas and Mark and Luke and Timothy and the saints who were in Caesar's household, than we are with our very best friends now.

Think of knowing Mary, the mother of Jesus, as well as you know your own mother and of having for intimate friends Martha and Mary and Lazarus of Bethany and Mary Magdalene and the unknown disciples who on the first Easter morning walked with their risen Lord on the way to Emmaus!

Think of talking with Zacchaeus and blind Bartimaeus, the daughter of Jairus and the wild man out of whom the legion of devils were cast.

And the blind man in the 9th chapter of John—how good it will be to shake hands with him and tell him some of the good things we have so often thought about his courage.

And Joseph of Arimathaea, Nicodemus and the boy who had the five loaves and two fishes. And the sick woman who touched the hem of His garment; the widow who gave the two mites and the Philippian jailor who got the old-time religion in an unmistakable way; the first leper who was cleansed, and all the rest. How much we shall miss, if we miss that meeting in the air.

8. Think of how glorious it will be to live for a thousand years in this world with our blessed Master and be closely associated with Him; with bodies that will not wear out or grow old, always in perfect health, and with faculties for enjoyment a thousand times higher than we possess now.

The millennium will be the greatest time ever known, for it will be the golden age of man. Poverty, sickness, war and pestilence will be unknown. There will be no Devil to cause human suffering and woe.

Then think of the delight of coming back into this world where we have had so much trouble and hardship and poverty and sickness, to live under such glorious circumstances as will then prevail.

A man told a friend of mine that, when a boy, he footed it for nearly a hundred miles over the old National Road. It was in August, the weather hot and dusty, and the boy penniless, homeless and disheartened. He had on a pair of cowhide shoes, and his feet became so sore that over much of the way he could only hobble along in great pain. A little while ago he went over the same road in an elegant automobile, and he never so enjoyed a ride in his life. The weather was fine, and he had nothing to do but sit there and drink in the beauty of the day and think of how much better off he was than when he went limping over that same road, a poor, helpless, sore-footed boy.

Well, it will be something like that with us in the millennium, perhaps, only vastly more glorious when we come back to have a good time here.

9. It will also mean to be richly rewarded for all we have ever done or suffered for the Lord.

Near the close of his hard and strenuous life Paul said:

"Henceforth there is laid up for me a crown of righteousness, which the Lord, the righteous judge, shall give me at that day: and not to me only, but unto all them also that love his appearing."—II Tim. 4:8.

Here are other verses showing there is to be a reward:

"And when the chief Shepherd shall appear, ye shall receive a crown of glory that fadeth not away."—I Pet. 5:4.

"And, behold, I come quickly; and my reward is with me, to give every man according as his work shall be."—Rev. 22:12.

10. If we have a part in that meeting, we shall escape the Great Tribulation which is to come upon all the earth as soon as the members of the body of Christ are taken out of the world.

The body of Christ is now the salt of the earth and the light of the world. It is the army with which God now holds in check the principalities and powers of evil. It is therefore evident that, when this army is taken out of the world, the Devil will have unhindered sway and will immediately begin to make this world as much like Hell as he wants it to be. In speaking of this awful time, Jesus said:

"For then shall be great tribulation, such as was not since the begin-
ning of the world to this time, no, nor ever shall be. And except those
days should be shortened, there should no flesh be saved: but for the
elect's sake those days shall be shortened."—Matt. 24:21,22.

And here is what Daniel says of it:

". . . and there shall be a time of trouble, such as never was since
there was a nation even to that same time: and at that time thy people
shall be delivered, every one that shall be found written in the book."—
Dan. 12:1.

Human imagination is incapable of picturing the awfulness of this Great
Tribulation that is surely coming on the world and may begin this very
day—yes, even this very hour! Think of it! It is to be the worst time the
world has ever known or ever will know. A worse time than the Flood,
a worse time than the bondage of Egypt and a worse time than the
destruction of Jerusalem, when women and children were torn in pieces
and the very name of mercy was unknown; a worse time than the reign
of Nero; worse than during the Spanish Inquisition; worse than when
Cortes destroyed the Aztecs; worse than during the French Revolution
and the Commune and worse than during the Dark Ages; a worse time
than when men were skinned alive; worse than when they were pulled
asunder by horses; worse than when men, women and children were
thrown to hungry lions and worse than when they were dipped in pitch
and burned as torches.

Do you want to live in that kind of a time? Well, the only thing that
can surely save you from it is to have a part in that meeting in the air,
for no others who are living at that time can escape it, and that awful
time may be upon us within the next ten minutes; for it will begin at
the very moment the rapture takes place. There is now not a single
prophecy remaining to be fulfilled before the Lord may come and the
members of His body be caught up to meet Him in the air.

It stands to reason that the Tribulation must be the most awful time
known because, for the only time in all history, the Devil will then be
loose and have unhindered sway. Everything he can do that will add
to human woe will certainly be done. Governments will go to pieces,
and there will be no security of life and property. A man may be a
millionaire one day and a beggar the next. A very chaos of crime and
outrage of every kind will be turned loose. God will let the world and

the universe see for a time what it will mean to live under the Devil's rule and will let those who pass through the Tribulation see that the good they so long enjoyed was because of the presence of the good. Some of you people who throw your votes and influence in favor of whiskey and all kinds of hellishness that go with it may live to find out in the bitterness of the Tribulation just what is meant by sowing the wind and reaping the whirlwind.

It is supposed that the Tribulation will cover a period of seven years. God in His mercy will make it as short as possible. That the real church of God, believers, members of the body of Christ, are to be taken out of the world before the Tribulation, is as clearly taught in the Bible as that through the atonement made by Christ man may have salvation from sin.

What will it mean to the world? Every believer will be instantly taken out, homes will be rent in twain, husbands will be robbed of godly wives, children will be taken out and those left behind will wring their hands in grief. No doubt newspapers will print extra editions. Universal consternation will reign. The world will neither see the Lord nor will they see their loved ones go. Those who have died in the faith will be raised.

WATCH! BE READY!

The statement of Jesus shows that not all the people are to be caught up in the air in clouds, but one here and there:

"I tell you, in that night there shall be two men in one bed; the one shall be taken, and the other shall be left. Two women shall be grinding together; the one shall be taken, and the other left. Two men shall be in the field; the one shall be taken, and the other left."—Luke 17:34-36.

This makes it look as if the number caught up in the air would not be large. When will the meeting in the air occur? In regard to this Jesus said:

"But of that day and that hour knoweth no man, no, not the angels which are in heaven, neither the Son, but the Father. Take ye heed, watch and pray: for ye know not when the time is."—Mark 13:32,33.

But He also said, after speaking of conditions that would prevail about that time:

"So likewise ye, when ye shall see all these things, know that it is near, even at the doors."—Matt. 24:33.

Will the world come to an end when Jesus comes and takes away the members of His body? No, not for at least one thousand years, perhaps longer. The millennium must come after Jesus comes, and must have its beginning at the close of the Great Tribulation.

The real truth is, that great event will not bring destruction to anything that is good, but will, on the contrary, introduce an era of the greatest progress and prosperity the world has ever known. The coming of Christ will bring the millennium—the Golden Age of man in this world—when the arts and sciences and everything else that man ought to delight in, will flourish as never before; and never until Jesus comes will the knowledge of the glory of God cover the earth as the waters cover the sea.

To say that the second coming of Christ is a pernicious thing to preach is the same as saying it would be a calamity for God to rule. It will be the culmination of the redemption of this world, and to say that it would put an end to all progress is as foolish as to say that putting a roof on a house would ruin it and throw the carpenters out of work.

There is nothing more clearly declared in the Bible than that Christ will come and reign on earth during the millennium, when all will be restored that was lost by the Fall. Then, and only then, will God's will be done on earth as it is in Heaven. The scribes and Pharisees thought that business was going to be endangered by Christ's first coming. The only business that will be hurt by the second coming of Christ will be the Devil's business. At the time of His coming there will be no general resurrection or judgment.

At the close of the millennium reign of Christ, the Devil will be loosed out of the pit for a season and look for the first time upon a world without sin. He will tempt people. They will be as foolish as now and yield to his lies and subtlety. He will gather his host and come against the saints to battle. Fire will fall from Heaven and consume them. Then takes place the resurrection of the wicked dead. Then the judgment of the great white throne, with Christ to judge.

There is this about it, however: We are living nearer to it than anybody ever lived before; and when it does come, it is going to come in a moment—in the twinkling of an eye—and the only safe course for us to pursue is to be ready for the Bridegroom when He comes.

"Take ye heed, watch and pray: for ye know not when the time is. For the Son of man is as a man taking a far journey, who left his house,

and gave authority to his servants, and to every man his work, and commanded the porter to watch. Watch ye therefore: for ye know not when the master of the house cometh, at even, or at midnight, or at the cockcrowing, or in the morning: Lest coming suddenly he find you sleeping. And what I say unto you I say unto all, Watch."—Mark 13:33-37.

We are not told when Jesus will come, but we are told that His coming is sure, and we are charged to watch for it. How it would affect our lives and make hard things easy to bear, if we would only do this, and always be doing this.

Don't you know how eagerly you get ready for company that you love, when you receive word that they are surely coming? How you clean house and want to have everything in the very best of order! If we were continually looking for the coming of Jesus, we would be as careful to keep our lives as clean as you would be to have your homes clean if you were expecting company. The certainty of His coming would also be a constant source of comfort and inspiration to us, if we believed it to be near.

The Lord does not come to the world at the time of the rapture, but only reveals Himself to the members of His body. At the time of His resurrection He was only seen by those who believed on Him. Pilate and the high priest and those who crucified Him did not know that He was risen. So it will be at the time of the rapture. The world will not know that He has been here and will have no knowledge of Him until He comes with the members of His body at the close of the Tribulation.

What an awful thing, then, to have the glorious privilege of living in this dispensation with all that it means and miss getting into the body of Christ by refusing to become a Christian. The preacher owes it to his people to look into these things that he may show them their great privilege and warn them of the awful things that may come upon them if they miss their chance and have to go through the Great Tribulation. The preacher who has never qualified himself to preach a sermon on the sure and certain coming of his Master will have to answer for an awful breach of trust when he stands before Him.

Our fleet of battleships made its remarkable trip around the Horn and around the world and again dropped anchor at home on schedule time, almost to the minute, in spite of storm and the fickleness of wind and wave.

If the calculations of men can be wrought out so precisely, certainly we have the right to expect that God will execute His plans with absolute precision in whatever task He sets for Himself. Certainly we can think of nothing so improbable as that He would complete His program for creation on schedule time and yet would so tie His own hands by failure to anticipate and provide for all possible emergencies and contingencies that the train of His purpose for redemption would be so delayed or nearly wrecked that it would almost have to be abandoned.

Do not think it for a moment. God's purpose can no more be kept back a minute than the heavenly bodies can be delayed a minute. In redemption God is working by the clock as surely as in creation, and His chariot of salvation is not marked late a single minute.

"COME, LORD JESUS!"

MONROE PARKER
1909-1994

ABOUT THE MAN:

When you meet Monroe "Monk" Parker you meet both an educator and an evangelist, Ph.D. and personal soul winner—a great mind and hot heart!

Parker was a pre-med student at Birmingham Southern College in Birmingham, Alabama, because so many of his family were in medicine. By the same token—in Parker's background was a long history of preachers.

But saving grace does not run in family bloodlines.

Parker attended church and Sunday school regularly but was not converted until he was nineteen. The same week, in his church, he heard Dr. Bob Jones, Sr. tell about a one-year-old school he had organized to teach and train preacher boys. Parker knew this was where God wanted him.

He went to Bob Jones College, where he was called to preach. After graduating, Parker entered evangelism. After five years in the field he returned to BJU to assume directorship of religious activities, a position that eventually led him to become assistant to Dr. Bob Jones, Sr. Even then he conducted ten revivals a year.

In 1949 he re-entered full-time evangelism, a ministry that was interspersed with a pastorate in Decatur, Alabama and presidency of Pillsbury Conservative Baptist Bible College for eight years. Under his leadership, the student body grew 20% annually.

Besides conducting hundreds of campaigns and preaching in scores of high schools, colleges, Bible institutes and seminaries and over many radio stations, Parker has taught in Bible colleges and in seminaries, organized an association of independent Baptist churches in Alabama, served as president of the Minnesota Baptist Convention, developed and built the Christian Dells Bible Camp and Conference Grounds near Decatur, Alabama, and serves now as General Director of Baptist World Mission. He also serves on a host of boards.

You kind of gasp for breath when you read the ministries God has given him, but you also breathe a grateful "Amen!" for the man and his ministry.

Dr. Parker is a preacher of unusual ability, has keen insight into the Word of God, and is loyal to every fundamental.

Aye, we need some more Ph.D.'s like "Monk" Parker!

X.

When Jesus Comes...

MONROE PARKER

"And if I go and prepare a place for you, I will come again, and receive you unto myself: that where I am, there ye may be also."—John 14:3.

"I will come again." One of the sublimest truths revealed in the Bible is that Jesus Christ is coming back to this world. Yes, our Lord Jesus, who was crucified, dead and buried, and who arose from the dead and sits at the right hand of God the Father making intercession for us, is coming back. That is not just a speculation, no empty dream, but a truth revealed by the out-breathed promises of the Almighty and omniscient God. It is a scriptural doctrine.

Everybody who believes the Bible believes in the second coming of Jesus Christ, but there are certain elements of the teaching about which there are differences of opinion even among orthodox Christians. For instance, there are the different views about the millennium.

I. THERE WILL BE A GOLDEN AGE

Let us see now, what is the millennium? *Mille* means "thousand"; *annum* means "years"; *millennium*, "a thousand years." This is purely scriptural. There will be a thousand years of righteousness on the earth. The prophets have looked down through the annals of future time to a golden day, the millennium, a thousand years of justice.

There Will Be Peace

There will be a golden day. The wolf and the lamb lying down together will take place when Jesus comes. In Isaiah, chapter 11, beginning at verse 6, we read,

"The wolf also shall dwell with the lamb, and the leopard shall lie

*down with the kid; and the calf and the young lion and the fatling
together; and a little child shall lead them."*

This is a picture of peace. The Scripture does not say that a little child
shall sing a song or quote a verse of Scripture in Sunday school. Of
course, children may do this, but this Scripture does not mean that.
It means that a little child shall lead a lion, and the lion will not harm
the child because peace will prevail in the world.

*"And the cow and the bear shall feed; their young ones shall lie down
together: and the lion shall eat straw like the ox."*

Think of it. Peace in this world! Even the ferocious and carnivorous
lion shall be as docile and tame as a kitten and shall "eat straw like
the ox."

Peace. No war in all the world. While this world is under the curse
of sin, it is impossible for men to avert war permanently. War began
when Satan rebelled against God. No sooner was man created than
Satan attacked God by striking at man, for he was a special object of
God's love. There has been war in the world from that day to this. War
is a diabolical institution with a diabolical origin and purpose. It will cease
only when Jesus Christ comes and casts Satan into the bottomless pit.
Man cannot end war because he cannot defeat Satan, who is the source
of war.

God instituted human government; and in so doing, He said, "Whoso
sheddeth man's blood, by man shall his blood be shed" (Gen. 9:6).
The same law which says, "Thou shalt not kill," provides the death penal-
ty for those who kill. Government has a God-given right to take life.
Of course, God will deal with governments for the misuse or abuse of
this right. As Christians, we are exhorted to be subject to civil authorities,
for the "powers that be are ordained of God" (Rom. 13:1). And until
Jesus Christ returns to put all things under His dominion, there will be
wars and rumors of wars.

Wars will come, and fight we must! Man may bring temporary peace,
but he is as powerless to end war permanently as he is to stop the wind
from blowing or the sun from shining.

Do not call me a pessimist. I tell you, when Jesus comes He is going
to change things.

*"And he shall judge among the nations, and shall rebuke many peo-
ple: and they shall beat their swords into plowshares, and their spears*

into pruning hooks." They will not need these instruments of war, for *"nation shall not lift up sword against nation, neither shall they learn war any more."*—Isa. 2:4.

Peace! World peace! Why? Because Jesus is going to reign, and He is the Prince of Peace.

The Curse Will Be Taken Away

The curse that is now on the world will be taken away when Jesus comes. When Adam and Eve ate the fruit from the forbidden tree in the Garden of Eden, God not only placed a curse upon the fallen pair and upon the serpent, but He said to Adam, "Cursed is the ground for thy sake" (Gen. 3:17).

When God said that, in my imagination I can see luxuriant gardens turn to wildernesses. I can see verdant valleys as they become deserts. Thorns appear upon rose bushes, and all nature begins to groan and travail under the curse of sin. But when Jesus comes that curse will be removed.

"The wilderness and the solitary place shall be glad for them; and the desert shall rejoice, and blossom as the rose. It shall blossom abundantly, and rejoice even with joy and singing: the glory of Lebanon shall be given unto it, the excellency of Carmel and Sharon, they shall see the glory of the Lord, and the excellency of our God. Strengthen ye the weak hands, and confirm the feeble knees. Say to them that are of a fearful heart, Be strong, fear not: behold, your God will come with vengeance, even God with a recompence; he will come and save you. Then the eyes of the blind shall be opened, and the ears of the deaf shall be unstopped. Then shall the lame man leap as an hart, and the tongue of the dumb sing: for in the wilderness shall waters break out, and streams in the desert. And the parched ground shall become a pool, and the thirsty land springs of water: in the habitation of dragons, where each lay, shall be grass with reeds and rushes. And an highway shall be there, and a way, and it shall be called The way of holiness; the unclean shall not pass over it; but it shall be for those: the wayfaring men, though fools, shall not err therein. No lion shall be there, nor any ravenous beast shall go up thereon, it shall not be found there; but the redeemed shall walk there: And the ransomed of the Lord shall return, and come to Zion with songs and everlasting joy upon their heads: they

shall obtain joy and gladness, and sorrow and sighing shall flee away."—Isa. 35.

This beautiful chapter, in which every verse is a precious promise from Almighty God, has never been fulfilled. There is going to be a golden age when Jesus comes.

"Behold, the days come, saith the Lord, that I will raise unto David a righteous Branch, and a King shall reign and prosper, and shall execute judgment and justice in the earth. In his days Judah shall be saved, and Israel shall dwell safely: and this is his name whereby he shall be called, THE LORD OUR RIGHTEOUSNESS."—Jer. 23:5,6.

II. HE WILL COME BEFORE THE MILLENNIUM

Now I have said that there are different views about the millennium. The amillennialists (so called because a means "without") do not believe there is to be a millennium. Although there are many orthodox scholars and saints who hold this view, I am convinced that at least a fifth of the Bible is prophecy pointing to such an age. The amillennialist must either spiritualize or ignore altogether such passages of Scripture as those cited above.

There are those who hold that the millennium began about the time of Constantine and continued for a thousand years. There is nothing to support this view. The Catholics believe this to have been a golden age because Catholicism flourished at that time. History teaches us that these centuries were "Dark Ages."

There are some who believe that we are living in the millennium now. We shall not take time or space to deal with this obviously unfounded and unsubstantiated view.

The postmillennialists have the idea that the world will grow better and better until gradually a golden age will dawn and that after the millennium Jesus will return to find a converted world waiting for Him.

I personally am a premillennialist, believing that Jesus will come before the millennium. I do not see how there can be a millennium of peace without the Prince of Peace.

We read in Revelation 20:6:

"Blessed and holy is he that hath part in the first resurrection: on such the second death hath no power, but they shall be priests of God and of Christ, and shall reign with him a thousand years."

If those who have part in the first resurrection are going to reign with Christ during the thousand years, the first resurrection must take place before the thousand years. It is clear that the first resurrection takes place when Jesus comes. He must come before the thousand years.

In Matthew 24 we read:

"But as the days of Noe were, so shall also the coming of the Son of man be. For as in the days that were before the flood they were eating and drinking, marrying and giving in marriage, until the day that Noe entered into the ark, And knew not until the flood came, and took them all away; so shall also the coming of the Son of man be."—Matt. 24:37-39.

Jesus is coming in a time when things are as they were in the days of Noah. Therefore, He will not find a converted world waiting for Him. These and many other passages of Scripture make it obvious that His coming is premillennial.

III. HIS COMING PERSONAL AND BODILY

The second coming of Jesus will be personal and bodily. In John 14:3 He said to His disciples, "I will come again." When He ascended into Heaven as His disciples stood looking after Him, two angels appeared to them and said, "Ye men of Galilee, why stand ye gazing up into heaven? this same Jesus, which is taken up from you into heaven, shall so come in like manner as ye have seen him go into heaven" (Acts 1:11). "This same Jesus," the personal, literal Son of God, the One who was nailed to the cross, the One who died with a broken heart, "shall so come in like manner as ye have seen him go."

He disappeared in the clouds; He will come back in the clouds. We read in Revelation 1:7, "Behold, he cometh with clouds; and every eye shall see him, and they also which pierced him: and all kindreds of the earth shall wail because of him." He disappeared from the Mount of Olives; He will come back there. "And his feet shall stand in that day upon the mount of Olives, which is before Jerusalem on the east" (Zech. 14:4). The Lord Jesus Christ Himself will personally appear in this world again.

Paul said:

"For the Lord himself shall descend from heaven with a shout, with the voice of the archangel, and with the trump of God: and the dead

in Christ shall rise first: Then we which are alive and remain shall be caught up together with them in the clouds, to meet the Lord in the air: and so shall we ever be with the Lord."—I Thess. 4:16,17.

IV. HIS COMING TWOFOLD

The coming of Jesus will be twofold, one great event in two phases, one great drama in two acts. The first act of the drama, known as **the Rapture,** is the coming of Jesus **for** His church. The second act will take place at least seven years after the first act. The second act is known as **the Revelation** and is the coming of Christ **with** His church. In the first act, He comes in the air, and the church is caught up to meet Him. In the second act, He comes to the earth and sets up His millennial throne and reigns a thousand years.

I have stated that there will be a seven-year interval between the two acts of this great drama. In Revelation the duration of this period is set forth in the very number of months and of days that elapse between the two phases of His coming. Also in the ninth chapter of Daniel, God sets forth in prophecy seven weeks in which certain things are to be accomplished. These are weeks of years, not days—literally "seventy-sevens." One of these weeks, which is a period of seven years, is yet in the future and will take place just before Jesus comes "to bring in everlasting righteousness."

All the signs of the times that we hear so much about point not to the rapture of the church but beyond the rapture to the revelation or His glorious appearing. The signs of the times point to the second act of the drama. No signs are related to the first act. However, the fact that signs are pointing toward the second act makes the first act, or the rapture, more impendent because, of course, the first act precedes the second one by at least seven years.

V. HIS COMING IMMINENT

The second coming of Jesus is imminent, likely to happen at any time. I do not say dogmatically that He is coming soon, though He may. I expect Him to. But then He may not. Nobody knows when it will be. We are charged to watch. Do you expect Him to come today or tonight? You do not? "Therefore be ye also ready: for in such an hour as ye think not the Son of man cometh" (Matt. 24:44).

VI. TRIBULATION PRECEDES PEACE

When Jesus comes and takes His own out of the world, there will be

Great Tribulation on earth. In speaking of this period in Matthew 24:21, 22, Jesus said:

"For then shall be great tribulation, such as was not since the beginning of the world to this time, no, nor ever shall be. And except those days should be shortened, there should no flesh be saved: but for the elect's sake those days shall be shortened."

It is not possible for human imagination to visualize the horrors of the Great Tribulation. This awful period may begin at any hour. Think of it! It is to be the worst time the world has ever known or ever shall know; a worse time than the Flood; worse than the Spanish Inquisition or the French Revolution or the Commune; worse than the Dark Ages. The Great Tribulation is to be worse than the time when men were pulled asunder by horses; worse than the time when men and women and children were thrown to the hungry lions on the sands of the arena. It will be worse than the reign of Diocletian or Nero; worse than the time when people were dipped in pitch and burned as torches. It is to be a time of war and famine and death and persecution and hatred and fear and fire and storm; a time when Satan is to have unhindered sway over the world; a time when God will pour out the wine cup of His wrath upon the world. The bottomless pit will be opened, and all Hell will break loose on the face of the earth. This dreadful period will culminate in the bloodiest battle in all the ages—the battle of Armageddon.

"Immediately after the tribulation of those days shall the sun be darkened, and the moon shall not give her light, and the stars shall fall from heaven, and the powers of the heavens shall be shaken: And then shall appear the sign of the Son of man in heaven: and then shall all the tribes of the earth mourn, and they shall see the Son of man coming in the clouds of heaven with power and great glory."—Matt. 24:29,30.

Christ shall reign on the earth, on the literal throne of David, in Jerusalem, and the golden glory of God will fill the earth as the waters cover the sea.

VII. WHEN THE GOLDEN AGE BLENDS INTO A GOLDEN ETERNITY

At the close of the millennium, the Devil, who will have been bound during the thousand years, shall be loosed for a little season. He will go about like a roaring lion seeking whom he might devour and will cause a stormy sunset at the close of the golden day. This will be a time of testing, but God will lay hold on the Devil and cast him into the "lake of fire and brimstone, where the beast and the false prophet are, and [he] shall be tormented day and night for ever and ever" (Rev. 20:10).

After Satan is cast into Hell, the wicked dead are raised and judged at the great white throne judgment. After this the "City Four-square," with its jewel foundations, its gates of pearl, its streets of flashing gold, will come down from God out of Heaven. Then the eternal order begins.

Will You Be Ready?

Now Jesus has been here, and He said He was coming back. He told us to watch for Him. He said that we should pray, "Thy kingdom come." Do you really want Him to come soon? Suppose that right now as you are thinking on this subject Jesus should come. Would you meet Him in the sky? Would you be caught up with the hosts of others to meet the Lord? You can be ready if you will. That is why Jesus died. He would not have toiled and struggled under the burdens He carried; He would not have been crowned with thorns and spit upon and cursed and mocked and laughed at and scourged and crucified, if He had not wanted to see you saved. Thank God for Jesus Christ! Thank God that He came into this world. And thank God that He is coming back. He said, "I will come again."

A little boy followed his mother to the gate one day and said, "Mother, please take Bobby."

"No, Bobby," she said, "I cannot take you because I am going to the hospital for an examination. I might have an operation. I do not know when, but I am coming back. I will come on the train. When you hear the whistle blow, remember that Mother might be on the train."

That evening the train whistle sounded, and little Bobby was out in the yard with a bound. "Daddy, Mother's coming! Mother's coming!" he cried.

"How do you know, Bobby?"

"Well, she said she was coming when the whistle blows."

But she did not come. The next day the whistle sounded, and once again Bobby ran to meet his mother; but she failed to come. But Bobby said, "I know she is coming. She said she was."

One day, surely enough, she came back.

O my friends, CHRIST IS COMING! CHRIST IS COMING! You say, "How do you know?" He said He would. Will you be ready when Jesus comes?

ROBERT GREENE LEE
1886-1978

ABOUT THE MAN:

R. G. Lee was born November 11, 1886, and died July 20, 1978.

The midwife attending his birth held baby Lee in her black arms while dancing a jig around the room, saying, "Praise Gawd! Glory be! The good Lawd done sont a preacher to dis here house. Yas, sah! Yes, ma'am. Dat's what He's done gone and done."

"God-sent preacher" well describes Dr. Lee. Few in number are the Baptists who have never heard his most famous sermon, "Payday Someday!" If you haven't heard it, or read it, surely you have heard some preacher make a favorable reference to it.

From his humble birth to sharecropper parents, Dr. Lee rose to pastor one of the largest churches in his denomination and head the mammoth Southern Baptist Convention as its president, serving three terms in that office. Dr. John R. Rice said:

"If you have not had the privilege of hearing Dr. Lee in person, I am sorry for you. The scholarly thoroughness, the wizardry of words, the lilt of poetic thought, the exalted idealism, the tender pathos, the practical application, the stern devotion to divine truth, the holy urgency in the preaching of a man called and anointed of God to preach and who must therefore preach, are never to be forgotten. The stately progression of his sermon to its logical end satisfies. The facile language, the alliterative statement, the powerful conviction mark Dr. Lee's sermons. The scholarly gleaning of incident and illustration from the treasures of scholarly memory and library make a rich feast for the hearer. The banquet table is spread with bread from many a grain field, honey distilled from the nectar of far-off exotic blossoms, sweetmeats from many a bake shop, strong meat from divers markets, and the whole board is garnished by posies from a thousand gardens.

"Often have I been blessed in hearing Dr. Lee preach, have delighted in his southern voice, and have been carried along with joy by his anointed eloquence."

XI.

Jesus Is Coming to Earth Again

R. G. LEE

"Which also said, Ye men of Galilee, why stand ye gazing up into heaven? this same Jesus, which is taken up from you into heaven, shall so come in like manner as ye have seen him go into heaven."—Acts 1:11.

"For the Lord himself shall descend from heaven with a shout, with the voice of the archangel, and with the trump of God: and the dead in Christ shall rise first: Then we which are alive and remain shall be caught up together with them in the clouds, to meet the Lord in the air: and so shall we ever be with the Lord. Wherefore comfort one another with these words."—I Thess. 4:16-18.

As to Christ's second coming, let us consider:

I. THE REALITY OF HIS RETURN

No one can read and believe the Bible and not believe in the second coming of Christ—when "...the Lord himself shall descend from heaven with a shout, with the voice of the archangel, and with the trump of God..." (II Thess. 4:16)—when the same Jesus who was taken up from the disciples into Heaven will so come in like manner as they saw Him go into Heaven (Acts 1:11). This is the personal, literal, visible return of the Lord Jesus Himself—not some new movement for the uplift of humanity, not some sweeping revival, not some gifts from Christ, not some catastrophe when God makes the wrath of man to praise Him. As Jesus went away, so will He come. They saw Him leave. They will see Him return. "Behold, he cometh with clouds; and every eye shall see him..." (Rev. 1:7). As all the predictions regarding His first advent, when the world coldly received Him as a babe on a pallet of straw, were literally fulfilled, so shall all the predictions regarding His second coming be just as literally fulfilled.

Clearly, definitely, unmistakably, is the second coming taught in the Word of God. Only the doctrine of the atonement is a more prominent Bible truth than the truth concerning the return of the Lord Jesus. In the New Testament, the second coming is mentioned 318 times. When the first coming is mentioned one time, the second coming is mentioned eight times. Only by ignorant spiritualizing or carelessly ignoring or looking upon these passages as interpolations, or by wrenching language out of its setting and rendering it meaningless, can one throw out of court the mass of evidence that Scripture presents. Christ's promise to return is the promise of promises—the crown and consummation of all promises. It is the coronation of all evangelistic hopes, the consummation of prophecy. Christ's promise is unmistakably divine, true, final. He is coming!

Nature and grace alike proclaim a returning glorified Messiah. Nature calls for Him to rectify her unveiling disorders, to repair her shattered structures, to restore her oppressed energies, to verify her sublime testimony to the Creator, so long questioned and overlooked. But grace sends forth a mightier call. If the whole creation groans and travails together in pain for the manifestation of the Son of God—how much more those sons of God themselves. As we have whole chapters—Matthew 24, Luke 21, Mark 13—given over to the teaching of the second coming, so we have whole books, such as First and Second Thessalonians, devoted to this important subject.

The first epistle to the Thessalonians is the first written and deals with the truths God would first have taught. Man teaches the second coming of the Lord last. Many churches today consider it *incidental*. The churches of the first century considered it *fundamental*. They were certain about the certainty of it. Men think often of Jesus' birth, of His life, of His crucifixion—and many biographies are written. Men think often of Jesus' resurrection, His ascension. We have days to celebrate these great events. But no one has ever suggested to have a day set apart to remember that He is coming again.

Yet His coming again is the next great event in the life of the Son of God. While it is perfectly scriptural to think of all the great facts connected with our salvation as wrought out by Him in the past, the Holy Spirit directs the attention of all believers to the future and assures us that He is coming again.

To one who accepts the authority of the Scriptures, the testimony of Jesus to His own second coming is of outstanding significance. What Jesus said in self-disclosure is of utmost importance. Note how total was the teaching of Christ about Himself. There are 316 separate items of teaching by our Lord. There are 198 items which are about His own person. This degree of self emphasis is amazing. When we study the 198 references to Christ made by Himself, we find 130 contain specific emphasis upon His own person. These statements reveal the self-consciousness of Jesus.

To get the quickest contact with our Lord's thought about Himself, let us classify in groups:

(1) Jesus spoke of Himself as "The Son of Man" 44 times.

(2) He called God "My Father" in an exclusive sense 20 times.

(3) He affirmed His unique and exclusive relationship to God 10 times.

(4) He pointed to His death, as divinely ordained or having redemptive significance, 25 times.

(5) He fore-announced His resurrection from the dead 17 times.

(6) He promised to be spiritually present while physically absent from His disciples 3 times.

(7) He set up His person as the supreme motive of life, calling men to do and to suffer in His name and for His sake, 17 times.

(8) He claimed supreme moral and religious authority 33 times.

(9) He claimed to be the final Judge who would determine the everlasting destiny of men 12 times.

(10) He claimed or exercised authority over nature and manifested supernatural knowledge 43 times.

(11) He rejoiced when men believed in Him and grieved in their unbelief 4 times.

(12) He accepted the title "Son of God" 9 times.

(13) He claimed the title of "Son of God" 3 times.

(14) Five times He affirmed He held a unique position as the Lord and Master of men.

(15) Forty-four times He claimed for Himself supreme significance as one in whose person centered the ultimate purpose of God.

Concerning the second coming, let us think of:

II. THE REASON FOR HIS RETURN

"But I would not have you to be ignorant, brethren, concerning them

which are asleep, that ye sorrow not, even as others which have no hope."—I Thess. 4:13.

The reason is that light may be shed upon the death of the believers and that hope may live in the Christian heart. God does not want us to be ignorant. The Bible is written that we may not be ignorant of great things we need to know.

Six times in the New Testament, Paul says: "I would not have you to be ignorant."

"Now I would not have you ignorant, brethren, that oftentimes I purposed to come unto you, (but was let hitherto,) that I might have some fruit among you also, even as among other Gentiles."—Rom. 1:13.

"Moreover, brethren, I would not that ye should be ignorant, how that all our fathers were under the cloud, and all passed through the sea."—I Cor. 10:1.

"Now concerning spiritual gifts, brethren, I would not have you ignorant."—I Cor. 12:1.

"For we would not, brethren, have you ignorant of our trouble which came to us in Asia, that we were pressed out of measure, above strength, insomuch that we despaired even of life."—II Cor. 1:8.

"For I would not, brethren, that ye should be ignorant of this mystery, lest ye should be wise in your own conceits; that blindness in part is happened to Israel, until the fulness of the Gentiles be come in."—Rom. 11:25.

And God would not have us to be ignorant of the second coming of Christ and all the signs and events related thereunto.

"But I would not have you to be ignorant, brethren, concerning them which are asleep, that ye sorrow not, even as others which have no hope. For if we believe that Jesus died and rose again, even so them also which sleep in Jesus will God bring with him. For this we say unto you by the word of the Lord, that we which are alive and remain unto the coming of the Lord shall not prevent them which are asleep."—I Thess. 4:13-15.

It is terrible to be ignorant of some great things: to know botany and be ignorant of Jesus—the Lily of the Valley; to know astronomy and be ignorant of Jesus—the Bright and Morning Star; to know biology and not know the life of Jesus; to know the ages of rocks—and be ignorant of the Rock of Ages; to know mathematics and be ignorant of how to add to faith virtue, knowledge, temperance, patience, godliness, kindness, love; to know about winds and be victims of passions greater than they; to have one's name written on checks and not on the Lamb's Book of Life; to be ignorant of the second coming is tragic.

Now think of:

III. THE RETURN

"The Lord himself shall descend from heaven." There will be no substitute. The One who comes is none other than the Lord Jesus Christ. As the first coming was literal in every sense, so His second coming will be literal in every sense. There will be a personal, visible, bodily, glorious reappearing of Jesus Christ.

1. Christ's spiritual presence is not the second coming, for the Bible says: "The Lord himself." Christ's presence is a reality, but that is distinct from His visible second coming. If His second coming is spiritual, then the same law of interpretation will make the first coming spiritual. "Every eye [not every mind] shall see him."

2. Death is not the second coming, for the Bible says: "The Lord himself." When a Christian dies, Christ does not descend from Heaven with a shout. No dead person arises. Nobody is caught up in the clouds. Nobody meets the Lord in the air. No such events take place until Christ returns. No such events occur at death. Therefore, the second coming cannot mean death. Substitute the word *death* in Philippians 3:20 and in Matthew 16:28 and see how ridiculous the statement and how nonsensical the teaching that the death of a Christian is the second coming of Christ. "For our conversation is in heaven; from whence also we look for [death] the Lord Jesus Christ." No! ". . . from whence we look for the Saviour, the Lord Jesus Christ."

". . . There be some standing here, which shall not taste of death, until they see [death] coming in his kingdom." Nonsense! Death and Christ are not synonymous. ". . . till they see the Son of man coming in his kingdom."

3. Conversion is not the second coming of Christ, for the Bible says: "The Lord himself." The regeneration of a sinner is as the wind. "The wind bloweth where it listeth, and thou hearest the sound thereof, but canst not tell whence it cometh, and whither it goeth: so is every one that is born of the Spirit" (John 3:8). But this is the first event in a sinner becoming a Christian. Glorious it is when a sinner is saved—when drunkards become sober, when infidels become believers, when liars become truthful, when people born once are born again. But the salvation of a sinner is not the second coming.

4. Great events in history are not the second coming of Christ, for the Bible says: "The Lord himself."

Pentecost is not the substitute for the coming of Christ, even though there are those who say that the predictions regarding Christ's return were fulfilled on that day. Many of the promises regarding the second coming were made after the day of Pentecost, when the Holy Spirit came. And none of the events of I Thessalonians 4:16,17 occurred on the day of Pentecost. On that momentous day, there was no resurrection of the dead, no believers caught up in the clouds to meet the Lord in the air.

The Lord *Himself* is coming bodily, visibly, really, actually, corporeally, gloriously, personally. More startling than the scenes of Pentecost, more momentous than the fall of Jerusalem, more significant than the indwelling of the Spirit, more beautiful than the conversion of a sinner, more to be desired than our departure to be with the Lord will be the literal, visible, bodily return of Christ.

When Christ comes, there will be:

IV. THE RESURRECTION

". . .the dead in Christ shall rise first" (I Thess. 4:16).

Those who die out of Christ are not blessed and holy. They must stay in their graves another one thousand years. Then after the Tribulation period and after the millennium, they will be raised and brought in judgment before the great white throne where they will receive the condemnation of Hell.

*"Blessed and holy is he that hath part in the first resurrection: on such the second death hath no power, but they shall be priests of God and of Christ, and shall reign with him a thousand years."—*Rev. 20:6.

". . . *Blessed are the dead which die in the Lord. . . . ."—*Rev. 14:13.

Dr. Herschel Ford says:

> There are sleeping Christians in many different places of the earth. The majority are in manmade graves. However, many Chris-

tians have gone down into the seas...many have been burned to death...some have been lost in the wild places of the earth, and their bones have been picked clean by the birds of the air...some have suffered and died in the deserts and their bones have been left to bleach in the broiling sun...some have been torn to pieces in explosions...some have flown away in airplanes and have never been found. None of this matters to Jesus, for He knows everything. He knows where they are, and He will show forth His power over death when He comes, for His loved ones will rise from everywhere and not one of them shall be lost.

When I attend the funeral of a Christian, I can truly say to him, "Goodby. I will see you with Jesus after a little while." We can say this of all who know Jesus, for we know that it is well with them.

Now, when the dead are taken up, this is the first resurrection—it is not a resurrection *of* the dead but a resurrection *from* the dead. The lost dead will be left in their graves, but the saved ones will be raised incorruptible.

There will be order and program in this resurrection from the dead. Paul outlines this order: "But every man in his own order: Christ the firstfruits; afterward they that are Christ's at his coming" (I Cor. 15:23).

Christ, the firstfruits. Then they that are Christ's at His coming. The victory of I Corinthians 15:54-58 will be accomplished:

"So when this corruptible shall have put on incorruption, and this mortal shall have put on immortality, then shall be brought to pass the saying that is written, Death is swallowed up in victory. O death, where is thy sting? O grave, where is thy victory? The sting of death is sin; and the strength of sin is the law. But thanks be to God, which giveth us the victory through our Lord Jesus Christ. Therefore, my beloved brethren, be ye stedfast, unmoveable, always abounding in the work of the Lord."

Don't overlook:

V. THE RAPTURE

"Then we which are alive and remain shall be caught up together with them in the clouds, to meet the Lord in the air: and so shall we ever be with the Lord."—I Thess. 4:17.

Every Christian on the earth will hear the commanding shout and will rise up to meet Him. The saved will be taken away before the Great

Tribulation overtakes a godless world. The unsaved will be left on earth to go through that awful period. Whether one has been saved a long or a short time, every Christian will be caught up. The living Christians and the dead Christians shall be caught up together and taken away.

Philip was caught away in the book of Acts:

"And when they were come up out of the water, the Spirit of the Lord caught away Philip, that the eunuch saw him no more: and he went his way rejoicing."—Acts 8:39.

This rapture of the living Christians will be simultaneous with the resurrection of the righteous dead. Paul is particular to say that "we which are alive," we who are left unto the coming of the Lord, shall in no wise precede them that are fallen asleep. These "fallen asleep" are the dead Christians who are raised in the first resurrection. Both will be translated together—and will meet the descending Lord in the air. The rapture of the living Christians will be preceded by a "change" in their condition. "Behold, I shew you a mystery; We shall not all sleep, but we shall all be changed" (I Cor. 15:51). It will be a change from corruption to incorruption. "For this corruptible must put on incorruption, and this mortal must put on immortality" (vs. 53). And all this will take place "in a moment, in the twinkling of an eye, at the last trump."

After the rapture, there will be:

VI. THE REUNION

We shall be caught up together. Together! That is just another way of spelling *reunion*. If we are not to be reunited to our redeemed loved ones—those whom we have loved and lost—then for what purpose is this Scripture? When would there be any comfort? When would there be any consolation? This epistle was written that Christians sorrow not as those who have no hope.

As Jacob saw Joseph and was with him after twenty years, so shall we be reunited with our redeemed loved ones. As Naomi was known when she went home again from the land of Moab, so shall we be known in the reunion at Christ's coming again.

We read in the first book of the Bible:

"Abraham died and was gathered to his people";
"Isaac died and was gathered to his people";
"Jacob died and was gathered to his people."

"He died in a good old age and was gathered to his people and they buried him."

What people? Their friends, their comrades, their old companions.

"Gathered unto his people" can hardly mean burial with his people, for the burial is mentioned after it. It comes between the dying and the burial. And we note that when the time of Moses' death had come this phrase is solemnly used: "The Lord said unto him, Get thee up into the mountain and die in the mount, *and be gathered to thy people!*"

Now, Miriam was already buried in the distant desert. Aaron's body lay on the slopes of Mount Hor. The little mother who made the ark of bulrushes long ago found a grave in the brick fields of Egypt.

Do the words teach that Moses came back to his people in this life all unseen when he was "gathered to his people"? Did the expression mean and does it mean that he came back to Miriam's body in the desert and to Aaron's body asleep on Mount Hor and that he lay down again by the side of the little mother in the brick fields of Egypt? No—never. Since he was to *die* and *then,* after dying, be "gathered to his people," it means that into the glory whence they had gone, he was to see them and be with them once again, and *know* them.

Then, without doubt, there will be:

VII. THE RECOGNITION

"So shall we ever be with the Lord." At the second advent of the Lord Jesus, there will be a glorious reunion of the redeemed—a reunion made wonderful by recognition.

In all lands, in all ages, under all forms of religion, the fact of recognition in the future world is received. Is it God implanted? Then it is rightfully implanted.

Cicero who lived before Christ's day said:

> Oh, glorious day when I shall retire from this low and sordid scene to associate with the divine assemblage of departed spirits . . . with my dear Cato, the best of sons and the most faithful of men. It was my sad fate to lay his body on the funeral pile. If I seemed to bear his death with fortitude, it was by no means because I did not feel sensibly the loss I had sustained. It was because I was supported by the consoling reflection that we should not be long separated.

Homer, great man to the Greeks, tells us of Ulysses meeting his mother in the spirit world and recognizing her. Virgil represents Aeneas as meeting with his friends over there and talking with them. Socrates was nerved to drink the hemlock because of the thought of meeting the friends who had gone before.

Notice David. There is a sick child in the house of David the king. He sits weeping in the deep shadows. He does not eat; his hunger has been swallowed up in grief too deep for words. He cannot sleep. Nature's great balm that "knits up the raveled sleeve of care" has fled from his eyes. David lies prostrate on his face, until the palace seems a house of many dirges, a house of gloom. What are all these courtly attendants when none of them can cool the fever fires in the body of the child? What are victorious armies when all the soldiers in his kingdom cannot make one little fluttering heart grow stronger? What are conquered provinces when all the revenue cannot buy away the grim figure of death from the bedside of the babe that is sick unto death?

A week passes by, dragging its weary length along. Then there is a great silence in the house. The shutters are closed. People talk in whispers and walk on tiptoe. Then in that great house two little eyelids are gently closed; two little hands are folded over a little bosom that heaves not a sigh; two little feet are at rest; one little heart is forever still.

Then the servants, hushed, awed and hesitant, come to speak the sad tidings to David the king. But they cannot make up their minds to tell him—and at the door they stand, whispering. David hears them and, looking up, asks: "Is the child dead?" "Yes, he is dead!" David rises, washes himself, puts on new apparel, and sits down to eat.

What power hushed that tempest? What strength has lifted up that king whom grief had dethroned? What lifted him from the ashes and gave him the oil of joy for mourning? It was the thought that he would come again into the possession of his child. No grave diggers could hide him. The wintry blasts of death could not put out that bright light. In that fair city where the hoofs of the pale horse never strike the pavement, he would clasp his lost treasure. So David wipes the tears, chokes back his grief and exclaims, "I shall go to him." What, let us ask, would it mean to David to go to his child if he did not know him?

This meeting of redeemed loved ones and friends is one of the many glorious hopes of the resurrection at the return of the Lord. We shall know those who have gone before. This is the glorious hope of the resurrection at the return of the Lord.

"For we know in part, and we prophesy in part. . . . For now we see through a glass, darkly; but then face to face: now I know in part; but then shall I know even as also I am known."—I Cor. 13:9,12.

"Beloved, now are we the sons of God, and it doth not yet appear what we shall be: but we know that, when he shall appear, we shall be like him; for we shall see him as he is. And every man that hath this hope in him purifieth himself, even as he is pure."—I John 3:2,3.

It is not strange that the apostle said, *"Comfort ye one another with these words."* Surely it is most comforting. And the comfort is a fountain *in* which and *at* which there is no drouth.

Let us give thought to:

VII. THE REIGN OF CHRIST ON EARTH

This is no incident nor accident, but the purpose of God. This kingdom, ordained from the beginning, is no post-creation afterthought of God but a pre-creation thought in His mind from all eternity.

Ordained from the beginning, this reign of Jesus on this earth is the green, flower-scented oasis in the desert of Time. Purposed of God, this kingdom reign of Christ is not Heaven—as some seem to think. But is not Heaven the culmination of time? Is Heaven not beyond the kingdom—when Time is no more? When the judgment of the great white throne is passed and the eternal ages have been flung open, that, as Dr. Len G. Broughton wisely says, is Heaven. "And this gospel of the kingdom shall be preached in all the world for a witness unto all nations; and then shall the end come" (Matt. 24:14).

Hear the Prophet Zechariah:

"And his feet shall stand in that day upon the mount of Olives, which is before Jerusalem on the east, and the mount of Olives shall cleave in the midst thereof toward the east and toward the west, and there shall be a very great valley; and half of the mountain shall remove toward the north, and half of it toward the south. And ye shall flee to the valley of the mountains; for the valley of the mountains shall reach unto Azal: yea, ye shall flee, like as ye fled from before the earthquake in the days of Uzziah king of Judah; and the Lord my God shall come; and all the saints with thee." — 14:4,5.

This refers to the earthly kingdom. Thus shall the King come—and men shall see Him. And not Him only but all the vast domain of His kingdom. The Devil shall be chained and sealed in a pit to deceive the nations no more until the thousand years are past.

The kingdoms of the earth, now glaring at each other across chasms of suspicion and ill will, shall learn war no more—shall be held together by Jesus Christ, who shall reign in all the affairs of the earth—and we shall have a new earth. This is the Word of God who says, "I make all things new." Jesus shall come and set His face against the powers of darkness to reign over the united kingdoms of earth.

This kingly administration of Jesus will be personal, and not just spiritual.

Dr. Len G. Broughton says:

> Language cannot be made any plainer than that which is used descriptive of Christ's second coming and the establishment of His kingdom. If His second coming is spiritual, and the kingdom which He is coming to establish is likewise spiritual, then the same law of interpretation will make His first coming spiritual. Oh, what a calamity this would be! It would rob the manger of its poetry and pathos. It would stop the song of the angel chorus on the morning of His birth. It would annul the matchless teaching, by precept and example, of our blessed Lord. It would climb the slopes of Calvary and hide away the blood of the covenant. It would pass over as a myth the story of the sepulchre, and frown with scorn upon the glories of Olivet. If the second coming of Jesus is spiritual, the sublimest picture contained in the gallery of inspired truth is destroyed, that picture of the disciples assembled together on the day of His ascension when the invisible chariot of God, let down from Heaven, caught up the Saviour, and bore Him away to His faraway home in the glory.

When Jesus comes, the pattern prayer of the saints, "Thy kingdom come, thy will be done on earth as it is in heaven," will be heard. Jesus, the rejected, will seize the reigns of government and rule in beneficent power and victory.

After the rapture of the living Christians and the resurrection of the dead Christians—all of whom shall be given glorified bodies as they are caught up together to meet the Lord in the air—the unrighteous dead and the unrighteous living are left. The unrighteous dead shall sleep on in their graves until the thousand years of the reign of Christ are past.

Immediately following the rapture of the saints at the first is the period of THE Great Tribulation. The Devil is in absolute control. The Holy Spirit's day has passed. Christ has not yet come to earth. He is in the clouds with His saints from whence they enter into Heaven. This is followed by the "judgment-seat-of-Christ" judgment, where rewards are given and ranks assigned.

But on the earth is not only the absence of the Holy Spirit, but the presence of the Devil.

"Therefore rejoice, ye heavens, and ye that dwell in them. Woe to the inhabiters of the earth and of the sea! for the devil is come down unto you, having great wrath, because he knoweth that he hath but a short time."—Rev. 12:12.

The Devil was first cast out of the Mount of God:

"By the multitude of thy merchandise they have filled the midst of thee with violence, and thou hast sinned: therefore I will cast thee as profane out of the mountain of God: and I will destroy thee, O covering cherub, from the midst of the stones of fire."—Ezek. 28:16.

The Devil was next cast out into the air:

"Wherein in time past ye walked according to the course of this world, according to the prince of the power of the air, the spirit that now worketh in the children of disobedience."—Eph. 2:2.

When Jesus comes "in the air," the Devil is cast down to the earth. "Inhabiters of the earth, the Devil is come down to you." And, because of the Devil having power and great wrath, utterly unopposed, knowing his time is short, he will rule with a high hand.

Describing this terrible Tribulation, John writes in the Revelation:

"And in those days shall men seek death, and shall not find it; and shall desire to die, and death shall flee from them."—Rev. 9:6.

And concerning those days, Matthew writes:

"For then shall be great tribulation, such as was not since the beginning of the world to this time, no, nor ever shall be. And except those days should be shortened, there should no flesh be saved: but for the elect's sake those days shall be shortened."—Matt. 24:21,22.

This Tribulation will make the worst famine seem as a feast, the world's worst wars seem as children's parties. But when Christ and His bride are united in the air, then Christ will come to earth and the Devil will be cast into the bottomless pit.

Here he must stay for one thousand years.

"And I saw an angel come down from heaven, having the key of the bottomless pit and a great chain in his hand. And he laid hold on the dragon, that old serpent, which is the Devil, and Satan, and bound him a thousand years, and cast him into the bottomless pit, and shut him up, and set a seal upon him, that he should deceive the nations no more, till the thousand years should be fulfilled: and after that he must be loosed a little season. And I saw thrones, and they sat upon them: and judgment was given unto them: and I saw the souls of them that were beheaded for the witness of Jesus, and for the word of God, and which had not worshipped the beast, neither his image, neither had received his mark upon their foreheads, or in their hands; and they lived and reigned with Christ a thousand years. But the rest of the dead lived not again until the thousand years were finished. This is the first resurrection. Blessed and holy is he that hath part in the first resurrection: on such the second death hath no power, but they shall be priests of God and of Christ, and shall reign with him a thousand years."— Rev. 20:1-6.

Since the millennium is to be a time of righteousness and peace, it is absolutely necessary that Satan be removed from the earth. How can you have a golden age without getting rid of the Devil? Satan, too strong to be overcome by any human power, will be locked up by the omnipotent Christ.

The arrest of Satan before the millennium! Thus the most notable arrest the universe has ever known is here described. An angel makes the arrest. The earth could enjoy no rest with Satan unbound. For one thousand years "that old serpent which is the Devil and Satan" will remain in the prison of the pit. Satan's freedom has filled the earth with disease, death, decay, destruction, sin, sorrow, suffering, pain, pang, groan, moan, tears, tragedy, dying, sighing, crying, war. But during his confinement, the earth will enjoy a Sabbath of rest. A thousand years of peace in a Satanless world! Think of it—and rejoice!

Jesus brings His bride back to the earth and will not allow Satan to roam the earth. Then will come the bridal party to the "new earth."

*"And the Lord shall be king over all the earth: in that day shall there be one Lord, and his name one."—*Zech. 14:9.

"His eyes were as a flame of fire, and on his head were many crowns; and he had a name written, that no man knew, but he himself. . . . And

out of his mouth goeth a sharp sword, that with it he should smite the nations: and he shall rule them with a rod of iron: and he treadeth the winepress of the fierceness and wrath of Almighty God. And he hath on his vesture and on his thigh a name written, KING OF KINGS, AND LORD OF LORDS."—Rev. 19:12,15,16.

Satan is silenced. This is what we call the millennium.

It is the answer to the prayer of Christ, which was given as our pattern: "Thy kingdom come, thy will be done, on earth as in heaven." This could never occur until Satan is out of the way.

With Satan bound, Christ shall sit upon His throne—and rule.

"And speak unto him, saying, Thus speaketh the LORD of hosts, saying, Behold the man whose name is The BRANCH; and he shall grow up out of his place, and he shall build the temple of the LORD: even he shall build the temple of the LORD; and he shall bear the glory, and shall sit and rule upon his throne: and he shall be a priest upon his throne: and the counsel of peace shall be between them both."— Zech. 6:12,13.

"And the LORD shall be king over all the earth: in that day shall there be one LORD, and his name one."—Zech. 14:9.

"Then the moon shall be confounded, and the sun ashamed, when the LORD of hosts shall reign in mount Zion, and in Jerusalem, and before his ancients gloriously."—Isa. 24:23.

"And I will cut off the chariot from Ephraim, and the horse from Jerusalem, and the battle bow shall be cut off: and he shall speak peace unto the heathen: and his dominion shall be from sea even to sea, and from the river even to the ends of the earth."—Zech. 9:10.

"Yea, all kings shall fall down before him: all nations shall serve him."—Ps. 72:11.

"I saw in the night visions, and, behold, one like the Son of man came with the clouds of heaven, and came to the Ancient of days, and they brought him near before him. And there was given him dominion, and glory, and a kingdom, that all people, nations, and languages, should serve him: his dominion is an everlasting dominion, which shall not pass away, and his kingdom that which shall not be destroyed. And the kingdom and dominion, and the greatness of the kingdom under the whole heaven, shall be given to the people of the saints of the most

High, whose kingdom is an everlasting kingdom, and all dominions shall serve and obey him."—Dan. 7:13,14,27.

"He shall be great, and shall be called the Son of the Highest: and the Lord God shall give unto him the throne of his father David: And he shall reign over the house of Jacob for ever; and of his kingdom there shall be no end."—Luke 1:32,33.

"Therefore being a prophet, and knowing that God had sworn with an oath to him, that of the fruit of his loins, according to the flesh, he would raise up Christ to sit on his throne."—Acts 2:30.

If those promises are not fulfilled, then the Word of God is false. But they shall be kept. God's Word is true.

During the thousand years—while Satan is bound and Jesus reigns— justice will prevail without partiality.

"Behold, the days come, saith the LORD, that I will raise unto David a righteous Branch, and a King shall reign and prosper, and shall execute judgment and justice in the earth."—Jer. 23:5.

"Behold, a king shall reign in righteousness, and princes shall rule in judgment."—Isa. 32:1.

There will be a new and fruitful earth:

"The wilderness and the solitary place shall be glad for them; and the desert shall rejoice, and blossom as the rose. It shall blossom abundantly, and rejoice even with joy and singing: the glory of Lebanon shall be given unto it, the excellency of Carmel and Sharon, they shall see the glory of the Lord, and the excellency of our God."—Isa. 35:1,2.

"And the desolate land shall be tilled, whereas it lay desolate in the sight of all that passed by. And they shall say, This land that was desolate is become like the garden of Eden; and the waste and desolate and ruined cities are become fenced, and are inhabited."—Ezek. 36:34,35.

"Behold, the days come, saith the Lord, that the plowman shall overtake the reaper, and the treader of grapes him that soweth seed; and the mountains shall drop sweet wine, and all the hills shall melt."— Amos 9:13.

The ferocious nature of animals and their instincts will be changed:

"The wolf also shall dwell with the lamb, and the leopard shall lie down with the kid; and the calf and the young lion and the fatling

together; and a little child shall lead them. And the cow and the bear shall feed; their young ones shall lie down together: and the lion shall eat straw like the ox. And the sucking child shall play on the hole of the asp, and the weaned child shall put his hand on the cockatrice' den."—Isa. 11:6-8.

"The wolf and the lamb shall feed together, and the lion shall eat straw like the bullock: and dust shall be the serpent's meat. They shall not hurt nor destroy in all my holy mountain, saith the Lord."—Isa. 65:25.

There will be no more war:

"And he shall judge among the nations, and shall rebuke many people: and they shall beat their swords into plowshares, and their spears into pruninghooks: nation shall not lift up sword against nation, neither shall they learn war any more."—Isa. 2:4.

Through the years men have talked of "learning war no more"— have talked of the time when the earth would be filled with righteousness and peace. Some men think they can bring about such a desirable age through education, United Nations, social betterment, scientific achievements, reformation, preaching, missionary work and other human agencies.

It will take more than all the things all men can do to straighten this old world out. Human plans and human hands and human powers cannot do it. There is only one—Jesus Christ, to whom God hath given all power in Heaven and in earth.

There shall be perfect safety:

"And I will make with them a covenant of peace, and will cause the evil beasts to cease out of the land: and they shall dwell safely in the wilderness, and sleep in the woods."—Ezek. 34:25.

"But they shall sit every man under his vine and under his fig tree; and none shall make them afraid: for the mouth of the LORD of hosts hath spoken it."—Micah 4:4.

There shall be long life:

"There shall be no more thence an infant of days, nor an old man that hath not filled his days: for the child shall die an hundred years old; but the sinner being an hundred years old shall be accursed."—Isa. 65:20.

Every one in the world will know Christ to begin with.

"And they shall not teach every man his neighbor, and every man his brother, saying, Know the Lord: for all shall know me, from the least to the greatest."—Heb. 8:11.

"For the earth shall be filled with the knowledge of the glory of the LORD, as the waters cover the sea."—Hab. 2:14.

The saints, even we, shall reign:

"Do ye not know that the saints shall judge the world? and if the world shall be judged by you, are ye unworthy to judge the smallest matters?"—I Cor. 6:2.

"And the things that thou hast heard of me among many witnesses, the same commit thou to faithful men, who shall be able to teach others also."—II Tim. 2:2.

"And I saw thrones, and they sat upon them, and judgment was given unto them: and I saw the souls of them that were beheaded for the witness of Jesus, and for the word of God, and which had not worshipped the beast, neither his image, neither had received his mark upon their foreheads, or in their hands; and they lived and reigned with Christ a thousand years."—Rev. 20:4.

Jerusalem shall be the center of worship:

"Thus saith the LORD of hosts; It shall yet come to pass, that there shall come people, and the inhabitants of many cities: and the inhabitants of one city shall go to another, saying, Let us go speedily to pray before the LORD, and to seek the LORD of hosts: I will go also. Yea, many people and strong nations shall come to seek the LORD of hosts in Jerusalem, and to pray before the LORD. Thus saith the LORD of hosts; In those days it shall come to pass, that ten men shall take hold out of all languages of the nations, even shall take hold of the skirt of him that is a Jew, saying, We will go with you: for we have heard that God is with you."—Zech. 8:20-23.

"But in the last days it shall come to pass, that the mountain of the house of the LORD shall be established in the top of the mountains, and it shall be exalted above the hills; and people shall flow unto it. And many nations shall come, and say, Come, and let us go up. . .to the house of the God of Jacob; and he will teach us of his ways, and

*we will walk in his paths: for the law shall go forth of Zion, and the
word of the LORD from Jerusalem."*—Micah 4:1, 2.

For one thousand years, Jesus will place everything good in the world
and keep everything bad out of it. Christ will "appear the second time
without sin, unto salvation"—not tinting the earth and seas and skies
with the transient beauty of the sunrise, but raising the dead, changing
the living, judging the world, glorifying His people, and establishing
His everlasting kingdom of "righteousness, peace, and joy, in the
Holy Ghost."

What our science could not do, He will do. What our theology and
preaching could not do, He will do. What our parliaments and senates
could not do, He will do. What our educational systems could not do,
He will do. What our armies and navies could not do, He will do.

And that day will be the watcher's looked-for day, the purchaser's
redemption day, the builder's completion day, the husbandman's harvest
day, the servant's reckoning day, the master's payday, the Son's
manifestation day, the bride's wedding day, the King's coronation day.

I heard Dr. John Roach Straton in New York once, quoting in part
another, set forth some of the glories of the millennial reign of Christ
in these words:

> Think of the sudden collapse of all the haunts of sin, the rooting
> out of the nests and nurseries of iniquity, the clearing away of the
> marshes and bogs of crime, where every type of damning pestilence
> is bred, and the changes that must hence come; think of the sum-
> mary abolition of all infamous cliques, combinations and rings—
> political rings, whiskey rings, municipal rings, state rings, railroad
> rings, mercantile rings, communistic rings, oath-bound rings and
> a thousand kinds of other rings—all the children of wickedness,
> hindering just law, suppressing moral right, crippling honest in-
> dustry, subsidizing legislation, corrupting the press, robbing the
> public treasuries, eating up the gains of honorable occupation,
> perverting public sentiment, spotting and exorcising men who can-
> not be made the tools of party, transmuting selfish greed and ex-
> pediency into principle, razing the dominion of virtue and in-
> telligence, subordinating the common weal to individual aggran-
> dizement, and setting all righteous administration at defiance.
> Think of the universal and invincible dragging forth to divine
> justice of every blatant infidel, perjurer, liar, profane swearer,
> drunkard, drunkard-maker, whoremonger, hypocrite, slanderer,
> trickster, cheat, thief, murderer, trader in uncleanness, truce-
> breaker, traitor, miser, oppressor of the poor, bribe-taking legislator,

time-serving preacher, mal-practitioner, babe-destroyer, friend-robber, office-usurper, peace-disturber, life-embitterer.

Think of the instantaneous going forth into all the world of a divine and unerring force, which cannot be turned or avoided, but which hews down every fruitless tree, purges away all chaff from every floor, negatives all unrighteous laws, overwhelms all unrighteous traffic, destroys all unrighteous coalitions, burns up every nest of infamy and sin, ferrets out all concealed wickedness, exposes and punishes all empty pretense, makes an end of all unholy business, and puts an effectual stop to all base fashions, all silly conceits, all questionable customs, and all the hollow shams and corrupt show and fastidiousness of what calls itself society, transferring the dominion of the almighty dollars to Almighty Right and reducing everything in human life, pursuits, manners and professions to the standard of rigid truth and justice.

Let us consider *seriously:*

IX. THE READINESS

"Then shall two be in the field; the one shall be taken, the other left. Two women shall be grinding at the mill; the one shall be taken, and the other left. Watch therefore: for ye know not what hour your Lord doth come. But know this, that if the goodman of the house had known in what watch the thief would come, he would have watched, and would not have suffered his house to be broken up. Therefore be ye also ready: for in such an hour as ye think not the Son of man cometh."—Matt. 24:40-44.

"Be ye also ready, for in such an hour as ye think not the Son of man cometh."

"Then shall the kingdom of heaven be likened unto ten virgins, which took their lamps, and went forth to meet the bridegroom. And five of them were wise, and five were foolish. They that were foolish took their lamps, and took no oil with them: but the wise took oil in their vessels with their lamps. While the bridegroom tarried, they all slumbered and slept. And at midnight there was a cry made, Behold, the bridegroom cometh; go ye out to meet him. Then all those virgins arose, and trimmed their lamps. And the foolish said unto the wise, Give us of your oil; for our lamps are gone out. But the wise answered, saying, Not so; lest there be not enough for us and you: but go ye rather to them that sell, and buy for yourselves. And while they went to buy,

the bridegroom came; and they that were ready went in with him to the marriage: and the door was shut. Afterward came also the other virgins, saying, Lord, Lord, open to us. But he answered and said, Verily I say unto you, I know you not. Watch therefore, for ye know neither the day nor the hour wherein the Son of man cometh."—Matt. 25:1-13.

The emphasis is on *". . . they that were ready went in."*

Some are not ready for love. Some are not ready for opportunity. Some are not ready for life. Some are not ready for death. Some are not ready for eternity.

Readiness—and "not be ashamed before him at his coming." That is our need. But to have joy when He comes! When He comes, we will be gladly waiting or sadly fearing.

How great was the joy in the Bethany home when they knew the Lord Jesus was coming! Did Martha hope He would not come because she had spring cleaning to do? Did Mary hope He would not come— because she had so many letters to write? Did Lazarus hope He would not come—because he was so engrossed with business? No! It was their joy to know the Lord was coming, for Christ put everything right.

By your desire for the appearing of your Lord, you can judge the state of your spiritual life.

The immigrant comes to these shores. He works to earn money to pay the passage of his beloved. When that ship comes in, he is on the dock. When the gangplank is lowered, he is at the barrier waiting for her to come through the customs. That is the attitude the Christian should have toward the coming of his Lord.

Do you want the Lord to come back? If you are an unsaved sinner, you do not want Him to come. You will be left when He appears, because He comes to take those who love Him, who have His Spirit in their hearts, who are His by faith. If you are a backslidden Christian, you do not want Him to come, because you will be embarrassed and ashamed. If the love of the world has grown so warm in your heart that the love of your Lord has grown cold, you do not want Him to come because you are tied up with this world and have no desire to see Him.

Do you want the Lord to come back? John saw all the glories of the end time. Then he cried with heartfelt personal longing, "Even so, Lord Jesus, come quickly."

I want Him to come for a good many reasons. I do not have much hope, so far as this world is concerned, that everything is ever going to be at peace again. I want the Lord to come back because I would like to know my children are safe with Him.

I want Him to come because I am tired of all the chaos, unrest and uncertainty, all the fumblings of government and the greed and envy of men. I am sickened of pictures of naked babies with swollen stomachs, stretching out thin, emaciated arms for a crust of bread in the streets of the cities of Asia. I am tired of pictures of blasted homes and falling bombs and boys with arms and legs lost on the field of battle. I want the Lord to come because He will set up a reign of righteousness on the earth.

But most of all I want Him to come because I want to see Him. I have never seen Him with these eyes, but with the eyes of faith I saw Him once when I knelt at the old fence corner and trusted Him. Perhaps I haven't always been faithful, but He has been, and I want Him to come because I want to tell Him I love Him. I want Him to come; do you? Then why stand ye gazing up? Witness and watch and work, and someday—pray God someday *soon*—we'll see Him in whom our souls delight, and be like Him forevermore.

"Behold, what manner of love the Father hath bestowed upon us, that we should be called the sons of God: therefore the world knoweth us not, because it knew him not. Beloved, now are we the sons of God, and it doth not yet appear what we shall be: but we know that, when he shall appear, we shall be like him; for we shall see him as he is. And every man that hath this hope in him purifieth himself, even as he is pure."—I John 3:1-3.

CURTIS HUTSON
1934-

ABOUT THE MAN:

In 1961 a mail carrier and pastor of a very small church attended a Sword of the Lord conference, got on fire, gave up his route and set out to build a great soul-winning work for God. Forrest Hills Baptist Church of Decatur, Georgia, grew from 40 people into a membership of 7,900. The last four years of his pastorate there, the Sunday school was recognized as the largest one in Georgia.

After pastoring for 21 years, Dr. Hutson—the great soul winner that he is—became so burdened for the whole nation that he entered full-time evangelism, holding great citywide-areawide-cooperative revivals in some of America's greatest churches. As many as 625 precious souls have trusted Christ in a single service. In one eight-day meeting, 1,502 salvation decisions were recorded.

As an evangelist, he is in great demand.

At the request of Dr. John R. Rice, Dr. Hutson became Associate Editor of THE SWORD OF THE LORD in 1978, serving in that capacity until the death of Dr. Rice before becoming Editor, President of Sword of the Lord Foundation, and Director of Sword of the Lord conferences.

All these ministries are literally changing the lives of thousands of preachers and laymen alike, as well as winning many more thousands to Christ.

Dr. Hutson is the author of many fine books and booklets.

XII.

The Second Coming of Christ

CURTIS HUTSON

The Promise, the Person, the Program, the Preparation

"But I would not have you to be ignorant, brethren, concerning them which are asleep, that ye sorrow not, even as others which have no hope. For if we believe that Jesus died and rose again, even so them also which sleep in Jesus will God bring with him. For this we say unto you by the word of the Lord, that we which are alive and remain unto the coming of the Lord shall not prevent them which are asleep. For the Lord himself shall descend from heaven with a shout, with the voice of the archangel, and with the trump of God: and the dead in Christ shall rise first: Then we which are alive and remain shall be caught up together with them in the clouds, to meet the Lord in the air: and so shall we ever be with the Lord. Wherefore comfort one another with these words."—I Thess. 4:13-18.

Several years ago a preacher preaching on the radio brought a series of prophetic messages. During that series he kept referring to his prophetic messages.

One day a lady, recognizing him on the street, ran to him and said, "O Brother _____ , I really do enjoy those *'pathetic'* messages you have been bringing."

Some *prophetic* messages may indeed be *pathetic*, especially when we make the mistake of date-setting and trying to pinpoint the very hour of Christ's return.

It is difficult, if not impossible, to get correct every detail of Bible prophecy. At best, we only get a general view of the landscape.

For instance, when I return from a revival meeting my wife asks me about that church. I tell her it was a brick church.

"What kind of brick?"

"I don't know. All I remember is red brick. I don't recall whether they were common brick or scratched surface."

"Were there any trees in the yard?"

"Yes, a number of trees."

"How many?"

"I don't remember."

"What kind of trees?"

"I don't remember that. I know there were several large ones."

You see, I got a general view of the landscape but not all the details. I had a good idea what the church looked like, but I could not be exact about all the details.

So it is with Bible prophecy. And one makes a mistake when he tries to pinpoint **everything.**

It is a mistake to try to set an exact date when the Lord will return.

Several years ago I heard a preacher say the Lord would return before 1980, and if He didn't he would quit the ministry. I do not know if he did, but I know he was wrong to set a date.

I have heard others name the Antichrist, and so far no one has been correct. If I understand the Bible, the Antichrist will not be revealed until after the rapture of the church; therefore, his identity will not be known until after the first phase of the second coming of Christ (II Thess. 2:3-8).

While we may not know every detail, we do know the Lord is coming, and we have a general view of the landscape. I will say more about that in "The Program of His Coming."

In this message I will cover four thoughts: "The Promise of His Coming," "The Person of His Coming," "The Program of His Coming" and "The Preparations for His Coming."

I. THE PROMISE OF HIS COMING

There are twenty times as many references in the Old Testament to the second coming of Christ as there are to His first coming. In all of Paul's epistles he refers to baptism only thirteen times, while he speaks of the second coming more than fifty times. Among the last words Jesus uttered before He left this world were:

"Let not your heart be troubled; ye believe in God, believe also in me. In my Father's house are many mansions: if it were not so, I would have told you. I go to prepare a place for you. And if I go and prepare

a place for you, **I will come again,** *and receive you unto myself; that where I am there ye may be also."*—John 14:1-3.

At His ascension, in Acts 1:10 the Bible states, "...two men stood by them in white apparel." And verse 11 records their statement: "Ye men of Galilee, why stand ye gazing up into heaven? this same Jesus, which is taken up from you into heaven, shall so come in like manner as ye have seen him go into heaven."

It is believed that these men in white apparel were angels and that they said, "This same Jesus...shall so come in like manner as ye have seen him go into heaven." How did He leave? Visibly. He will return visibly. He left in a body; He will return in a body. He left from the Mount of Olives; He will return to the Mount of Olives (Acts 1:12; Zech. 14:4).

Philippians 3:20 says, "Our conversation is in heaven; from whence also we look for the Saviour, the Lord Jesus Christ." Hebrews 9:28 states, "...and unto them that look for him shall he appear the second time without sin unto salvation."

The Bible is filled with promises of Jesus' coming. In Revelation 22—once in verse 7, once in verse 12 and again in verse 20—Jesus says, "Behold, I come quickly," "Behold, I come quickly," "Surely I come quickly...." And the Bible closes with the Apostle John saying, "Even so, come, Lord Jesus. The grace of our Lord Jesus Christ be with you all. Amen" (Rev. 22:21).

Friends, one verse in every thirty in the New Testament refers to the second coming.

A Bible-believing preacher brought a tremendous sermon on the second coming. When he had finished one of these modernistic, potato-string-backbone, rosewater-squirting preachers who start nowhere and end up in the same place, said to him, "I want you to know that I can't get that out of the New Testament."

The wise old preacher replied, "You sure can't, buddy. It's in there to stay!"

Yes, the promise of the second coming of Christ is in the Bible to stay. There are 259 chapters in the New Testament and over 300 references to the second coming of Christ.

Now let me say a word about the Person of His coming.

II. THE PERSON OF HIS COMING

I mention this because there are different ideas concerning the second coming. Some say it is death. And at some funerals preachers imply that Jesus came for the individual. But when one dies, the opposite is true. The deceased goes to be with Christ. Second Corinthians 5:8 states, ". . .to be absent from the body, and to be present with the Lord." Paul said in Philippians 1:23, "I am in a strait betwixt two, having a desire to depart, and to be with Christ; which is far better." So the second coming is not the death of the believer.

When the Christian dies, his soul and spirit leave his body and go immediately to be with Christ: absent from the body, present with the Lord (II Cor. 5:8).

Others spiritualize the second coming and say it is when Jesus comes into your heart—that is, when you are saved. I knew a dear preacher who believed and taught that. He told me when I got saved Jesus came into my heart and that was the second coming. This teaching is not consistent with the Scripture. In I Thessalonians 4:16 the Bible describes the coming of Christ for His own: "For the Lord himself shall descend from heaven with a shout, with the voice of the archangel, and with the trump of God: and the dead in Christ shall rise first."

When Jesus Christ came into my heart, there was no shout, no voice of the archangel, no trump of God; and there was certainly no resurrection of the Christian dead. The second coming is different from Jesus' coming into one's heart. When a man accepts Jesus Christ as Saviour, Jesus does not literally, physically return to the earth. When one is saved, the Holy Spirit comes into that person to take up His permanent residence. Jesus dwells in us in the Person of the Holy Spirit, but He Himself is in Heaven seated on the right hand of the Father. "To him that overcometh will I grant to sit with me in my throne, even as I also overcame, and am set down with my Father in his throne" (Rev. 3:21).

Friends, Jesus is now in Heaven, seated at the right hand of the Father. He is in our heart in the Person of the Holy Spirit. Romans 8:9 says, "Now if any man have not the Spirit of Christ, he is none of his." First Corinthians 6:19 says, "What? know ye not that your body is the temple of the Holy Ghost which is in you, which ye have of God, and ye are not your own?" The Holy Spirit indwells the Christian. So the second coming of Christ is not death; it is not the new birth.

The second coming of Christ means the literal, physical, bodily return of Jesus Himself. Notice what He said in John 14:3: "And if I go and prepare a place for you, I will come again." He says in that same passage, "If it were not so, I would have told you."

When I hear these modernistic preachers deny the second coming, I mumble to myself, "If it were not so, He would have told us." Friend, Jesus Himself is coming!

In Acts 1:11 the angels said, ". . . this same Jesus. . . ." Not a spirit, not an angel, but "this same Jesus, which is taken up from you into heaven, shall so come in like manner as ye have seen him go into heaven."

It will be the same Christ who lived on this earth two thousand years ago. It will be the same Christ who healed the sick, unstopped the deaf ears, raised the dead, was crucified, buried and rose again. That same Jesus is coming again. His coming will be personal, bodily and literal.

The Bible says in I Thessalonians 4:16, "For the Lord *himself* shall descend from heaven."

III. THE PROGRAM OF HIS COMING

Now let me give you a bird's-eye view of the program of His coming.

When I first began to study the second coming, I noticed some verses that seemed contradictory. I say "seemed" because there are no contradictions in the Bible, for it is the inspired, inerrant, infallible Word of God. I give you two such verses. Revelation 1:7 says, "Behold, he cometh with clouds; and *every eye shall see him*." But Revelation 16:15 says, "Behold, I come as a thief. Blessed is he that watcheth, and keepeth his garments. . . ." Is He coming in the clouds and *every eye shall see* Him, as the Bible says in Revelation 1:7? Or will He come as a thief? When a thief comes *every eye* doesn't see him.

Recently several homes have been burglarized in our neighborhood, but no one has seen the burglar. *Every eye* doesn't see a thief. He slips in unexpected, gathers quickly what he came for, then leaves.

Revelation 16:15 states that Jesus is coming as a thief. Then Revelation 1:7 says, "Behold, he cometh with clouds; and *every eye shall see him*."

Another seeming contradiction is I Thessalonians 3:13: "To the end he may stablish your hearts unblamable in holiness before God, even our Father, at the coming of our Lord Jesus Christ *with all his saints.*" In the next chapter He talks about bringing some of the saints with Him and says other saints (resurrected saints) will be caught up together with them, to meet the Lord in the air. How is He coming with all His saints if some saints are going to be caught up to meet Him in the air?

These verses can be understood when you understand the program of His coming. His coming is in two phases. He first comes for His own (I Thess. 4:13-18). He later comes with His own to fulfill His promise to David and to Abraham. He will sit on David's throne in Jerusalem and rule the nations with a rod of iron.

The first phase of His coming is called the rapture of the church. The second phase we call the revelation.

When Jesus Christ comes for the church, He will come as a thief. He will gather His own—the born-again believers from all over the world—and as soon as they are gathered He will be gone.

When He comes with His own, at the revelation, then every eye shall see Him. "Behold, he cometh with clouds and every eye shall see him" (Rev. 1:7).

Now here is the program: He first comes for His own. That is the rapture of the church. Later He comes back with His own to fulfill His promise to Abraham and to David. He will sit down on David's throne and rule the nations with a rod of iron. That is the revelation. He first comes for us (the rapture of the church); He later comes with us (the revelation).

1. The Rapture of the Church

The word *rapture* is not in the Bible. However, it does describe a Bible experience. First Thessalonians 4:13-18 gives us a description of the rapture:

"But I would not have you to be ignorant, brethren, concerning them which are asleep, that ye sorrow not, even as others which have no hope. For if we believe that Jesus died and rose again, even so them also which sleep in Jesus will God bring with him. For this we say unto you by the word of the Lord, that we which are alive and remain unto the coming of the Lord shall not prevent [precede] them which are asleep."

The living Christians will not go ahead of those who are asleep—that is, those who are dead. Verse 16 gives the order.

"For the Lord himself shall descend from heaven with a shout, with the voice of the archangel, and with the trump of God: and the dead in Christ shall rise first. . . ."

When Jesus comes for His own at the rapture of the church, there will be a shout, the voice of the archangel; then there will be the sounding of the trumpet, and the dead in Christ shall rise first.

"Then we which are alive and remain shall be caught up together with them [those who have been resurrected] *in the clouds, to meet the Lord in the air: and so shall we ever be with the Lord. Wherefore comfort one another with these words."*

Jesus Christ could come for His own at any moment. There are no signs that precede His coming. The Bible does not say to watch for signs, but we are to watch for the Saviour, the Son.

For instance, Philippians 3:20 states, "Our conversation [citizenship] is in heaven; from whence also we look for the Saviour"—not looking for signs but for the Saviour.

Titus 2:13: "Looking for that blessed hope, and the glorious appearing of the great God and our Saviour Jesus Christ." Not looking for signs; looking for the Saviour.

Hebrews 9:28, ". . . and unto them that look for him shall he appear the second time without sin unto salvation." We are not told to look for signs but for the Son, the Saviour.

There are no signs that precede Christ's coming for His own. His coming is imminent and has been since New Testament times. The Apostle Paul thought Jesus Christ would come in his lifetime and said in I Thessalonians 4:17, "Then WE which are alive and remain . . . ." Paul thought he would be living when Jesus came.

Every Bible-believing Christian expects to be alive when Jesus comes.

This week in my office sat an 84-year-old man who had driven over 300 miles to visit with me. As he sat there suddenly his eyes closed and opened. The color left his cheeks. I thought he had a heart attack and was probably going to die in my office. In a moment he revived, smiled and said, "I thought I would be alive at the rapture, but I believe the Lord is calling me Home."

He wouldn't let me call a doctor. His daughter-in-law drove him home that afternoon; and early the next morning his son called to say, "I am glad you visited with Father yesterday. He went to be with the Lord last night."

Here was an 84-year-old man who thought he would be alive when Jesus came.

Since Dr. Rice has gone on to be with Christ, I have had a hundred letters or more stating, "I never thought Dr. Rice would die. I thought he would be living when Jesus came." Well, to be honest, I thought so too.

Paul thought Jesus would come in his lifetime. Said he: "WE which are alive and remain."

The coming of Christ for His own is imminent. It could happen any second. No signs have to be fulfilled. He could have come day before yesterday. He could have come last year. He could have come in Paul's time. **He may come today!** We are to live in constant expectancy of His coming.

While talking to five preachers, Robert Murray McCheyne, a great preacher of yesteryear, looked at one and asked, "Do you think Jesus will come today?"

His friend answered, "I think not."

To another he said, "Do you think Jesus will come today?"

He too replied, "I think not."

To the third he asked, "Do you think Jesus will come today?"

Again he heard, "I think not."

To the fourth he continued: "Do you think Christ will come today?"

This friend replied, "I think not."

Finally he asked the last one, "What about you? Do you think Christ will come today?"

His reply was the same, "I think not."

Then McCheyne turned to Matthew 24:44 and read without comment, "Therefore be ye also ready: for in such an hour as ye think not the Son of man cometh."

Jesus Christ could come today; and when He comes for His own, the trumpet will sound, there will be the shout of the voice of the archangel, the dead in Christ will be raised first, then we which are alive and remain shall be caught up together with them in clouds to meet the Lord in the air!

This does not mean that every believer will be given a cloud on which to ride. The expression "caught up in clouds" means clouds of people. Revelation 1:7 says, "Behold, he cometh with clouds." And Hebrews 12:1 states, "Wherefore seeing we also are compassed about with so great a cloud of witnesses . . . ."

Did you ever notice birds migrating south? As they pass over, there seemingly are thousands of them. They are often referred to as a great cloud of birds!

Friends, when Jesus comes and the dead are raised and believers are changed in a moment, in the twinkling of an eye, a great cloud of believers will be leaving Murfreesboro, Tennessee; a great cloud of believers will leave Chicago, Illinois; a great cloud of believers will be leaving New York City, Atlanta, Georgia, and on and on and on.

From all over the world **great clouds** of believers will be caught up. The trumpet will sound, the Christian dead will be raised, and we which are alive and remain will be caught up together with them in clouds to meet the Lord in the air.

When Jesus comes, the Christian dead will be raised and the living saints will be changed. Paul said in I Corinthians 15:51,52, "Behold, I shew you a mystery; We shall not all sleep [we won't all be dead], but we shall all be changed, In a moment, in the twinkling of an eye . . . ." Those who are asleep will be resurrected, and the living saints will be changed, "In a moment, in the twinkling of an eye."

I am told that the word *moment* comes from the same word from which we get our word *atom,* and means a space of time so small that it cannot be divided again. Say, friends, that is quick!

I have been told that the twinkle of an eye is much faster than the blinking or closing of the eye. We shall all be changed "In a moment, in the twinkling of an eye."

Continuing in I Corinthians 15, the Bible says, ". . . then shall be brought to pass the saying that is written, Death is swallowed up in victory. O death, where is thy sting? O grave, where is thy victory?" (vss. 54,55).

The saints who are changed in a moment, in the twinkling of an eye, will shout as they are caught away, "O death, where is thy sting?" They never feel the sting of death. They are alive when Jesus comes. The dead in Christ who are resurrected will shout, "O grave, where is thy victory?" Some will have been in the grave for thousands of years, but the grave will lose its hold. It will not be victorious over the child of God.

Jesus said in John 11:25,26, "I am the resurrection, and the life: he that believeth in me, though he were dead, yet shall he live: And whosoever liveth and believeth in me shall never die." Two groups: "He that believeth in me, though he were dead, yet shall he live"—the resurrection of the saints who die and go on to be with Christ before the second coming. And "he that liveth and believeth in me shall never die"—the person who is alive at Jesus' coming and has trusted Him as Saviour.

Here are the events on God's prophetic calendar: He comes for His own—the rapture of the church. The Antichrist is revealed on earth and has a successful reign for seven years, called "the seventieth week" of Daniel, "the day of Jacob's trouble" or "the Tribulation period." While the Tribulation period is taking place on earth, the saints will be judged at the judgment seat of Christ. They will later be married to the Lamb, described in the Bible as "the marriage of the Lamb" (Rev. 19:7-9). At the close of the Tribulation period, the saints, along with Christ, will come back to this earth and Jesus will sit down on David's throne and rule the nations with a rod of iron.

2. The Revelation

Now I share with you the covenant God made with Abraham, which has to do with land and people. The covenant He made with David has to do with the throne. "The Lord hath sworn in truth unto David; he will not turn from it; Of the fruit of thy body will I set upon thy throne" (Ps. 132:11).

Some say that is a spiritual throne, but David never had a spiritual throne. This king in Israel had an actual, literal, physical throne. And when Jesus Christ comes again with His saints, at the close of the Tribulation period, He will sit down on a literal, physical throne in Jerusalem. He will sit upon David's throne.

Notice the language of the promise: "The Lord hath sworn in truth unto David . . . ." Now, that is strong. But catch the rest of it, ". . . he will not turn from it." It makes no difference what anyone says or thinks, God has made the promise that "he will not turn from it; Of the fruit of thy body will I set upon thy throne."

He also made a promise to Abraham:

"Now the Lord had said unto Abram, Get thee out of thy country, and from thy kindred, and from thy father's house, unto a land that I will shew thee: And I will make of thee a great nation, and I will bless thee, and make thy name great; and thou shalt be a blessing: And I will bless them that bless thee, and curse him that curseth thee: and in thee shall all families of the earth be blessed."—Gen. 12:1-3.

Here God called Abram and his descendants to form a great nation through which He would bless the land. Later He confirmed this covenant in Genesis 13:14,15,

"And the Lord said unto Abram, after that Lot was separated from him, Lift up now thine eyes, and look from the place where thou art northward, and southward, and eastward, and westward: For all the land which thou seest, to thee will I give it, and to thy seed for ever."

Notice several things in this covenant. First, He said, "I will make of thee a great nation"—the nation Israel. Second, "I will bless thee." He spoke of temporal and spiritual blessing. Third, "I will. . .make thy name great." Abraham's name is one of the universal names. Fourth, He said, "And thou shalt be a blessing."

In Galatians 3:13,14 the Bible says,

"Christ hath redeemed us from the curse of the law, being made a curse for us: for it is written, Cursed is every one that hangeth on a tree: That the blessing of Abraham might come on the Gentiles through Jesus Christ; that we might receive the promise of the Spirit through faith."

God goes on to say, "I will bless them that bless thee." Then He promises, "I will. . .curse him that curseth thee." And adds, "In thee shall all families of the earth be blessed" (Gen. 12:3).

God has not yet completely fulfilled His promise to Abraham.

After the Six-Day War, many Bible students thought Jesus would come in the next few days or weeks. I heard preachers talk about how near the coming of Christ was. One went so far as to set a specific date.

Now, wait a minute. I think His coming is imminent. It could happen today. But people did not understand the covenant God made with Abraham.

Notice several things regarding this covenant.

Abraham and his descendants were to have all the land of Canaan. To Abraham He promised: "For ALL THE LAND which thou seest, to thee will I give it, and to thy seed for ever." After the Six-Day War the Jews did not have all the land. The boundaries of the land are given in Genesis 15:18, Ezekiel 47:19; 48:1. On the west side, the river of Egypt; to the east, the River Euphrates; north to Hamath; and to Kadesh on the south. The Jews never occupied all that land, and they do not have it today. And that promise to Abraham will not be fulfilled until they have all this land. And all Jews will be back in the land when the promise is fulfilled to Abraham. All Jews are not back today.

So they did not have all the land that was promised; and they were not all back. And when the Bible speaks of the regathering of Israel, it talks about giving them a new heart. So they were not all converted. The Bible talks about a nation being born in a day. All the nation of Israel will be saved. That has not yet come to pass.

Now, wait! They will not be saved as a nation. But each individual who makes up the nation will trust Christ as Saviour. They will look upon Him whom they have pierced. They will recognize that they have rejected the true Messiah. Then they will trust Him as Saviour, and a whole nation will be born in a day.

After the Six-Day War they did not have all the land.

They were not all back.

And they were not all converted as the Bible promises.

God also promised to give the land to Abraham himself. " . . . *to thee* will I give it, and to thy seed for ever" (Gen. 13:15). Abraham was not back in the land after the Six-Day War. When that promise is fulfilled, Abraham himself will be back in the land.

Christ was to be in the land with Abraham. Again, notice the expression in Genesis 13:15, " . . . to thee will I give it, and to *thy seed.*" Galatians 3:16 states, "Now to Abraham and his seed were the promises made. He saith not, And to seeds, as of many; but as of one, And to thy seed, which is Christ."

There is no question about to whom the seed refers. An interpretation is given here in Galatians 3:16: "He saith not, And to seeds, as of many; but as of one, And to thy seed, *which is Christ.*"

So there are five things that will be true when God fulfills His promise to Abraham.

1. The Jews will have all the land—every inch of it—that God promised.

2. All the Jews will be back in the land.

3. They will all be converted.

4. Abraham himself will be in the land.

5. Christ will be in the land with Abraham.

The covenant God made to Abraham is not yet fulfilled and will not be until Jesus Christ comes again at the close of the Tribulation. Then He will gather the nation of Israel and fulfill His promise to Abraham and His covenant to David.

The regathering of the nation Israel is repeatedly connected with the conversion of the entire remnant of the nation and the beginning of the reign of Christ (Isa. 11:1-12; Ezek. 34:12-14; Jer. 23:3-6; 33:14-17; Matt. 24:29-31).

Notice the order in Matthew 24:29-31:

"Immediately after the tribulation of those days shall the sun be darkened, and the moon shall not give her light, and the stars shall fall from heaven, and the powers of the heavens shall be shaken: And then shall appear the sign of the Son of man in heaven: and then shall all the tribes of the earth mourn, and they shall see the Son of man coming in the clouds of heaven with power and great glory."

Revelation 1:7 says, "Behold, he cometh with clouds; and every eye shall see him." We are talking now about the revelation, not about the time when He comes as a thief in the night for His own, but when He comes with clouds and every eye shall see Him.

"And he shall send his angels with a great sound of a trumpet, and they shall gather together his elect from the four winds, from one end of heaven to the other."

First, we have the Tribulation: "Immediately after the tribulation of those days" (vs. 29).

Second, we have the second coming of Christ, the revelation. "Then . . . they shall see the Son of man coming in the clouds of heaven with power and great glory" (vs. 30).

Third, we have the regathering of the Jews: "And he shall send his angels with a great sound of a trumpet, and they shall gather together his elect from the four winds, from one end of heaven to the other" (vs. 31).

Now, the promise God made to Abraham will be fulfilled after the Tribulation period, when Jesus comes to reign. The Jews will be regathered to the land. They will all be saved—a nation will be born in a day. They will have all the land. Abraham himself will be there. And Christ will be there with Abraham.

Jesus Christ is coming back to the earth literally and visibly, to fulfill not only His promise to Abraham but also His promise to David. "The Lord hath sworn in truth unto David; he will not turn from it; Of the fruit of thy body will I set upon thy throne" (Ps. 132:11).

This reign of Christ is described as the millennial reign, because it is a thousand years.

"And I saw thrones, and they sat upon them, and judgment was given

unto them: and I saw the souls of them that were beheaded for the witness of Jesus, and for the word of God, and which had not worshipped the beast, neither his image, neither had received his mark upon their foreheads, or in their hands; and they lived [they had been martyred; now they live; they were resurrected] *and reigned with Christ a thousand years. But the rest of the dead lived not again* [the unsaved dead were not resurrected] *until the thousand years were finished.* [A thousand years between the resurrection of the saved and the unsaved.] *This is the first resurrection* [of the saved]. *Blessed and holy is he that hath part in the first resurrection: on such the second death hath no power, but they shall be priests of God and of Christ, and shall reign with him a thousand years. And when the thousand years are expired, Satan shall be loosed out of his prison, And shall go out to deceive the nations which are in the four quarters of the earth."*—Rev. 20:4-8.

We call this thousand-year reign of Christ the millennial reign. We say we believe in the premillennial return of Christ—that is, we believe Christ is coming for His own before He comes back with His own to reign for a thousand years. That is premillennial.

I believe unfulfilled prophecy should be taken literally because prophecy that has been fulfilled thus far was literally fulfilled.

For instance, in Isaiah 9:6,7, the Bible says, "For unto us a child is born." That was literally fulfilled. "Unto us a son is given." That was literally fulfilled. The Bible goes on to say, "And his name shall be called Wonderful, Counsellor, The mighty God, The everlasting Father, The Prince of Peace. Of the increase of his government and peace there shall be no end, upon the throne of David, and upon his kingdom, to order it, and to establish it with judgment and with justice from henceforth even for ever. The zeal of the Lord of hosts will perform this."

Why should we take the first few expressions in this passage literally and not take literally the latter few expressions? If the Child was born and prophecy was literally fulfilled, then why are we not to believe that the remaining part of the prophecy will be literally fulfilled?

Yes, Jesus is actually, literally, physically going to return to the earth. He will sit down on David's throne. The great society which has been dreamed about for years will then be a realization rather than a dream. The curse brought on nature because of sin will then be removed. Wars will be no more. Righteousness will prevail on the entire planet. And happiness will be universal.

Several things that will happen when Christ comes to reign:

1. The curse that has been on the earth because of sin, will be removed.

"For we know that the whole creation groaneth and travaileth in pain together until now. And not only they, but ourselves also, which have the firstfruits of the Spirit, even we ourselves groan within ourselves, waiting for the adoption, to wit, the redemption of our body."—Rom. 8:22,23.

When Adam sinned, the land was cursed, man was cursed, and the animal kingdom was cursed. When Jesus comes to reign, the curse on the land will be lifted.

"The wilderness and the solitary place shall be glad for them; and the desert shall rejoice, and blossom as the rose. It shall blossom abundantly, and rejoice even with joy and singing: the glory of Lebanon shall be given unto it, the excellency of Carmel and Sharon, they shall see the glory of the Lord, and the excellency of our God."—Isa. 35:1,2.

Here the Bible teaches that the curse will be lifted from the land.

2. The curse will also be lifted from animal nature.

"The wolf also shall dwell with the lamb, and the leopard shall lie down with the kid; and the calf and the young lion and the fatling together; and a little child shall lead them. And the cow and the bear shall feed; their young ones shall lie down together: and the lion shall eat straw like the ox. And the sucking child shall play on the hole of the asp [a very poisonous snake], and the weaned child shall put his hand on the cockatrice' den. They shall not hurt nor destroy in all my holy mountain: for the earth shall be full of the knowledge of the Lord, as the waters cover the sea."—Isa. 11:6-9.

Try putting a leopard and a kid together today and see what happens! But during the reign of Christ, the leopard and kid shall lie down together. The wolf and the lamb shall dwell together. And "the calf and the young lion and the fatling together." Notice this: "and a little child shall lead them"—the wolf, the lamb, the leopard, the kid, the bear, the young lion and the fatling. Wild animals, such as lions and tigers, will be like house cats during the millennial reign of Christ.

3. During Christ's reign "the earth shall be full of the knowledge of the Lord, as the waters cover the sea."

When I was a little boy in a country church, I recall singing:

> **The kingdom is coming, O tell me the story,**
> **God's banner exalted shall be!**
> **The earth shall be full of His knowledge and glory,**
> **As waters that cover the sea.**

But I had no idea what it meant. When Jesus Christ comes to reign, the earth will be filled with the knowledge of the Lord.

4. The curse will be lifted from human bodies. Isaiah 35:5,6:

"Then the eyes of the blind shall be opened, and the ears of the deaf shall be unstopped. Then shall the lame man leap as an hart, and the tongue of the dumb sing: for in the wilderness shall waters break out, and streams in the desert."

According to Isaiah 65:20, men will live to be a thousand years old. "There shall be no more thence an infant of days, nor an old man that hath not filled his days: for **the child shall die a hundred years old.**" If a man dies at a hundred years old, he will be considered still a child! Man's life span will certainly be increased.

5. During the millennial reign of Christ, there will be no more poverty.

"And they shall build houses, and inhabit them; and they shall plant vineyards, and eat the fruit of them. They shall not build, and another inhabit; they shall not plant, and another eat: for as the days of a tree are the days of my people, and mine elect [Israel] shall long enjoy the work of their hands."—Isa. 65:21,22.

In Micah 4:4 the Bible says, "But they shall sit every man under his vine and under his fig tree; and none shall make them afraid: for the mouth of the Lord of hosts hath spoken it."

Friends, it will be a blessed time when Jesus returns to this earth, takes His rightful place on David's throne and rules the nations with a rod of iron.

6. Satan will be chained and bound during the reign of Christ.

"I saw an angel come down from heaven, having the key of the bottomless pit and a great chain in his hand. And he laid hold on the dragon, that old serpent, which is the Devil, and Satan, and bound him a thousand years, And cast him into the bottomless pit, and shut him up, and set a seal upon him, that he should deceive the nations no more, till the thousand years should be fulfilled."—Rev. 20:1-3.

Some say Satan is already bound. But a wise friend of mine said, "If he is bound, he is bound to me." When another fellow said, "He is already chained," someone suggested that if he is, he is on an awfully long chain.

No, Satan is not yet bound. He is called "the god of this world" (II Cor. 4:4). But when Jesus comes to reign, Satan will be chained, cast into the bottomless pit, a seal will be placed upon him, and he will deceive the nations no more, until the thousand years are finished.

A number of other things will happen during the reign of Christ. I can only mention them.

7. Jerusalem will be the center of worship and knowledge for the whole earth (Micah 4:1,2).

8. There will be no more wars. Men shall beat their swords into plowshares, according to Micah 4:3.

9. All Israel will know the Lord (Rom. 11:26).

10. Christ will reign on David's throne, the actual, literal throne from which David reigned. Then, finally:

11. Christians will reign with Him. Revelation 3:21 says, "To him that overcometh will I grant to sit with me in my throne, even as I also overcame, and am set down with my Father in his throne."

IV. THE PREPARATION FOR HIS COMING

In light of the fact that Jesus Christ is coming and could come for His own at any moment, I want to say two things:

First, if you have not accepted Jesus Christ as your personal Saviour, please trust Him today. There are two groups in the world today—the saved and the lost. If Jesus came in the next five minutes, everybody who has trusted Christ as Saviour would leave the earth.

Luke 17:34-36 says:

"I tell you, in that night there shall be two men in one bed; the one shall be taken, and the other shall be left. Two women shall be grinding together; the one shall be taken, and the other left. Two men shall be in the field; the one shall be taken, and the other left."

That is not spiritually speaking; that is actually, literally so. There will be two people at a mill grinding; one will leave, and the other will be left behind. There will be two people in a field working; one will leave, and the other will be left behind.

I have heard preachers spiritualize this passage and say that means that the new man inside will leave and the old body will be left behind. But the Bible does not teach that the bodies of Christians will be left behind. As a matter of fact, it teaches that the body will be changed, not left. Says Philippians 3:20,21:

"For our conversation [citizenship] *is in heaven; from whence also we look for the Saviour, the Lord Jesus Christ: Who shall change our vile body, that it may be fashioned like unto his glorious body."*

It says nothing about getting a new body and leaving the old one; it says *this* vile body will be changed.

I'm afraid some of our doctrine is based on words we have heard in song. I remember singing,

> **"This robe of flesh I'll drop, and rise**
> **To seize the everlasting prize."**

But we will not drop this robe of flesh and rise. This robe of flesh will be changed "In a moment, in the twinkling of an eye," and made exactly like Jesus' body.

First John 3:2, "Beloved, now are we the sons of God, and it doth not yet appear what we shall be: but we know that, when he shall appear, we shall be like him; for we shall see him as he is." So when the Bible says, "two men shall be in the field; the one shall be taken, and the other left," that does not mean the spiritual man inside the body will leave and the body will be left. It means exactly what it says: there will be two in a field; one will be taken and the other left.

When the trumpet sounds, the saved will be caught up to meet the Lord in the air and the unsaved will be left. The unsaved who are left could be divided into two groups: those who have heard the Gospel and had an opportunity to be saved and those who have never heard the Gospel and have not had an opportunity to be saved. Those who have heard the Gospel and could have trusted Christ as Saviour but rejected Him will have their destiny sealed. A person who heard the Gospel and had an opportunity to be saved before the rapture of the church will not have an opportunity to be saved after the rapture. But those who had never heard the Gospel will have such an opportunity.

Notice II Thessalonians 2:7,8:

"For the mystery of iniquity doth already work: only he who now letteth [hindereth] *will let* [hinder], *until he be taken out of the way. And then shall that Wicked be revealed, whom the Lord shall consume*

with the spirit of his mouth, and shall destroy with the brightness of his coming."

Verse 10 continues,

"And with all deceivableness of unrighteousness in them that perish; [notice] BECAUSE they received not the love of the truth, that they might be saved."

Why do they perish? Because they "received not the love of the truth, that they might be saved."

Now, notice verses 11 and 12: "And for this cause God shall send them strong delusion, that they should believe a lie: That they all might be damned who believed not the truth, but had pleasure in unrighteousness."

Here the Bible says those who heard the Gospel but "received not the love of the truth, that they might be saved," would be sent a strong delusion "because they received not the love of the truth, that they might be saved." They are sent a strong delusion "that they should believe a lie: That they all might be damned who believed not the truth, but had pleasure in unrighteousness."

There are two groups in the world at this moment: the saved and the lost. If Jesus comes in the next five minutes, the saved will be caught out; the unsaved will be left behind. The unsaved who have heard the Gospel and had an opportunity to be saved will be given a "strong delusion, that they should believe a lie: That they all might be damned who believed not the truth, but had pleasure in unrighteousness." When they had an opportunity to trust Christ, they rejected Him; therefore the Bible says their destiny is sealed. On the other hand, those who never heard the Gospel and never had an opportunity to be saved would be given such an opportunity during the Tribulation period.

This is not what some call a second chance for salvation because these precious people never had the first chance. During the Tribulation period, the Bible teaches that 144,000 born-again, blood-washed missionaries will preach the Gospel all over the world, and then many will be saved. In Revelation 7:14 the Bible speaks of those who "came out of great tribulation, and have washed their robes, and made them white in the blood of the Lamb." These are Tribulation saints, those who trust Christ during the Tribulation.

Let me remind you again that, if you have heard the Gospel and had an opportunity to trust Christ, you will not have an opportunity to be saved after the rapture of the church. If you have never trusted Christ as your personal Saviour, please trust Him today. In the words of Matthew 24:44, "Therefore be ye also ready: for in such an hour as ye think not the Son of man cometh." It could be today. If you are a Christian, then ". . . abide in him; that, when he shall appear, we may have confidence, and not be ashamed before him at his coming" (I John 2:28). Live for Christ that you may meet Him confidently and unashamed.

XIII.

Answering Those Who Teach Great Tribulation Comes Before Rapture

JOHN MEREDITH

Many devout and capable Bible scholars have come to see that there is a mistranslation of II Thessalonians 2:3, and that Paul was still explaining the rapture as he wrote this second letter to the Thessalonian church. The Greek text shows that the words "a falling away" are translated from *hee apostasia*, and Liddell and Scotts Greek Lexicon gives "department" or departure as one of the definitions of the word *apostasia*.

The Geneva Bible of 1537 gives this as "a departing." William Tyndale, in his 1539 Bible, speaks of it as "a departynge." Cranmer's Bible of 1537 also gives the same meaning of "departure." The first Bible to translate this "a falling away" is the King James Version.

Dr. E. Schuyler English, long editor of *Our Hope* magazine, said that this Scripture so intrigued him that he desired to know what others would say about it. Writing to several men whose standing as believers in the Bible as the Word of God is unquestioned and whose understanding of Greek enables them to speak with assurance, he received replies that helped to throw light on this important portion of Scripture.

There seems to be no doubt that Paul was telling the Thessalonians of the departure of the saints in the rapture and was not at this time making any reference to the apostasy. There are many words in our English language in which the prefix "apo" is used, and all of them utilize the meaning of the Greek *apo* in so doing.

The prefix *apo* means literally "from, away from, off." The word *apostle* means "one sent away." The Greek word *kalyptein* means "to cover or conceal." Using the prefix *apo* we have the word *apokalyptein* from which we get our word *apocalypse*, meaning "to uncover or unveil or disclose to view." This is our word for the writings of the Revelation.

The Greek word *stasia* means "standing or the place where one is standing." Combined with the prefix *apo*, it would be *apostasia* or "departure from where one is standing." If Paul were actually referring to the apostasy here, he would have used the expression *a-pisteuo*. This would be the word *pisteuo*, which means "faith, trust and obedience." By using the first letter of the Greek alphabet as a prefix, he would have given *pisteuo* a negative sense, or "no faith, no trust, no obedience." This is apostasy or a falling away from faith.

Dr. English reports that Dr. Clarence Mason of the Philadelphia School of the Bible replied to his inquiry as follows:

> I am greatly impressed by the evidence in favor of the translation "departure" without reading into it the thought of departure from the faith. It appears to me that it makes better sense to have *apostasia* and the manifestation of the man of sin to be descriptions of historical events, rather than a description of what those events cause. The departure of the saints with the Holy Spirit is a distinct historical event, as is the manifestation of the man of sin.

Dr. Allen A. MacRae of Faith Theological Seminary said in his reply that the noun *apostasia* occurs only twice in the New Testament, but that it is derived from the verb *aphisteemi,* of which various forms are found in the New Testament record. Of the fifteen times this verb occurs, eleven are translated "depart"; and the other four rendered "draw away," "fall away," "refrain from" and "withdraw oneself." "Only three of the occurrences have any reference to a departure from the faith."

Dr. Dwight Pentecost of Philadelphia School of the Bible, Dr. Kenneth Wuest of Moody Bible Institute and others agreed with Dr. English that the Greek text of II Thessalonians 2:3 should be considered as referring to the departure of the saints described in I Thessalonians 4:13-18.

Dr. Wuest said:

> The *hee apostasia* therefore cannot be either a general apostasy in Christendom which does precede the coming of Antichrist, nor can it be the particular apostasy which is the result of his activities in making himself the alone object of worship. . .I am driven to the inescapable conclusion that the *hee apostasia* in II Thessalonians 2:3 refers to the rapture of the church which precedes the Day of the Lord, and holds back the revelation of the Man of Sin who ushers in the world aspect of that period.

Dr. Wuest further said:

Had the translators included the definite article in their translation and used the word *departure,* thus allowing the student of the
English Bible to come to his own conclusion regarding the interpretation of what the departure is, as the context throws light upon
the expression, we would have been saved from the generally
accepted interpretation of this passage.

Paul's use of the definite article means that he was talking to the
Thessalonian Christians about "the Departure" or "The Rapture," of
which there is only the one he has just described in the latter part of
his first letter to them. So far as is known, the Thessalonian church knew
nothing of any coming apostasy, nor were they concerned with that
sort of trouble in their own church at that time.

The Thessalonian Christians were well informed as to the translation
of the saints in the rapture and were looking with expectation for the
coming of the Lord as a definite reality. When Paul, their teacher and
spiritual leader, spoke to them about *hee apostasia,* it would have meant
to them just what he was already talking to them about. From this they
understood that Antichrist, the "Man of Sin," could not be revealed
until the rapture or departure had removed the true believers from the
earth.

JOHN R. RICE
1895-1980

ABOUT THE MAN:

Preacher...evangelist...revivalist...editor...counselor to thousands...friend to millions—that was Dr. John R. Rice, whose accomplishments were nothing short of miraculous. Known as "America's Dean of Evangelists," Dr. Rice made a mighty impact upon the nation's religious life for some sixty years, in great citywide campaigns and in Sword of the Lord Conferences.

At age nine, after hearing a sermon on "The Prodigal Son," John went forward to claim Christ as Saviour. In 1916, with only $9.35 in his pocket, he rode off on his cowpony toward Decatur Baptist College. He was now on the road to becoming a world-renowned evangelist, although he was then totally unaware of God's will for his life.

There was many a twist and turn before Rice rode through the open door into full-time preaching—the army, marriage, graduate work, more seminary, assistant pastor, pastor—then FINALLY, where God planned to use him most—in full-time evangelism.

Dr. Rice and his ministry were always colorful (born in Cooke county, in Texas, December 11, 1895, and often called "Will Rogers of the Pulpit" because of their likeness and mannerisms)—and controversial. CONTROVERSIAL—and correctly so—because of his intense stand against modernism and infidelity and his fight for the Fundamentals.

Dr. Rice lived and died a man of convictions—intense convictions. But, like many other strong fighters for the Faith, Rice was also marked with a sincere spirit of compassion. Those who knew him best knew a man who loved them. In preaching, in prayer, and in personal life, Rice wept over sinners and with saints. But there is more...

Less than seventy-one hours before the dawning of 1981, one of the most prolific pens in all Christendom was stilled. Dr. John R. Rice left behind a legacy in writing of more than 200 titles, with a combined circulation of over 61 million copies. And through October of 1981, a total of 24,058 precious souls reported trusting Christ through his ministries, not counting those saved in his crusades nor in foreign countries where his literature has been translated.

XIV.

Jesus May Come Today!

JOHN R. RICE

PART I

I. CHRIST'S RETURN ALWAYS IMMINENT

That Jesus may come today is the blessed hope of the Christian. When He went away, two angels stood by the apostles and announced, ". . . this same Jesus, which is taken up from you into heaven, shall so come in like manner as ye have seen him go into heaven" (Acts 1:10,11).

The Saviour promised the grieving disciples the night before He was crucified, "And if I go and prepare a place for you, I will come again, and receive you unto myself; that where I am, there ye may be also."

Paul was inspired of God to write to the Thessalonians,

"For the Lord himself shall descend from heaven with a shout, with the voice of the archangel, and with the trump of God; and the dead in Christ shall rise first: Then we which are alive and remain shall be caught up together with them in the clouds, to meet the Lord in the air: and so shall we ever be with the Lord."—I Thess. 4:16,17.

Jesus may come today!

I do not mean that there are signs that show He is coming nor that we are in "the end of the age." I mean that Jesus may come today—just as He might have and was expected to come by devoted Christians in Bible times and ever since Pentecost.

The coming of Christ is imminent—that is, at hand. His coming was possible during apostolic times and down to the present. We do not know when He will come; but according to Scripture, the Lord's return is imminent and is to be constantly expected.

Christ's coming is the one great truth most emphasized in the New Testament. The greatest emphasis is not on the Antichrist nor on what will happen before he comes nor on the Tribulation time, but on this: "Watch therefore, for ye know neither the day nor the hour wherein the Son of man cometh."

To set any date, any year, any era for His return is to violate the clear teaching that Jesus may come at any time, might have come at any time since Pentecost or may come at any time in the centuries ahead.

If World War I or World War II or the re-establishment of the little state of Israel in Palestine or any other event must transpire and so be a sign of His coming, then His coming has not been imminent. The teachings of imminency and of signs are in direct opposition. Both cannot be true. So anything that contradicts the teaching of Christ's return being imminent is contrary to Scripture.

In the last few years a rash fad has arisen among many premillennialists who are teaching that Jesus will not come for His own until in the midst of the Tribulation, or after. That sad heresy arose because men ignored the imminency of Christ's coming. They ceased to look for Him as a matter of scriptural command and began to look at newspaper signs, world events. And the more they stressed signs, the more they forgot that He could have come at any moment.

If wars, heresies and other troubles and events were signs of the end of the age, as they taught, then when no rapture came their excuse was, "Well, perhaps we are about to enter the Tribulation without a rapture"! Thus they were led into a heresy, a hurtful and deceptive fad of false teaching. If Jesus can come at any moment and if we are commanded to constantly watch, then the Tribulation and the reign of the Antichrist cannot precede His coming.

Jesus may come today. He might have come at any time since New Testament days. But there are no signs by which anyone can accurately foretell when that event will happen.

Now let us consider some of the clear, scriptural proofs in what Jesus said—that His coming is imminent, the first thing on God's prophetic program, that it may be at any time.

In the Discourse on the Mount of Olives, recorded in Matthew 24, the Saviour emphatically warned the disciples that no one knew the time of His return but that all were to watch.

The first part of the Discourse may be somewhat complicated to the

casual reader by the fact that the Lord is addressing the Jews and partly had the fate of Jerusalem in mind. He spoke not only of the Great
Tribulation, when the Man of Sin will commit the abomination of desolation in Jerusalem, but also of the destruction of Jerusalem by Titus in
A.D. 70, which would follow much the same course. The first destruction of Jerusalem under Titus was a first fulfillment of the prophecies
of the later awful destruction under the Antichrist. He spoke to Jews,
some of whom would still be alive when the fall of Jerusalem would
take place and would flee for their lives. He had that in mind, along
with the future Great Tribulation when Jews would similarly flee for their
lives.

Between verse 15, when the prophesied abomination of desolation
should take place, and verse 35, is the story of Jews in the Tribulation
time and the return of Christ with His saints and angels to reign and
to set up His kingdom at Jerusalem. It is not the story of the rapture,
the first phase of Christ's coming.

However, beginning with verse 36, Christ had in view His second
coming as a whole event. And it is that first phase of His coming—
when Jesus will come in the air to receive His saints—of which we are
warned in Matthew 24:36-51.

When Jesus says, "But of that day and hour knoweth no man, no,
not the angels of heaven, but my Father only," He refers to the day
when the trumpet shall sound and the dead in Christ shall rise and we
shall be caught up together with Him to meet the Lord in the air. That
is so with the rest of the chapter.

Now note these emphatic statements which prove that Christ's coming was to be expected at any moment, that His coming was and is
imminent.

1. No One Knows When Jesus Will Come!

Read again the words of Jesus in Matthew 24:36, "But of that day
and hour knoweth no man, no, not the angels of heaven, but my Father
only." No man knows—not even the angels in Heaven—when Christ
will return.

In Mark's inspired account of the same Olivet Discourse, it is even
stronger. In chapter 13 we read,

"But of that day and that hour knoweth no man, no, not the angels
which are in heaven, neither the Son, but the Father. Take ye heed,
watch and pray: for ye know not when the time is."—Vss. 32,33.

The angels do not know, and while on earth even the Son Himself did not know, the time of the second coming! Surely He knows now. I think that knowledge of when He would come again was part of His glorious manifestation of deity which He laid aside when He took on the form of man and came into this world. But if the perfect, sinless Jesus, who had an infinite understanding of the Scriptures and knew everything about man, did not know the time of the second coming, then how presumptuous for any Bible teacher to pretend to know even approximately when He will return.

The Saviour gives solemn instruction and warning: "Take ye heed, watch and pray: for ye know not when the time is."

2. Jesus Illustrated the Unexpectedness of His Coming With Reference to Noah and Those Who Died in the Flood

Here in Matthew 24:37-39 Jesus says:

"But as the days of Noe were, so shall also the coming of the Son of man be, For as in the days that were before the flood they were eating and drinking, marrying and giving in marriage, until the day that Noe entered into the ark, And knew not until the flood came, and took them all away; so shall also the coming of the Son of man be."

Some have perverted this Scripture and made it teach that men could tell when Christ would return because people would sin like they did before the Flood. But Jesus said the exact opposite—that people before the Flood went ahead eating and drinking (no harm about that) and "marrying and giving in marriage" (which is normal and proper); but that they went on with this ordinary way of life, unsuspecting—"and knew not until the flood came, and took them all away." Then we have the solemn warning that just so suddenly, just so unexpectedly "shall also the coming of the Son of man be." The plain intent here is that no one can know when, but that Jesus could come at any moment and all ought to be watching.

3. Jesus Indicated That We Would Not Know Even a Few Hours in Advance of His Coming!

Jesus said, "Watch therefore: for ye know not what hour your Lord doth come" (Matt. 24:42).

Two men will go to work in the field—one a Christian, the other lost.

Both are utterly unaware that that very day Jesus will come. One will be taken, the other left.

Two women will be grinding at the mill, preparing meal that will be baked into bread that day—one saved and the other lost. Both will be utterly unwarned that Jesus will come that very day. One will be taken, the other left. Then Jesus gives the solemn warning in verse 42, "Watch therefore: for ye know not what hour your Lord doth come."

No one will know ahead of time. Therefore, all should watch for His imminent coming.

4. Jesus Illustrated the Imminence of His Coming by the Unexpected Thief

Illustrating further the utter unexpectedness of His coming, Jesus said in Matthew 24:43, "But know this, that if the goodman of the house had known in what watch the thief would come, he would have watched, and would not have suffered his house to be broken up."

As unexpected as the coming of a thief, so will Christ's coming be. The goodman of the house had no forewarning when the thief would come. So it will be when Christ returns to the earth. The goodman of the house did not know what watch of the night the thief would come. So it will be when Jesus comes.

He has now gone away. The world is in night. Suppose Jesus should come for His saints in the year 2000. If Christ should come in the year 2000, this night might have been divided up into four watches of 500 years each. The Roman night was so divided—the *evening* watch, the *midnight* watch, the *cockcrowing* watch, the *morning* watch. Jesus referred to this further in the inspired account of this Discourse: "Watch ye therefore: for ye know not when the master of the house cometh, at even, or at midnight, or at the cockcrowing, or in the morning" (Mark 13:35).

Jesus is saying that no one could know ahead of time whether He would come in the first 500 years or in the second 500 years or in the third 500 years or in the fourth 500 years. Oh, but let us be prepared and looking for His coming!

5. Jesus Likened His Imminent Coming to the Return of a Master at an Undisclosed Time

Jesus gave the following illustration of how earnestly we should watch for His coming:

"Therefore be ye also ready: for in such an hour as ye think not the Son of man cometh. Who then is a faithful and wise servant, whom his lord hath made ruler over his household, to give them meat in due season? Blessed is that servant, whom his lord when he cometh shall find so doing. Verily I say unto you, That he shall make him ruler over all his goods. But and if that evil servant shall say in his heart, My lord delayeth his coming; And shall begin to smite his fellow servants, and to eat and drink with the drunken; The lord of that servant shall come in a day when he looketh not for him, and in an hour that he is not aware of, And shall cut him asunder, and appoint him his portion with the hypocrites: there shall be weeping and gnashing of teeth."—Matt. 24:44-51.

In the above parable not a hint was given to the servant as to when his lord would return. There were no other foretold events by which the servant could estimate the time of his lord's return. But how urgently the Saviour pressed it on the hearts of all that His coming may be at any moment and that we should all be looking and ready.

Summing up the warnings of Jesus in the Olivet Discourse in Matthew 24, let us note the following verses again:

"But of that day and hour knoweth no man, no, not the angels of heaven, but my Father only."—Vs. 36.

"Watch therefore: for ye know not what hour your Lord doth come."—Vs. 42.

"Therefore be ye also ready: for in such an hour as ye think not the Son of man cometh."—Vs. 44.

And in Mark 13 note these verses:

"But of that day and that hour knoweth no man, no, not the angels which are in heaven, neither the Son, but the Father. Take ye heed, watch and pray: for ye know not when the time is."—Vss. 32,33.

"Watch ye therefore: for ye know not when the master of the house cometh, at even, or at midnight, or at the cockcrowing, or in the morning: Lest coming suddenly he find you sleeping. And what I say unto you I say unto all, Watch."—Vss. 35-37.

In all the Olivet Discourse the intent is to warn His disciples and all other Christians of all ages that He might come at any moment, that His coming will be unexpected and without warning. We are commanded to watch and pray, to obey and be ready. We have clear proof that Christ's coming is always at hand and is never foreseeable nor predictable.

6. The Resurrected Saviour Told the Apostles That the Time of His Return Is Unknowable

After Jesus rose from the dead, He appeared to the disciples and continued with them forty days "speaking of the things pertaining to the kingdom of God." He commanded them to wait in Jerusalem for the enduement with power. And the apostles—all of them Jews—naturally anxious about the restoration of the kingdom of Israel, asked, "Lord, wilt thou at this time restore again the kingdom to Israel?" (Acts 1:6). Then Jesus gave them a memorable answer that should help settle this matter of His imminent coming for all of us: "It is not for you to know the times or the seasons which the Father hath put in his own power" (Acts 1:7).

The time of Christ's second coming and the attendant events are not to be known! God did not intend men to know "the times or the seasons," the years or the eras, which He had hidden.

So even the approximate time is not only unknown but unknowable. And when we seek to find a time and declare it, we go against the express command of God. Those who, reading the book of Daniel, make a day mean a year, will find their folly fruitless. Those who measure passages in the great pyramid and make an inch mean a year, will find they cannot learn from that the time of Christ's coming. Those who scan the newspapers and look for signs will find that they still do not know the times and seasons which God has put absolutely and solely in His own hands!

And how presumptuous to dig into the future to try to learn things which God has intentionally hidden! That is the sin of the fortunetellers, of the spiritualist mediums, of the astrologers.

II. RAPTURE OF THE SAINTS, CAUGHT UP TO MEET THE LORD AT HIS COMING, IS TO BE FIRST EVENT OF THOSE PROPHESIED IN SCRIPTURE

Many Scriptures foretell future events—the Great Tribulation . . . the reign of the Antichrist . . . the setting up of David's throne upon which Christ shall reign . . . His millennial kingdom . . . the last rebellion . . . the great white throne judgment. . .the making of a new Heaven and a new earth, and others. But when an order is indicated, in every case the rapture is prophesied as the first event to occur. No other prophesied event is to happen before Christ's coming in the air to receive His saints. Consider the following Scriptures:

1. Rapture First in II Thessalonians 2:1-3

In Paul's second letter to the Thessalonians we find that these saints had gotten an idea somewhere that the day of the Lord, including Christ's judgment of the nations and His reign on earth, was to occur immediately. So Paul writes to tell them that the first thing on God's calendar is the rapture; then other things will follow in course.

"Now we beseech you, brethren, by the coming of our Lord Jesus Christ, and by our gathering together unto him, That ye be not soon shaken in mind, or be troubled, neither by spirit, nor by word, nor by letter as from us, as that the day of Christ is at hand. Let no man deceive you by any means; for that day shall not come, except there come a falling away first, and that man of sin be revealed, the son of perdition."

In verse 2 the term "the day of Christ" should be "the day of the Lord." This refers to specific events, including Christ's coming back with His saints to reign, the destruction of the Gentile world powers, etc., but Paul says that cannot come until two other things take place. One is indicated in verse 1—". . .by the coming of our Lord Jesus Christ, and by our gathering together unto him." Paul is anxious for them not to think about "the day of the Lord" but about Christ's coming and our gathering to Him. Then he says that great time of judgment will not come until two things happen: ". . .except there come a falling away first, and that man of sin be revealed, the son of perdition."

There must be a "falling away first." Many have supposed that this "falling away" referred to some moral declension, to some spiritual apostasy. But we are not convinced. We believe, with Dr. E. Schuyler English and many other scholars, that this would be better translated ". . .except there come a departure first," or literally, the catching away of Christians at Christ's coming. That is first on God's program! Then after that shall "that man of sin be revealed, the son of perdition."

Christ's coming certainly does not need to wait for spiritual apostasy nor moral declension. The world has been in a moral declension since Adam and Eve were cast out of the Garden of Eden. In the first century there was a great falling away, and in a few years all the great churches known and mentioned in the Bible passed out of existence. But these other prophesied events cannot come "except there come a falling away first." One day the power of gravity will be broken, and we will be caught up to meet the Lord in the air. That comes first.

2. In Revelation the Rapture Is Indicated Before Other Prophesied Events

The first chapter of the book of Revelation is introduction. Chapters 2 and 3 are messages to seven churches, without any particular future prophecy. From chapter 4 on through to the end is prophecy of the future.

Chapter 4 begins,

"After this I looked, and, behold, a door was opened in heaven: and the first voice which I heard was as it were of a trumpet talking with me; which said, Come up hither, and I will shew thee things which must be hereafter. And immediately I was in the spirit: and, behold, a throne was set in heaven, and one sat on the throne."—Vss. 1,2.

Verse 1 is important because it is the only verse in the Revelation that can possibly refer to the rapture of the saints. The rapture is here figured and pictured when a door was opened and John was caught up into Heaven in the spirit and saw things Christians will see when they are caught up to meet Christ in the air and taken to Heaven.

Chronologically, the rapture of the saints in Revelation comes before any other prophesied event. If the rapture be not pictured in Revelation 4:1, it is not pictured at all in this book of prophecy of future things. So Revelation 4:1 surely pictures that blessed rapture which is to come before all other prophesied events.

3. It Is Intimated in Many Parables of Jesus That His Coming Is the First Event in God's Program

The parable of the ten virgins in Matthew 25 indicates that no prophesied event must come before the Saviour returns for us. While both foolish and wise virgins slumber and sleep, nothing happens—until suddenly the bridegroom comes!

That is indeed the very point of the parable, for Jesus sums up the moral of the parable in these strong words: "Watch therefore, for ye know neither the day nor the hour wherein the Son of man cometh."

The Saviour, our heavenly Bridegroom, is coming to catch away His bride. As individuals, we should be as bridesmaids who prepare for the coming of the Bridegroom, for no one knows when He may come. The rapture is the first clearly promised event in God's schedule of future events!

Likewise, in the parable of the talents in Matthew 25, no prophesied events are indicated before the man traveling into a far country returns to ask an accounting of his servants on how they used their talents.

The parable of the pounds in Luke 19:11-27 indicates, too, that the coming of Christ to catch away His servants into the air and to reward them at the judgment seat of Christ, is next on God's schedule. No one knows when it will be, but it is imminent.

In the parable of the marriage feast in Matthew 22:1-14, it is abundantly clear that Christians are servants who should invite sinners to be ready for the marriage. As far as prophesied events are concerned, Christ's coming to receive His saints in Glory and there to have the wedding supper, is next on God's program.

Many other parables bear out this teaching.

III. THE LORD'S SUPPER—A CONTINUAL REMINDER TO EXPECT CHRIST'S COMING

The second coming is related to almost every great doctrine of Christianity. So it is not surprising that the Lord's Supper is given, with particular instructions, to remind us of Christ's second coming.

In I Corinthians 11:26, by divine inspiration Paul says, "For as often as ye eat this bread, and drink this cup, **ye do shew the Lord's death till he come.**"

The Lord's Supper has a double meaning. The bread and the cup, picturing the broken body and shed blood of our Saviour in His crucifixion, is also a pointer to remind us of Christ's second coming. An air of expectancy should be around the communion table. There we remember Christ's sacrifice for us. And there we look forward to His coming.

The instance here is more powerful when we remember that Paul begins his discussion of the Lord's Supper by saying, "For I have received of the Lord that which also I delivered unto you, That the Lord Jesus the same night in which he was betrayed took bread. . . ." In the Gospels of Matthew, Mark and Luke, Jesus said, "This do in remembrance of me." But Paul tells us that the Lord Jesus revealed to him that He had in mind remembrance of Christ **in view of His second coming.**

When the New Testament quotes the Old Testament we often find a more detailed picture of truth than that given in the Old Testament. When in the Sermon on the Mount Jesus said, "It has been said . . . but I say unto you," He enlarged upon the Old Testament meaning. Men are still forbidden to commit adultery, but Jesus included even lust in the heart as adultery.

Here the same principle is involved. Paul brings to mind what Jesus said, but adds that Jesus taught him what kind of a remembrance a Christian should have of the Lord's Supper. They were to "SHEW THE LORD'S DEATH TILL HE COME."

So Christians at Corinth were encouraged, as Christians now are encouraged, to remember that Christ's coming is at hand. This thought should bless our hearts when we take of the bread and the cup.

Does not this indicate that the general New Testament teaching is that Jesus may come at any moment and that Christians in Bible times momentarily expected His return as imminent?

IV. NEW TESTAMENT CHRISTIANS WERE CONSTANTLY TAUGHT TO EXPECT CHRIST'S RETURN IN THEIR LIFETIME

New Testament Christians took to heart Christ's warning about His return and looked for Him in their lifetime. They were systematically taught by the apostles to expect Christ to return at any moment.

1. From the Day of Their Salvation, the Thessalonians Waited for Christ's Return

In the first letter of Paul to the Thessalonian Christians, it is noticeable that each of the five chapters closes with a reminder of the second coming—the last verse in each of the first three chapters, the last six verses in chapter 4, and verse 23 in chapter 5.

In I Thessalonians 1:9,10 we note that Paul had won these converts to Christ by teaching them to turn to God from idols and to wait for Jesus to come.

*"For they themselves shew of us what manner of entering in we had unto you, and how ye turned to God from idols to serve the living and true God: And **to wait for his Son from heaven,** whom he raised*

from the dead, even Jesus, which delivered us from the wrath to come."

One of the simplest elements of New Testament faith was that, from the time of their conversion, Christians were taught to look for Christ's coming. Were they wrong to "wait for his Son from heaven"? No, they were taught to do what Jesus had commanded all of us to do—to watch, not knowing the day nor the hour when Christ will come.

Paul wrote to the Christians at Thessalonica that he was praying they might be preserved, even in body, until the coming of the Lord Jesus Christ! In I Thessalonians 5:23, writing by God's infallible inspiration, this is what Paul said: "And the very God of peace sanctify you wholly; and I pray God your whole spirit and soul and body be preserved blameless unto the coming of our Lord Jesus Christ."

He was praying that these Thessalonians should be wholly set apart for God. When Paul prayed that their whole spirit, soul and body would be preserved "blameless unto the coming of our Lord Jesus Christ," he was praying that Christ would come in the lifetime of those Thessalonian Christians. Every day Paul was praying for Christ's return. He hoped earnestly that He might come before a single one of the Christians at Thessalonica should die and his body should decay!

This is a fair sample of the teaching of apostles and prophets in Bible times. New Testament Christians were taught, by divine inspiration, to expect Christ to come in their lifetime.

Christ's coming is imminent. No one knows when He will come. He might have come at any time since Pentecost; He may come today; or He may come at any time in the future.

2. Christians at Rome Were Taught That Christ Would Soon Return and Bruise Satan Under Their Feet

Writing under the infallible direction of the Holy Spirit to the Christians at Rome, Paul reminded them that all of creation is out of joint and groans and travails, waiting for Christ to come.

They were taught that all of us are waiting for the adoption, to wit, the redemption of our bodies which will take place at the rapture (Rom. 8:23). The dead shall be raised incorruptible, and we shall be changed. So these at Rome were encouraged to expect Jesus to come and change their vile bodies.

In Romans 16:20 Paul says, "And the God of peace shall bruise Satan under your feet shortly." This is an allusion to the promise given Eve in Genesis 3:15, that the Seed of the woman—Jesus Christ—should bruise the serpent's head. That bruising did not take place at Christ's first coming, but it will take place at Christ's second coming. And Paul wrote that that would occur "shortly"! The idea surely is that Christians should have a sense of expectancy, gladly holding to the blessed hope that Christ would come and it could be very soon.

3. Philippian Christians Also Waited for Christ's Coming

The apostles taught everywhere in New Testament times that Christians should watch for the return of the Saviour. We find in Philippians 3:20,21 this same doctrine:

"For our conversation is in heaven; from whence also we look for the Saviour, the Lord Jesus Christ: Who shall change our vile body, that it may be fashioned like unto his glorious body, according to the working whereby he is able even to subdue all things unto himself."

Christians at Philippi were premillennialists. They did not set any signs for Christ's coming, nor did they expect the Great Tribulation to occur first. But they looked for the Saviour, the Lord Jesus Christ, who would change their vile bodies and one day would change ours.

Note that it was the rapture they looked for—the resurrection of the Christian dead and the changing of the Christian living. But the inference is that they expected Christ to come while they were alive; and it was not the resurrection but the change they expected! "We shall not all sleep, but we shall all be changed."

4. To the Seven Churches of Asia Minor Jesus Repeatedly Said, "I Come Quickly"

The book of Revelation is God's message to His servants concerning the things which must shortly come to pass (Rev. 1:1). The book is partly addressed to seven particular churches in Asia Minor, but of course it is to all Christians.

Three times in the last chapter the Lord gave to John the promise, "Behold, I come quickly."

The first time is in verse 7—"Behold, I come quickly: blessed is he that keepeth the sayings of the prophecy of this book."

The second time is in verse 12—"And, behold, I come quickly; and my reward is with me, to give every man according as his work shall be." Here we are specifically told that it is the coming of Christ to catch up His saints and to take them away to the judgment seat of Christ where rewards will be assigned, according to I Corinthians 3:14 and II Corinthians 5:9,10.

The third time is in verse 20—"He which testifieth these things saith, Surely I come quickly. Amen." In the same verse is the divinely inspired and recorded response in the heart of John: "Amen. Even so, come, Lord Jesus"!

"I come quickly"—Jesus said it three times. The point is, He will come suddenly—not necessarily soon, but quickly, suddenly. His coming will be as sudden as a flash of lightning. It will be as sudden as "the twinkling of an eye."

John the Beloved was anxious to see Him. And the old man on the Isle of Patmos was inspired to write down his plea, "Amen. Even so, come, Lord Jesus"—the proper response of a Christian to the thought of Christ's coming. We are taught to pray for and to expect His coming at any moment.

Surely all these examples show that New Testament Christians confidently hoped for Christ to come in their lifetime. They did not pretend to know when. They set no dates nor times for His coming but simply obeyed the word of the Lord Jesus and looked for Him.

V. APOSTLE PAUL PERSONALLY EXPECTED CHRIST TO COME IN HIS LIFETIME

Paul himself obeyed the command of the Lord Jesus and the command He passed on to others: he confidently hoped and prayed for Christ's coming in his lifetime.

A good proof of this is I Thessalonians 4:13-18:

"But I would not have you to be ignorant, brethren, concerning them which are asleep, that ye sorrow not, even as others which have no hope. For if we believe that Jesus died and rose again, even so them also which sleep in Jesus will God bring with him. For this we say unto you by the word of the Lord, that WE WHICH ARE ALIVE AND RE-MAIN unto the coming of the Lord shall not prevent them which are asleep. For the Lord himself shall descend from heaven with a shout, with the voice of the archangel, and with the trump of God: and the dead in Christ shall rise first: THEN WE WHICH ARE ALIVE AND REMAIN shall be caught up together with them in the clouds, to meet

the Lord in the air: and so shall we ever be with the Lord. Wherefore comfort one another with these words."

Two groups are mentioned here—"them which are asleep" and "we which are alive and remain unto the coming of the Lord." Paul put himself with those whom he expected would be alive when Jesus came.

First, Paul said, would be the resurrection of the Christian dead: "And the dead in Christ shall rise first: Then WE which are alive and remain shall be caught up together with them in the clouds, to meet the Lord in the air. . . ." In saying "WE," Paul included himself as one of those who would be alive and remaining until the coming of the Lord.

Was Paul foolish in this expectancy? No—he was obeying Jesus Christ and looking daily for Him. He set no dates, nor did he pretend to know the time of His return.

In I Corinthians 15 Paul has much to say by divine inspiration about the blessed resurrection of the Christian dead. Here, too, he shows that he expected to be alive when Jesus came.

"Behold, I shew you a mystery; We shall not all sleep, but we shall all be changed, In a moment, in the twinkling of an eye, at the last trump: for the trumpet shall sound, and the dead shall be raised incorruptible, and we shall be changed."—Vss. 51,52.

When Paul said, "We shall not all sleep, but WE shall all be changed," he expected to be among those whose bodies did not fall asleep in death. He said that "the dead shall be raised incorruptible, and WE shall be changed."

At Christ's coming there will be two classes: the dead who will be raised and the Christians living who will be changed. Paul expected to be with those who would be alive when he said, ". . . WE shall be changed."

We repeat our question: Was Paul foolish to expect to be living when Jesus came? No. He was being obedient. He set no dates, nor did he pretend to know when He would come. He knew that Christ's second coming was imminent—that is, that Jesus might come at any time, that nothing was prophesied to come before Christ's return for His saints. So he lived in happy expectation.

Just before Paul was put to death, he seemed to have it revealed to him that he would die, so he wrote,

"For I am now ready to be offered, and the time of my departure is at hand."

But even so, he thought that Timothy and others to whom he wrote would probably be alive, so he continued:

"I have fought a good fight, I have finished my course, I have kept the faith: Henceforth there is laid up for me a crown of righteousness, which the Lord, the righteous judge, shall give me at that day: and not to me only, but unto all them also that love his appearing."—II Tim. 4:6-8.

Paul said in effect, "I am going on ahead to receive my crown because I have fought a good fight. But the Lord will lay up a crown for every one of you who love His appearing, and one day when He shall appear you will receive crowns, too." Paul did not definitely say that Christ would come in their lifetime, but he expected it to happen.

PART II

The Imminence of Christ's Return Proves He Is COMING WITHOUT SIGNS

Now the imminence of Christ's return proves certain facts. By getting settled this great principal truth—He may come at any moment, the time is unknown, cannot be foretold, but it is the first prophesied event of the future—we may keep straight on other important truths regarding Christ's coming.

Since no one knows when Jesus will return, then there can be no signs of Christ's coming.

Down through the ages many honest and well-meaning preachers have preached on signs of Christ's return.

Martin Luther thought the corruption and power of the papacy was a sign of Christ's soon return.

Many thought that the Reign of Terror in France indicated the end of the age. World War I, World War II, the rise of Russian communism, the re-establishment of the little nation Israel, the increase in modernism in major denominations, the rising of the National Council of Churches, along with earthquakes, famines, meteor showers, floods and pestilences, nuclear bombs, etc., have been looked upon as signs of Christ's coming. I, too, without setting any dates for Christ's return, once felt that there were increasing signs that Christ would soon appear to take away His own. But I found that I was preaching only guesses, guesses that I could not prove by the Bible; that this kind of teaching tended away from the one thing the Lord emphasized the most—His imminent second coming.

I. ANY GENUINE SIGNS TO INDICATE CHRIST'S COMING WOULD NECESSARILY SET APPROXIMATE DATES AND SO VIOLATE CHRIST'S PLAIN COMMAND

I drive along the highway and see highway signs. Driving west from Chicago on Highway 30, one sign says, *WHEATON 8 MILES*. A little further on, a sign reads, *GLEN ELLYN CITY LIMITS*. I know that Glen Ellyn is three miles from Wheaton. I drive on further west and see a sign that says, *WHEATON CITY LIMITS*. Obviously highway signs are intended to tell one when he approaches and when he arrives at a particular place.

Signs of Christ's coming would be setting dates, at least approximate dates, but Jesus said, "But of that day and hour knoweth no man, no, not the angels of heaven, but my Father only" (Matt. 24:36). Again He said, "It is not for you to know the times or the seasons, which the Father hath put in his own power" (Acts 1:7).

I flew from Washington, D.C., to Chicago. As we left, the hostess announced, *"You are on United Airlines Flight 811 to Chicago. Flying time will be approximately one hour and forty-five minutes."* As we neared Chicago, the hostess announced again, *"We are now approaching O'Hare Field. Please fasten your seat belts. We are due to land in approximately twelve minutes."* On a scheduled flight, where one is expected to know the time of arrival, such specific announcements may be expected.

But Christ's coming is exactly the opposite. No one knows when. He might have come a thousand years ago; He may come today; or He may not come for centuries yet. The time is hidden. Therefore, it would be impossible to have any signs pointing to the time of Christ's return since that return is imminent, always at hand, but never foretold.

Christ's coming may be properly illustrated by another kind of journey. Let us suppose that this journey occurs in wartime. It has been determined by the high command of America's armed forces that on a certain city a bomb must be dropped, both for the heartening of our own people and for the discouragement and disruption of military plans in that city.

Suppose General Doolittle is put in charge of this and that a carefully selected group of flyers are assembled. Each person's background is checked, his loyalty established beyond question, his flying skill proved. These men are asked to volunteer for a dangerous mission, the nature of which they do not know. After they volunteer, they are to be flown to an isolated airfield for training. They must learn to take off in bombers from a carrier deck, which is much shorter than would usually be needed. They must have intensive training. None are allowed to know where this isolated field is. They will not be allowed to tell their families, nor can they write letters or have any communication with others. To maintain utmost military secrecy, they are to be kept in absolute isolation during this training period.

Now these flyers are all put on board a transport plane. In the night it takes off for its unknown destination. All the windows are darkened. Not a single person aboard but the pilot and co-pilot knows his destination. Will it take one hour's flight or five?

Suppose these men fly from Seattle to an isolated airfield in Arizona for their final training. Each guesses and tries to decide from any clues he can remember or imagine, where they will be going, how long they will be en route, when they will land. BUT NOBODY KNOWS! One hour, two hours, three hours, four hours, five hours, six hours, seven hours may go by. They have been expecting to land at any moment for the last six hours.

Finally, apparently without any preliminary warning, the plane sits down on the far-off field. There is absolutely no way anyone besides the pilots could know at what time they would arrive.

So it is about the coming of the Lord Jesus. All of us are going swiftly on our way toward that great day—a glad day for faithful Christians; a terrifying day for others. When Christ will come is known only to the Commanding Officer. We can safely trust ourselves in His hands. He has told us it is not for us to know when His coming will be. So, with absolutely no warning, in a moment, in the twinkling of an eye, Jesus will come to catch us up to meet Him.

One simply cannot have signs of Christ's coming and have Christ's coming imminent, always at hand, unpredicted and unpredictable.

II. JESUS MIGHT HAVE COME BEFORE ANY SUPPOSED SIGN OF HIS COMING COULD HAVE HAPPENED!

Let me illustrate why no particular event could possibly be a sign of

Christ's coming. Suppose that the rise of the papacy and the corruptions and oppression that came with it were signs of Christ's soon return, as some of the Reformers taught. But Paul truly expected Christ to come in his lifetime. All New Testament Christians were taught to look for, to wait for Christ's coming (I Thess. 1:10; 5:23; Phil. 3:20). Since Jesus could have come long before the rise of the papacy, then the rise of the papacy could not possibly have been a sign of Christ's soon coming.

Were World War I and World War II signs of Christ's coming? That could not possibly be, since Jesus might have come, and He had taught millions of Christians to expect His coming, before these wars occurred. So the rise of communism and atheism in Russia; the founding of the little nation Israel by a handful of unconverted Jews in 1947; the rise of the National Council of Churches, dominated by modern unbelievers—these could not possibly be signs of Christ's coming because His return could have been at any time, even centuries before these so-called "signs" came into being.

III. SO-CALLED SIGNS OF CHRIST'S RETURN
HAVE ALWAYS FAILED

The Millerites, who started the Seventh-day Adventist movement, taught that Christ would come in October of 1843. They had seen falling meteors. The earnest farmer, Miller, had searched the Scriptures and, reading Daniel 8:14, had made a day mean a year (which it never does in the Bible) and thought that surely Christ would come. But He did not come. The good farmer did his calculations again: he figured he had missed it by one year. Surely the following year Jesus would come on October 22, 1844. But He did not come then.

When I was a lad, I went to a free show in the opera house in Gainesville, Texas. There, along with many pictures, a lecture was given on the theme, "Thousands Now Living Will Never Die."

"Pastor" Russell, founder of Millennial Dawn, the Watchtower Society, Jehovah's Witnesses or whatever you may call them, announced that Jesus would come in 1914. But 1914 came and went and Jesus still has not come. Those of his persuasion say that Jesus came in the spirit!

Years ago I was in seminary with a brilliant young man. He knew the truth of Christ's coming, but he began to preach sensational sermons on signs. Later he fell into the British-Israelite delusion and set out to prove that, according to the Great Pyramid, Jesus was coming soon. By measuring certain passages, counting an inch to a year, he determined that Jesus would come on September 16, 1936, if my memory serves me right about the date. But this day came and went. Jesus did not come. The man was discredited. He went into worse heresies, landed in prison and finally forsook Christianity and the Bible altogether.

I believe, with most premillennial scholars, that the Man of Sin, mentioned in II Thessalonians 2:3 and prophesied in the book of Daniel and in Revelation, will restore in some form the Roman Empire. It seems that the beast in Daniel 7:7,8, picturing the first Roman Empire, and the beast in Revelation 13:1-10 are basically the same. If so, then the Antichrist will restore the Roman Empire. I think Revelation 17 has definite references to Rome, particularly to the city of Rome, and to a great false religion which seems to be the Roman Catholic Church.

Then, if we should find a man arising, a dictator, who will set out to restore the Roman Empire and who seems to be making strong progress to that end, would not that mean that Jesus would come soon to take away His own? Would that not mean that soon Daniel's seventieth week would begin, the Man of Sin would be revealed, and this age would come to its rapid close?

Those were my thoughts when Mussolini made himself dictator and when he announced that he would restore the Roman Empire, when he seized Ethiopia and joined with Hitler to rule Europe. So I began to preach that Mussolini might prove to be the Antichrist and that Christians ought to take the rise of Mussolini as a sign of Christ's coming.

But it did not work out that way. The Axis (originally Nazi Germany and Fascist Italy) lost the war. Mussolini was discarded by his people, then hanged up feet first with his mistress, his body abused and murdered by the throng that hated him. Italy lost Ethiopia, lost her dream of empire. I found that I was preaching guesses instead of the Word of God. I was teaching people to expect Christ's return on what newspapers said instead of using the Bible as the guideline.

Preaching signs has always failed, and it always will. God is against this heresy. It grows out of desire to know more than God has revealed.

Bible teachers and preachers want to be sensational, want to prove that they know more than others, want to get a following for themselves. Perhaps these good men, often sincere men, want to shock and alarm lost sinners into getting saved. But in doing so they use unjustifiable means, make statements they cannot prove. Trying to see into the future, to know the things that God has deliberately hidden from men, is wrong in principle. When He said, "It is not for you to know the times or the seasons which the Father hath put in his own power," He was speaking of prophesied future events.

Announcing signs of Christ's coming has brought reproach upon the great truth of the Lord's premillennial return.

I heard Dr. George W. Truett, famous and mighty preacher but not a profound Bible student, speak slurringly of premillennialists. He gave Jehovah's Witnesses and Seventh-day Adventists as examples of premillennialists! These premillennialists who preach speculations, signs and public events bring reproach on the cause of Christ and on the great truth of Christ's literal, personal return.

IV. "SIGN OF THY COMING" OF MATTHEW 24:3 WILL APPEAR LONG AFTER THE RAPTURE, AT THE CLOSE OF THE TRIBULATION TIME; THIS SIGN IS OF CHRIST'S RETURN WITH HIS SAINTS TO REIGN

As Jesus sat on the Mount of Olives, His disciples asked Him, "Tell us, when shall these things be? and what shall be the sign of thy coming, and of the end of the world?" (Matt. 24:3). That little phrase, "the sign of thy coming," has been misused by many an honest preacher.

Jesus answered them in the same chapter:

"Immediately after the tribulation of these days shall the sun be darkened, and the moon shall not give her light, and the stars shall fall from heaven, and the powers of the heavens shall be shaken: And then shall appear the sign of the Son of man in heaven: and then shall all the tribes of the earth mourn, and they shall see the Son of man coming in the clouds of heaven with power and great glory."—Vss. 29,30.

Note that after the Tribulation people shall see the Son of Man assembling the hosts of Heaven, including raptured saints, to return to the earth. They will see Him coming in the clouds of Heaven with power and great glory, followed by armies of angels. He will ride upon a white horse and will be crowned with many crowns (Rev. 19:11-16).

But when that sign in Heaven appears, it will be long after the rapture, even at the close of the Tribulation period. All of us who are saved will have been in Heaven with the Saviour and will be preparing now to return with Him for His reign on earth. So "sign" mentioned here

will not occur before Christ comes for His saints. No Christian now living will be here on earth to see it. Rather, we will be with Jesus and
preparing to return with Him after our honeymoon in Heaven.

The Scripture says, "Jews require a sign" (I Cor. 1:22). When Christians are taken out at the rapture after Christ comes for His own, then
we begin Daniel's seventieth week, prophesied in Daniel 9:25-27. The
Antichrist will make a covenant with the many Jews who will be in the
land of Palestine. They will rebuild their Temple, start their sacrifices
and worship. In the midst of that week of seven years, the Man of Sin
will enter into the Temple, claim to be God, demand the worship of
men; and he will thus commit the abomination of desolation, prophesied
by Daniel (See Dan. 9:27, Matt. 24:15, II Thess. 2:2-4).

We are clearly told that the "falling away" or departure, the rapture
of the saints, must come before the Man of Sin can be revealed. Then
the Antichrist will reign a definite period of forty-two months or three
and a half years or 1,260 days according to many, many prophecies
(Dan. 7:25; 12:7,11; Rev. 11:2,3; 12:6,14; 13:5).

In this "time of Jacob's trouble" when the Antichrist will be hating
and punishing Jews, it will be altogether proper that a sign should
appear for the Jews at the close of the Tribulation period. There will
be no mystery about how long the Tribulation will be. It is already plainly
set and prophesied. And a sign will only be an encouragement to Jews
then alive on the earth and other Christians who will have been converted during the Tribulation time.

But the sign mentioned in Matthew 24:3 and 24:30 will not appear
before Jesus comes. Verse 29 tells us it will appear after Jesus comes
for His saints and at the end of the Tribulation time.

Likewise, the "parable of the fig tree" in Matthew 24 applies to those
who will be left here when Jesus comes and takes away His own. Those
in the Tribulation time will see the sign of the Son of Man in Heaven,
will see the Lord coming in clouds and glory, will see the angels of God
collecting Jews from all over the world and bringing them back
miraculously to Palestine. And to anyone alive on the earth during the
Tribulation, Jesus said, "When ye shall see all these things, know that
it is near, even at the doors."

But that "sign" of the fig tree does not apply today. There are no
signs, can be no signs of when Christ will return. Those signs can only
occur *AFTER* Jesus comes. They refer to His revelation in power and

glory when He returns with His saints to set up His kingdom.

V. ANY SUPPOSED PROPHECIES OF SIGNS OF CHRIST'S COMING ARE MISUNDERSTOOD SCRIPTURES

All the Scriptures which have been quoted by zealous people as giving signs by which one could know when the Saviour's coming draws near are simply misunderstood.

1. Matthew 24:33 and Luke 21:28 Do Not Refer to the Rapture

We have mentioned that Jesus spoke of certain things—the sign of the Son of Man in Heaven, the regathering of Jews out of all nations by the angels—when He said, "So likewise ye, when ye shall see all these things, know that it is near, even at the doors" (Matt. 24:33). However, this does not speak of the rapture, that coming of Christ into the air to receive His saints. Rather, it speaks of the time "immediately after the tribulation of those days" (vs. 29). During and after the Great Tribulation there will be signs but none before the rapture.

A similar statement by the Saviour is given in Luke 21:28, "And when these things begin to come to pass, then look up, and lift up your heads; for your redemption draweth nigh." Here Jesus speaks of the great distresses that shall occur during the Tribulation time:

"And then shall they see the Son of man coming in a cloud with power and great glory. And when these things begin to come to pass, then look up, and lift up your heads; for your redemption draweth nigh."— Luke 21:27,28.

When we put the preceding verse with it, we see without any doubt that Jesus here spoke of His coming in power with His saints and angels, after the Great Tribulation. He did not speak here about His rapture, when He will catch away His saints into the air.

2. Jesus Said Wars, Famine, Pestilence Are Not Signs of the End

Strangely enough, people constantly use wars, famines, pestilences and earthquakes as signs of Christ's coming, although He clearly said they would not be a sign of the end. Read again Matthew 24:6,7:

"And ye shall hear of wars and rumours of wars: see that ye be not troubled: for all these things must come to pass, but the end is not yet.

For nation shall rise against nation, and kingdom against kingdom: and there shall be famines, and pestilences, and earthquakes, in divers places."

People say that wars and rumors of wars are signs of the end, but Jesus said, ". . . all these things must come to pass, BUT THE END IS NOT YET." Wars and rumors of wars, earthquakes, famines, pestilences ARE NOT signs of the end. Rather, they are characteristics of the whole age! Jesus had just been warning of the coming destruction of Jerusalem. Wars were as characteristic of Christ's day as of ours. The whole course of this age is marked by the curse of God on nature and the distresses of human strife and war. But these are not signs of Christ's coming.

3. "Perilous Times" in II Timothy 3:1-9 Characterize the Whole Age

"Perilous times" are foretold for "the last days" in II Timothy 3:1-9. But to use these perilous times as a sign that we are at the end of the age wholly misinterprets the passage. In verse 5 Timothy is commanded, ". . . from such turn away," and verses 6 to 9 show that the people discussed lived in the time of Paul and Timothy.

Besides, the term "the last days" never meant the end of this gospel age. Rather, it means the whole New Testament age. See Acts 2:16,17 where Peter says that Pentecost is in the period called by Joel "the last days," and Hebrews 1:1,2 where it is said that God has spoken to us "in these last days. . .by his Son," and I John 2:18 where we are told "it is the last time." "The latter times" in I Timothy 4:1 also meant this whole New Testament age. "The last days" in II Peter 3:3 also refers to this whole New Testament age.

4. In Daniel "the Time of the End" Refers to the Great Tribulation

Often fervent speakers quote from Daniel 12, verses 4, 9 and 10 which, says Daniel, was to "shut up the words, and seal the book, even to the time of the end," and "the words are closed up and sealed till the time of the end," and "none of the wicked shall understand; but the wise shall understand."

But "the time of the end" or its equivalent is used in Daniel nine times (Dan. 8:17,19; 9:26; 11:35,40,45 and 12:4,6,9). IN EVERY CASE

IT REFERS TO THE GREAT TRIBULATION PERIOD WHICH IS, FOR THE JEWS, "THE TIME OF THE END"—that is, it will end definitely the seventy weeks determined upon the Jewish people as foretold in Daniel 9:24. But the Great Tribulation takes place AFTER Christ comes for His saints. There can be no signs until after Christ comes and raptures His saints. Then there will be signs during and after the Great Tribulation, looking toward His return with saints and angels literally to the earth to set up His kingdom.

5. There Is No "Laodicean Age" to Indicate Christ's Coming

An unfortunate interpretation of Scripture by Plymouth Brethren and by notes in the very fine Scofield Reference Bible has made the messages to the seven churches of Asia in Revelation, chapters 2 and 3, represent different periods of this age. But the seven churches were literal churches, all existing at the time the book of Revelation was written. The Bible itself has not a word to say about their being types representing ages of church history. That is a matter of human fancy, and it is unfortunate that anybody would ever make a doctrine out of it or take it as inspired. The Bible never says modernism, formalism and worldliness in the churches are marks of the closing age. The messages to these seven churches have meaning for us, as do all the Scriptures, but the Bible does not teach that these churches represent periods of church history. So to say that "we are in the Laodicean age" is to propagate a man's doctrine which has not a word of substantiation in the Scripture.

Notice in the Scofield Reference Bible these paragraph headings before the several messages to the seven churches of Asia:

(1) the message to Ephesus. The church at the end of the apostolic age; first love left.

(2) the message to Smyrna. Period of the great persecutions, to A.D. 316.

(3) the message to Pergamos. The church under imperial favor, settled in the world, A.D. 316 to the end.

(4) the message to Thyatira. A.D. 500-1500: the triumph of Balaamism and Nicolaitanism; a believing remnant (vss. 24-38).

(5) the message to Sardis. The period of the Reformations; a believing remnant (vss. 4,5).

(6) the message to Philadelphia. The true church in the professing church.

(7) the message to Laodicea. The final state of apostasy.

Again let me stress that these divisions making these seven churches—all existing in the days of John the apostle, all addressed in these letters, written at the same time—typical of different ages and eras of church history, is purely a work of human fancy, of men's invention. The good men who have accepted this fanciful arrangement and who believe that the seven churches represented seven ages of church history surely do not realize how presumptuous their position is. Consider the following facts:

First, if any one of these classifications beside the first one be accurate, then Jesus could not have come until after 316 A.D. Paul, then, was a fanatic, a religious nut, to be looking for Jesus to come in his lifetime.

Second, Jesus Christ would not have been quite honest when He urged those Christians left here on earth to watch every day for His coming.

Third, if John Nelson Darby, Dr. C. I. Scofield or any other person has found out some other great fact of prophecy which was not made clear to New Testament Christians in the Scriptures, then the Bible itself was not complete, and we must have some other source of information about the future aside from the Scriptures.

Of course all of these suppositions are unthinkable. Here are two concepts which emphatically clash, which are altogether contradictory: that we may expect Christ to come at any moment, without any warning; that the age until Christ's coming is marked out in seven divisions which anyone may follow—I say those two ideas utterly contradict.

The seven supposed divisions in Revelation, chapters 2 and 3, are simply human fancy gone astray.

Every one of those churches existed when the book of Revelation was written. The messages came to people then alive. These messages have meaning for us, but they do not have any prophetic intent beyond the group to whom they were particularly addressed.

Some characteristics of those seven churches exist today in various churches and groups. Some are as devoted as the best Christians in Ephesus; some are as backslidden and cold as the lukewarm ones at Laodicea.

No Bible student that we know of professes to find anywhere in the Bible a clear statement that these seven churches really represent the consecutive eras of church history. The late Dr. H. A. Ironside, greatly trusted Bible teacher, said:

The seven lamp stands are said to symbolize the seven churches of Asia, but there was a mystery connected with them. While some have tried one key and some another (and there have been all kinds of efforts made to interpret this mystery), no solution was found until some devout students of Scripture weighing this portion said, "Might it not be that inasmuch as this section of the book presents 'the things which are,' God has been pleased to give us here a prophetic history of the church for the entire dispensation?"

Then Dr. Ironside explained that they fitted the ages of church history to the seven churches and decided that the key would fit the lock! On that so flimsy a basis, without any direct scriptural statement, we are told that before Christ could return to the earth the period of church history must involve seven ages or eras represented by these seven churches. We are told that Christ could not have returned before these eras are completed. And that now we are in the Laodicean, or last, days. Thus good people make of none effect the clear teaching of Jesus that no one knows when He will return, and they unconsciously make mockery of those who obey the Saviour by looking for and expecting Him, even as they expected Him in Bible times. And these commit also the grievous assumption that they know that He will return within a certain limited time. Thus they arrogantly go beyond Scriptures with a man-made doctrine which is heresy.

Again let me state it: There is no "Laodicean Age" to indicate Christ's coming.

6. "As Ye See the Day Approaching" Refers to Destruction of Jerusalem

Some have supposed that Hebrews 10:25 refers to the second coming of Christ. There the inspired apostle gives instruction: "Not forsaking the assembling of ourselves together, as the manner of some is; but exhorting one another: and so much the more, as ye see the day approaching." Those who would find signs of Christ's coming say that this Scripture promises that we can "see the day approaching."

But that would contradict the clear statements of the Saviour, that Jesus will come as a thief in the night, that no one can know the day nor the hour of His coming.

What then does this Scripture mean? What day could the Hebrew people see approaching?

The answer is, they could see the coming destruction of Jerusalem.

The Epistle to the Hebrews was written to Jews a little before the destruction. Jesus had warned, "And when ye shall see Jerusalem compassed with armies, then know that the desolation thereof is nigh" (Luke 21:20). A similar warning had been given in Luke 19:41-44 and in Matthew 24:2. Jews living in Jerusalem could "see the day approaching" of the prophesied destruction of Jerusalem, when not one stone of the Temple would be left upon another and the city would be trodden under the foot of the Gentiles, and they, the Jews, would be scattered to all nations.

If one reads the Epistle to the Hebrews with this thought in mind, he will be tremendously impressed with the way God turns the hearts of the Jews away from the Jewish Temple, away from the Jewish priesthood, away from the ceremonies of the Mosaic Law, and from the old to the new covenant. We are told that Christ is better than the angels, better than the Jewish high priest of the Levitical priesthood. The whole book is preparing the Hebrews for the destruction of Jerusalem, with its Temple, priesthood and separate nation.

Now chapter 10 is particularly written to reconcile Jews to the doing away with animal sacrifices. The inspired writer says, "For it is not possible that the blood of bulls and of goats should take away sins" (vs. 4). He says, "Sacrifice and offering and burnt-offerings and offerings for sin thou wouldest not, neither hadst pleasure therein; which are offered by the law" (vs. 8). Again he says, "And every priest offering oftentimes the same sacrifices, which can never take away sins" (vs. 11).

Then there is the wonderful promise that, according to the new covenant, God writes His law in the hearts of the people, forgives their sins and remembers them no more. Then comes that dramatic statement about the end of the sacrifices: "Now where remission of these is, there is no more offering for sin" (vs. 18).

The offerings are over. The Temple sacrifices are no more needed. Christ Himself has superseded the Levitical priesthood. Then verse 25 says, "Not forsaking the assembling of ourselves together, as the manner of some is! but exhorting one another: and so much the more, as ye see the day approaching." The Hebrew people saw approaching the destruction of Jerusalem, as foretold by the Saviour.

Verses 26 to 31, immediately following, are really God's explanation of the terrible, terrible destruction and bloodshed when the city was destroyed, when, according to Josephus, 1,100,000 Jews were killed and a remnant scattered over the world. Read the passage and see how it fits:

"For if we sin wilfully after that we have received the knowledge of the truth, there remaineth no more sacrifice for sins, But a certain fearful looking for of judgment and fiery indignation, which shall devour the adversaries. He that despised Moses' law died without mercy under two or three witnesses: Of how much sorer punishment, suppose ye, shall he be thought worthy, who hath trodden under foot the Son of God, and hath counted the blood of the covenant, wherewith he was sanctified, an unholy thing, and hath done despite unto the Spirit of grace? For we know him that hath said, Vengeance belongeth unto me, I will recompense, saith the Lord. And again, The Lord shall judge his people. It is a fearful thing to fall into the hands of the living God." — Heb. 10:26-31.

These are the days of vengeance of which Jesus prophesied in Luke 21:20-24. The inhabitants of Jerusalem could foretell when the destruction of Jerusalem approached.

"And when ye shall see Jerusalem compassed with armies, then know that the desolation thereof is nigh. Then let them which are in Judaea flee to the mountains; and let them which are in the midst of it depart out; and let not them that are in the countries enter thereinto. For these be the days of vengeance, that all things which are written may be fulfilled. But woe unto them that are with child, and to them that give suck, in those days! for there shall be great distress in the land, and wrath upon this people. And they shall fall by the edge of the sword, and shall be led away captive into all nations: and Jerusalem shall be trodden down of the Gentiles, until the times of the Gentiles be fulfilled."

Jews in Jerusalem could "see the day approaching" for the destruction of Jerusalem. But we today cannot see the day approaching for Christ's coming.

Only by misinterpretation of Scripture can one find any signs pointing to the time of Christ's return.

XV.

The Premillennial Question

Compiled by REV. DENZEL B. MILLER

One of the prominent questions of the day is: Will the church go through the Tribulation? Some of the world's greatest Bible teachers were premillennial.

There is no remedy for the deadly plague of modernism like the blessed hope of the premillennial coming of the Lord. Postmillennialism is a natural breeding ground for modernism; for, like modernism, it denies plain statements in the Word of God. Under the guise of "spiritualizing," it makes the eternal Word of the eternal God of none effect.

DR. HARRY IRONSIDE:

In his book, *The Lamp of Prophecy* (pp. 128,129), the late Dr. H. A. Ironside says:

"Some years ago it was my great privilege to sit at the feet of Dr. A. T. Robertson as he gave a course of lectures on the epistle to the Colossians directly from his Greek Testament in Calvary Baptist Church in New York City. He was conducting a ministerial conference, and it was my privilege in that conference to give a series of addresses from my English Bible (because I am not scholar enough to give them from a Greek Testament and most folk are not scholars enough to follow me if I were), and I was rather gratified to see the great man sitting down before me every day. I recognized Dr. Robertson as undoubtedly the outstanding Greek scholar in America, if not of the world; and yet that dear, kindly man of God sat and listened to a poor insignificant person like myself, and he was just as gracious and just as attentive as anyone could possibly be.

"I went through the two letters to the Thessalonians; and at the close of the last address, Dr. Robertson came to me and said, 'Well, this is the first time that I have ever listened to anyone go carefully through those epistles from the premillennial standpoint, and I must say that my judgment has gone with you through the entire series. I have never definitely declared myself as a premillennialist, but I think if I had my life to live over again I would be much more positive concerning this, for I have never in my ministry known a premillennialist who was a modernist.'

"One is often asked how to understand prophecy. The answer is: Just read it and believe it. It is as simple as that. The Bible has a way of saying what it means and meaning what it says."

(*Nearing the End,* taken from the Preface)

DR. WILLIAM PETTINGILL:

Why the Church Must Escape

"The church will not pass through the Great Tribulation, nor into any part of it. The Great Tribulation is a visitation of the wrath of God in judgment upon His enemies. The church of Christ is His body, the fullness of Him that filleth all in all (Eph. 1:22,23). In Christ, by the reckoning of God, the church has already passed through God's judgment for sin on the cross of Calvary. To subject the body of Christ again to the billows of God's wrath would be unjust, and it is unthinkable that a righteous God could permit such a thing. We have been, by our relation to Christ, 'delivered. . .from the wrath to come' (I Thess. 1:9,10).

"The church is also the bride of Christ (Eph. 5:31,32), bone of His bone and flesh of His flesh, and they together are 'one flesh' (Gen. 1:23,24). To put the church through the Great Tribulation would be to subject Christ Himself the second time to the visitation of God's wrath. It is impossible, and cannot be. 'Shall not the Judge of all the earth do right?' (Gen. 18:25).

"And we have in Revelation 3:10 a definite statement showing that the church will be kept out of the Great Tribulation. Literally translated, the verse says: 'Because thou hast kept my enduring Word, I also will keep thee from the hour of trial, which shall come upon all the world, to try them that dwell upon the earth.' This is plainly a reference to the Great Tribulation; and it is a promise to those who have kept His enduring Word, 'the word of the Lord [which] endureth for ever' (I Pet. 1:25).

"The true church, the born-again ones, have kept His Word. Not that they have obeyed it perfectly (we do nothing perfectly), but we have not discarded it as the modernist does. We have 'a little strength,' and have kept His Word, and have not denied His name (Rev. 3:8); and therefore, when the 'hour of trial'—the day of God's wrath and of the wrath of the Lamb—when it comes, we shall be taken out and kept from it. He who cannot lie has said it, and He will do it. Blessed be His name forever!"

(*Nearing the End,* pp. 53-55)

The greatest Bible teachers in the world today are premillennial in belief.

DR. LEE ROBERSON:

"Let us notice that the rapture of the saints will occur before the Tribulation begins. There are some premillennialists who would try to say that the church goes through the Tribulation, and then Christ comes. If this be so, then His coming would not be sudden and unannounced. It would not be as a thief in the night.

"We are to watch for the coming of Christ and not for the Tribulation. His coming for the redeemed will precede the awfulness of the Tribulation time . . . . The Tribulation begins when the church is caught up and the Holy Spirit taken out of the world. The Great Tribulation is a time of judgment upon a Christ-rejecting world. We are going to be taken out, and then the judgment will fall."

(From *Some Golden Daybreak,* pp. 21,24)

DR. M. R. DE HAAN:

"One of the burning questions of the day and one which is arousing unusual interest is: Will the church go through the Tribulation? Strange as it may seem, although Scripture shows that the very essence of the blessed hope is the hope of escaping the Tribulation, there are thousands of sincere and well-meaning Christians who have been misled into believing that the church, the bride of Christ, will have to go through that awful day. Such are the trickeries of the enemy.

"The more important a doctrine is, the more Satan seeks to confuse God's people. It is easy to understand why he hates the truth of the imminent return of the Lord Jesus, for there is nothing in the world that will cause men to live watchfully and carefully as much as the expectation of His 'any moment' return. This confusion among Christians has made it difficult to interest the unsaved in salvation, since they look at these differences and confusion among Christians and do not believe that salvation is real."

(*The Second Coming of Jesus,* pp. 45,46, Zondervan Publishing Company. Used by permission.)

If the church goes through the Tribulation, then we have no "blessed hope" to look forward to, but dark days of Tribulation. If the church goes through half of the Tribulation, then Jesus could not return at any moment. The modernists and the liberals would like for us to believe this.

In the Old Testament, Enoch, representing the church, escaped the Flood because he was translated to Heaven. So will the church escape the Tribulation by being translated to Heaven. Noah went through the Flood, as Israel will go through the Great Tribulation.

No part of the true church will pass through any part of the Tribulation. The Lord spewed out the church of Laodicea because they were neither cold nor hot. This is a picture of the rapture when the modernistic and false church will be left behind. It would not be right for God to punish the true church, and the Tribulation is punishment for the false church and the unsaved. *The church is part of the body of Christ, and the body cannot go through the Tribulation.*

The Bible teaches that the church will not go through any part of the Tribulation. Why cannot Christians accept the plain teachings of the Word of God instead of arguing their own beliefs? *The following Bible passages give conclusive proof that the church will go through no part of the Tribulation.*

Jeremiah 30:7
Matthew 24:29,30
Luke 21:28,31,36
I Thessalonians 1:10
I Thessalonians 5:9-11
Revelation 3:10

(From *Bible Believing Baptist Beacon.*)

For a complete list of books available from the Sword of the Lord, write to Sword of the Lord Publishers, P. O. Box 1099, Murfreesboro, Tennessee 37133.